Praise for FTSE

'FTSE is a story which should inform and fascinate anyone interested in capital markets.'

Sir Donald Brydon CBE, chairman of the Sage Group and former chairman of the London Stock Exchange Group

'An inspiring success story; how a clear vision, relentless commitment and two great British brands combined to create a global leader.'

Rona Fairhead, Baroness Fairhead CBE, former chief executive of the Financial Times Group and former Minister of State at the Department for International Trade

'Richly detailed, and written with an attractively light touch, bringing out personalities as well as indices, this is an important contribution to our understanding of how the modern City has developed.'

David Kynaston, social historian and author of *City of London: The History* and *Austerity Britain 1945–1951*

'Mark Makepeace takes us on a 35-year journey from a sedentary world of top hats, long lunches and fixed commissions to a dynamic global marketplace dominated by computers and algorithms, a marketplace of infinite choice. In the process he not only tells the story of a brilliant British company that kept pace with this dizzy change but he charts the development of financial markets transformed within a generation by the forces of technology and globalization.'

John Makinson, founder of Makinson & Cowell, former CFO of Pearson, and former CEO of Penguin

'FTSE and Mark have had a ring-side seat for every major change in the UK stock market - and have been active players in many of the deals and mergers that have re-shaped the sector internationally. It is a fascinating story of a crucial phase in the investment landscape.'

John Ridding, CEO of the Financial Times Group and former editor of the Financial Times, Asia

FTSE

The inside story of the deals, dramas and politics that revolutionized financial markets

FTSE

*The inside story of the deals, dramas and politics that
revolutionized financial markets*

MARK MAKEPEACE

with

JAMES ASHTON

NICHOLAS BREALEY
PUBLISHING
London · Boston

First published by Nicholas Brealey Publishing in 2020
An imprint of John Murray Press
A division of Hodder & Stoughton Ltd,
An Hachette UK company
1
Copyright © Mark Makepeace 2020

This book is for information or educational purposes only and is not intended to act as a substitute for medical advice or treatment. Any person with a condition requiring medical attention should consult a qualified medical practitioner or suitable therapist.

A CIP catalogue record for this title is available from the British Library

Hardback ISBN 9781529330021
Export Trade Paperback ISBN 9781529336016
eBook ISBN 9781529330052

Typeset by KnowledgeWorks Global Ltd.

Printed and bound in Great Britain by Clays Ltd, Elcograf S.p.A.

John Murray Press policy is to use papers that are natural, renewable and recyclable products and made from wood grown in sustainable forests. The logging and manufacturing processes are expected to conform to the environmental regulations of the country of origin.

John Murray Press
Carmelite House
50 Victoria Embankment
London EC4Y 0DZ

Nicholas Brealey Publishing
Hachette Book Group
Market Place, Center 53, State Street
Boston, MA 02109, USA

www.nicholasbrealey.com

To my gorgeous wife, Rachel, and my wonderful children, Claire, Dom and Nic. I love you all.

Contents

About the Author

Mark Makepeace offers a unique perspective on the financial services industry. During a 35-year career he was founding Chief Executive of FTSE International and turned a small UK start-up into one of the largest and most successful global index providers – and one of Britain's most famous brands. In 1985, he arrived in the City at the London Stock Exchange as a clerk to co-ordinate Big Bang – and never left. He recently stepped down as Chief Executive of FTSE Russell and from his role as Executive Director responsible for the LSE's information services division.

James Ashton is a senior financial journalist who has covered some of the biggest economic and corporate stories of recent times. He was City Editor and Executive Editor of the *London Evening Standard* and *Independent* titles and before that City Editor of the *Sunday Times*. Today he is a business commentator and interviewer for the *Telegraph* and *Times* and produces his own influential leadership podcast, 'Leading with James Ashton'.

Foreword

As a member of the board of the London Stock Exchange in the 1990s, I came across Mark Makepeace as he led the development of our indexing activities. As the possibility of creating an index business came into focus, I argued strongly that he was the man to lead it. The representative of our joint venture partner the *Financial Times* disagreed. Now, looking back over 25 years later, I am glad that my judgement has been vindicated. As I returned as Chairman in 2015 I found that LSEG was almost unique among major exchange groups in wholly owning one of the world's leading index businesses; the business Mark Makepeace had proposed had become a huge profit generator.

My dictionary defines an index as 'a figure indicating the relative level of prices or wages compared with that of a previous date'. It is unlikely that the author of that statement would ever have envisaged the role that capital market indices play today in the way in which capital is allocated around the world. Initially, a barometer of the performance of an economy, an index today has taken on a spectrum of other roles and this has raised some major questions about the governance and processes of calculation involved.

Mark Makepeace has lived through this entire evolution with a front row seat and has laid out here a narrative of the drivers of that evolution. This is a personal and a corporate journey seen through both micro- and macro-lenses. It is also the story of a British global success.

It is a journey that owes much to changes in computing power. The arrival of the PC transformed the ability of investment managers to understand the risks in their portfolios in a quantitative manner. The arrival of huge computing power allowed the analysis of massive quantities of data to discover patterns of relationships invisible to the eyes of past investors. Over the last fifty years there has been a complete revolution in how savings are managed as a result.

I recall in the early 1970s, as young investment analyst, asking my boss why he had just bought 100,000 shares in Lucas Industries for the pension fund of the newly formed British Airways. He explained the merits of Lucas, but that was not the question to which I was seeking an answer. I wanted to know why he had chosen 100,000 and not some other number. The reply was deeply dissatisfying: it was a round number.

Now portfolios can be managed with precision and, in parallel, the consequences of the investment decisions can be accurately measured. Indices have become benchmarks which offer the user the ability to analyse deviations in performance in minute detail. They also reflect, and possibly encourage, the application of different and innovative investment strategies.

Mark Makepeace has shown how this evolution took place, the commercial decisions that were the drivers of change and the vision of the future which he, and others, led to create an index industry.

FTSE is today a far cry from the FT30 which was intended as a simple barometer of the health of the British economy. Its executives now influence how capital is raised, how much is raised and how flows move around the world.

It is as if the scoreboard at a cricket match is a determinant of how the game is played. Decisions about inclusions or non-inclusions in an index can cause large amounts of capital to move. This raises interesting questions about who is responsible for the decisions throughout that process and what accountability they have. Mark Makepeace cleverly discusses the impact on South Korea, China and Saudi Arabia of decisions that he and his team made. He rightly stresses the importance of good governance and transparency of process, in which FTSE has undoubtedly been a leader, but the trends towards regulation that he notes are only likely to become stronger.

The investment managers who track indices have laid out clearly what they are doing but, in doing so, are committing to a future where decisions are effectively made by someone else. Of course they could choose to renegotiate their mandates, but the reality is that this is very unlikely other than in circumstances of an exceptional nature. This all points to the increased importance of the index producers.

As Mark Makepeace points out, FTSE was early in the movement towards ESG with its innovative FTSE4Good series. Here we can all see the way in which indices can help lead the market and behaviour whilst simultaneously responding to new trends. The rise of ESG investing, the obligations on corporates to report their path to net-zero carbon use and issues around diversity will all play an increasing role in the evolution of the indices.

Looking forward, Mark Makepeace hints at the index producers turning into virtual investment managers. After all an index is composed of a portfolio of stocks. The boundaries between investment management and index production are likely to get increasingly blurred. At the same time, he highlights the growth in self-indexing. He also shows how these trends have been driven by giants such as Vanguard and BlackRock.

We are entering the 'Age of Data Wars' and index producers will be at its heart. The advent of new technologies such as machine learning and artificial intelligence are already propelling the investment management industry forward with a vigour similar to that which came from the advent of widely available computing power. Curating and manipulating data will become increasingly valuable activities and anyone who can add value to the data in a systematic way, and efficiently distribute the results, will have the foundations of a very interesting business model. Scale will also be important. It is interesting to speculate how different the world of 2070 will look as a consequence; the evidence of the changes since 1970 to date are that there is new and profound change to come.

Mark Makepeace has shown in this memoir how this is not just a story about high-level business growth but also about the way in which one individual has helped shape the future. He has shown how, in touching detail, his personal journey has been entangled with these big trends. Entanglement starts to raise questions about quantum physics too! For now though, the development of FTSE is both a successful personal and institutional story which should inform and fascinate anyone professionally interested in capital markets or personally in what happens to their savings. It is a story, full of life, chronicling markets over the last fifty years.

Sir Donald Brydon
London
2 July 2020

Abbreviations

Amex American Stock Exchange
BMR Benchmarks Regulation (EU)
BT British Telecommunications
CalPERS California Public Employees Retirement System
CAPS Combined Actuarial Performance Services (UK)
CBI Confederation of British Industry
CBOE Chicago Board Options Exchange
CDO Collateralized Debt Obligation
CEP Council on Economic Priorities
CFTC Commodity Futures Trading Commission (USA)
CMA Capital Market Authority (Saudi Arabia)
CME Chicago Mercantile Exchange
CNS Company News Service
CSRC China Securities Regulatory Commission
DJI Dow Jones Indices
DMGT Daily Mail and General Trust

EIRIS Ethical Investment Research Service
Epra European Public Real Estate Association
ESG Environmental, Social and Governance Practices
ETF Exchange-Traded Fund
FCA Financial Conduct Authority (UK)
FSA Financial Services Authority (UK)
GEIS FTSE Global Equity Index Series
RAFI Research Affiliates Fundamental Index
HSBC Hong Kong & Shanghai Banking Corporation
ICB Industry Classification Benchmark
ICEM International Federation of Chemical, Energy, Mine and General Workers' Unions
IDC International Data Corporation
IIA Index Industry Association
IOSCO International Organization of Securities Commissions

IPO Initial Public Offering

IRRC Investor Responsibility
Research Center (USA)

KOSPI Korea Composite Stock
Price Index

Libor London Inter-bank
Offered Rate

LIFFE London International
Financial Futures and Options
Exchange

LBS London Business School

LSE London Stock Exchange

LTOM London Traded Options
Market

MBA Master of Business
Administration

MBS Mohammed bin Salman
(Crown Prince of Saudi Arabia)

MiFID Markets in Financial
Instruments Directive (EU)

MPDS Market Price Display
Service

MSCI Morgan Stanley Capital
International (now trade name)

Nareit National Association of
Real Estate Investment Trusts
(USA)

OECD Organization for
Economic Co-operation and
Development

OPEC Organization of the
Petroleum Exporting Countries

PRI Principles for Responsible
Investment (UN)

RNS Regulatory News
Service (LSE)

RPC Restrictive Practices Court
(UK)

S&P Standard & Poor's

SEAQ Stock Exchange
Automated Quotations

SEC Securities and Exchange
Commission (USA)

SETS Stock Exchange
Electronic Trading Service

SGX Singapore Exchange

SME Small to Medium-size
Enterprise

Sonia Sterling Overnight Index
Average

SPDR Standard & Poor's-500
Depositary Receipts

SRI Socially Responsible
Investing

TCFD Task Force on
Climate-related Financial
Disclosures

TMX Toronto Stock Exchange

TPI Transition Pathway Initiative

UKLA UK Listings Authority

UNICEF United Nations
Children's Fund

Webs World Equity
Benchmark Shares

WHO World Health
Organization

WTO World Trade Organization

XFN Xinhua Financial Network

Timeline

1 July 1935
The FT 30 index
is launched

26 Nov 1962
The FT-Actuaries
All-Share (later
FTSE All-Share)
is launched

3 Jan 1984
The SE 100 (later
FTSE 100)
index is launched

21 Apr 2001
FTSE/Xinhua China 25,
an index of Chinese stocks
for international investors,
announced in partnership
with Xinhua News Agency

27 Feb 2001
FTSE4Good
Index launched

30 June 2000
FTSE All-World Index
goes live after acquisition
of Barings Emerging
Markets Indices

28 Nov 2005
FTSE RAFI (Research
Affiliates Fundamental
Index) series begins

28 Sep 2006
SGX (Singapore) launch
futures contracts on the
FTSE/Xinhua A50
(later FTSE China A50)

12 Dec 2011
LSE buys out the *FT*
from their FTSE joint
venture for £450 million

3 Dec 1984
British Telecom
privatization and
first day of share trading

27 Oct 1986
Big Bang

31 Dec 1986
The FT-Actuaries
World Index (later
FT/S&P World, then
FTSE World) is launched

29 Nov 1999
FTSE International buy
out Goldman Sachs
and S&P from the
FT/S&P World Index

16 Nov 1995
FTSE International, a
joint venture between
the *Financial Times* (*FT*)
and the London Stock
Exchange (LSE), begins trading

12 Oct 1992
The FTSE 250
is launched

2 Oct 2012
FTSE wins the
mandate for all of
Vanguard's international
equity benchmarks

26 June 2014
LSE buys the Frank
Russell Company
for $2.7 billion

30 May 2017
LSE acquires The Yield
Book and Citi Fixed
Income Indices for $685m

23 Mar 2020
Final inclusion of both
Saudi Arabia and China
A shares in FTSE's emerging
market indices

I
World vision

When television networks cut to the Oval Office on the evening of 11 March 2020, America was expectant. US presidents through history have reserved live, primetime addresses to the nation for the gravest of circumstances. John F. Kennedy spoke of the Cuban Missile Crisis, George W. Bush of the 9/11 terror attacks on New York's World Trade Center and Barack Obama of BP's *Deepwater Horizon* oil spill.

Designed to convey reassurance and solidity, the trans mission format sees the Leader of the Free World sitting behind the Resolute Desk, a present from Queen Victoria hewn from English oak, and before two further familiar emblems, the Stars and Stripes and the President's flag.

It was Donald Trump's only second such address. US networks are reluctant to hand over so much airtime for political reasons these days, and, in any case, the 45th President favours the immediacy of Twitter to communicate with citizens. But the USA was facing a national emergency because of COVID-19, the novel coronavirus that had spread around the world since first being detected in the Chinese city of Wuhan in late December 2019. On the day that the World Health Organization designated the outbreak as a global pandemic, Trump decided to speak out.

What is traditionally a careful, heavily scripted and statesmanlike broadcast quickly went wrong. 'Smart action today will prevent the spread of the virus tomorrow,' Trump said halfway through the nine-minute address, but by then the damage had been done. His stumbling delivery as he strayed from the autocue did little to allay American fears that the US government was not on top of things. The shock announcement of a 30-day ban on European travellers coming to the USA was muddled when Trump stated it would affect cargo arrivals and trade, which it would not.

The reaction was instant. After a 10-week build-up, rising fear solidified into panic over the following 24 hours. With fresh impetus, countries closed borders and schools. Sports bodies including the National Basketball Association suspended tournaments. Pictures of deserted tourist destinations, from Rome's Colosseum to the Broadway theatre district, were beamed around the world. Call it a slowdown, a lockdown, whatever: the world was pulling down the shutters for perhaps its greatest peacetime crisis.

The severity of the situation was measured nowhere better than on the world's stock markets, which fell like dominoes as alarm at Trump's outburst rolled around the globe. Airlines, tourism, the global supply chain and day-to-day business was under threat from drastically reduced demand. But most frantic traders glued to their desktop screens and fevered workers and homeowners scrolling through the news on their smartphones did not immediately clock how far individual shares had fallen. For them the story of this sharply deteriorating economic environment was told first through one or two numbers that in modern society and fast-moving money markets have come to codify confidence – or a lack of it.

Those single values are distilled from a miasma of data, the product of stock indices which are calculated many times per second from the average of a basket of prices. That is how Japan's Nikkei, which dived while Trump was still talking, put a value on what one asset manager quickly dubbed 'the most expensive speech in history'. It is how, later that same day, billions of dollars were sliced from the value of the Dow Jones Industrial Average, which entered bear market territory as it slid 10 per cent, and the S&P 500, which fell almost as far. And bang in the middle, where East meets West, tumbled one of the world's most famous share indices: the FTSE 100.

A british institution

The FTSE 100 is a modern British brand recognized the world over, like the Royal Family, the BBC or Sir Richard Branson's Virgin empire. They are just four letters on an electronic ticker tape, trading screen or radio bulletin. Yet in the space of a few decades FTSE – or Footsie, as it is commonly known – has become a byword for money, power, influence and – crucially after numerous financial crises – confidence.

On a daily basis, from when trading begins in London's Square Mile at 8am every morning, the value of the FTSE 100 is used as a shorthand for prosperity or hardship, part of the visual language of how well the world is doing. Green is for good, the colour of prices on the rise, and traders punching the air. Red is for decline and sometimes danger and heads clasped in hands, shaking in disbelief as trading concludes at 4.30pm.

In both the short and long term, FTSE read-outs spark a multitude of investment decisions and political manoeuvres. Its reach extends far beyond the high-pressure trading rooms of London, New York and Hong Kong to impact the wealth of nations and how much almost every worker will have to live on when they retire.

The flagship FTSE 100 Index has since 1984 compiled the performance of the UK's 100 largest listed companies into a single figure for all to see. It takes the price of each share – every one a small slice of ownership that is valued according to the company's prospects and how much dividend it is expected to pay out to its owners – and weights them according to the market value of their outstanding shares. As a capitalization-weighted – or cap-weighted – index, the giants of the FTSE

100 such as HSBC in banking and GlaxoSmithKline in phar-ma-ceuticals have greater impact on its value than firms that are fellow members but could be 5 per cent of their size. What began life with an arbitrary value of 1,000 points has so far peaked at 7,903.50 points during trading on 22 May 2018 after a long bull run of rising equity values. The FTSE 100 ended that day at 7,877.45 points, to date the highest close.

From its birth in Thatcherite Britain, it has kept pace with the changing financial markets better than the fashion for bowler hats and pinstripe suits that dominated the City at the time. Latterly, those 100 constituents – which face promotion or relegation once a quarter to ensure only the biggest remain as members – have taken on a more international flavour. The Footsie is now a global indicator.

It is one of many indices that have been housed within FTSE International, the company I founded in 1995 to capitalize on the FTSE 100's appeal and an increasing appetite for financial data. FTSE has grown to become a vital piece of trusted financial infrastructure, and since 2011 it has been wholly owned by the London Stock Exchange (LSE), changing its corporate name to FTSE Russell in 2014 when we acquired the American index provider Russell. In 25 event-packed years, FTSE – the company – has gone from a start-up of just nine people to a company big enough to be a member of the FTSE 100 in its own right.

Operating at the heart of the City of London, the FTSE 100 has become a magnet for international businesses seeking deep pools of capital and a kitemark of respectability. FTSE Russell's renown has travelled in the other direction, collating investments in emerging markets in every corner of the globe as well as the value of sovereign wealth. Today, this British start-up runs indices for everything – countries, asset classes, industries – by size and increasingly by investment style and strategy. FTSE can help investors measure the relative performance of Vietnam versus South Korea, energy stocks versus retail and equities versus bonds. Our indices help investors identify and manage risks within their portfolios, measure the performance and regulate the pay of fund managers, and keep track of the strategy they follow. Increasingly, indices are being used to replicate the work of 'active' managers in cheaper and more transparent 'passive' index funds. As capitalism has globalized and a data revolution has transformed the investment industry, FTSE leads its field and guides the fortunes of an astonishing $16 trillion of funds.

How – and why – FTSE works

An index is no more than a gauge of the value of the stock market. It tells us – every second – the stock market's view of the collective value of companies. This market is a crowd of investors – buyers and sellers – all coming together trying to predict the value of their investments, both now and in the future. Fear sparks panic and pulls the market down. Greed spurs buying frenzies and pushes the market up. Investors who can judge when best to buy or sell shares are rare because they must be better than the crowd, which is complex, constantly changing and constantly learning. The crowd feeds on analysis, information and news – fake and real – and tries to interpret the impact on industries and companies. The role of the index provider is to ensure that the index represents the market accurately, truthfully and without bias. We observe, we try to understand the mood of the crowd, but we stay on the sidelines – most of the time.

FTSE works because humans gravitate to order, making sense of information by grouping it into families to rank and review. This process has taken place for centuries in libraries where information used to be organized manually by index cards and today by huge computer databases. At the Library of Congress in Washington, DC, the largest library in the world, a collection of more than 168 million items including more than 39 million catalogued books and other print materials in 470 languages are carefully catalogued so they can be searched and studied. As a handy navigational tool, this book is indexed too.

The Internet giant Google's mission is to organize the world's information to make it universally accessible. Its search function has become ubiquitous and is used an estimated 2 trillion times per day. Google ranks web pages based on their usefulness and the expertise of sources. It says: 'The index is like a library, except that it contains more info than in all the world's libraries put together.' Google's search index contains hundreds of billions of web pages and is well over 100,000,000 gigabytes in size.

Financial indexation is not so large, but has grown exponentially. At the last count, the Index Industry Association (IIA) found that there are 2.96 million indices globally. It is an astonishing number, given that there are only 60,000 stocks in the world. And, as the number of stocks listed on stock exchanges around the world shrinks each year, the number of indices continues to grow exponentially. Today nearly all of the $74 trillion total invested internationally will make some use of a benchmark.

The growth can be explained by the changing use of financial indices. They started life as confidence barometers that swung whenever a catalyst for buying or selling shares (the equivalent of a Donald Trump tweet) took place. Then they were adopted by the investment industry as performance benchmarks in particular for mutual funds that pool money from a large number of investors and pick a series of stocks to back. Fund managers whose investment decisions outpaced a particular index – hence were above average – were feted for their wisdom and rewarded with great personal wealth as well as fresh assets to steer. Underperformers had some explaining to do and faced an outflow of funds.

But mushrooming demand over the last two decades is thanks to the trend for tracking the index, not beating it. Rather than singling out stocks to invest in, money managers – or the algorithms they rely on – spread their risk today by picking trends or topics they think will prosper in the long term. Exchange-traded funds (ETFs) – of which more in Chapter 6 – are baskets of stocks created to replicate the FTSE 100 or others but trade on an exchange just like an individual stock and account for about 10 per cent of all funds invested.

Their popularity is behind the tectonic shift from active to passive investing, where assets follow indices at lower cost than paying for less predictable human intervention. The value of passive funds has swung from 9 to 27 per cent in 12 years to 2019 according to data from financial analysts Morningstar, led by equities which have gone from 16 to 43 per cent over the same period. Passive funds are on track to exceed active funds in less than a decade according to many stock market analysts, with the USA leading the way. This trend throws up questions about the ethics and regulation of index providers that I will address in this book. Three fund managers have grown to dominate passive investing – BlackRock, Vanguard and State Street – of which more later, too. For its part, FTSE creates new indices to stimulate or meet market demand across a melting pot of asset classes. With coverage in more than 70 countries, covering 98 per cent of the investable equity market globally, it also creates bespoke indices for particular clients.

This range can be simplified. FTSE manages around 200 index families but within each the permutations are vast. Take real estate as an example. The FTSE Epra/Nareit Global Real Estate Index Series is designed for property investors whether they are interested in office, industrial, retail or residential bricks and mortar. It is a project jointly run with the respective experts in their region, the National Association of Real Estate Investment Trusts (Nareit) of the USA and the Brussels-based European Public Real Estate Association (Epra) who supply in-depth data about company performance.

This industry category does not necessarily behave in the same way as the broader equity market but typically pays consistent dividends so may attract investors who favour reliable income over hopes of growth.

Choosing property is not the end of the decision making. There isn't just one FTSE Epra/Nareit index: there are 17. Investors can select almost any property permutation, whether that is an index that tracks property in developed markets, in the Americas or across the globe excluding the USA. There is even an offshoot series of green property indices that upweights those stocks that score highly for green building certification and energy usage.

Revenues and rivals

Our business model has two strands. I liken it to the way copy-righting works in the music industry. On the one hand, you license the words of the song you have written. On the other, you take a small licensing fee every time the song is played or if someone records a new version.

First of all, we receive subscriptions fees from fund managers, asset owners, actuarial consultants and investment banks who use our data in the investment process, typically as a benchmark against which to measure investment performance or analyse risks to the investment portfolio. The world is increasingly data-driven so the volumes of information we provide have increased sharply. Renewal rates are extremely high, running at more than 90 per cent.

And then there is income from licensing the FTSE trademark for use in financial products. This is mainly to passive funds whose ETFs or mutual funds are linked to our indices. This activity builds on our reputation in data. Our cut is small, typically 0.01 per cent and rarely more than 10 per cent of the product issuer's fees, but is linked to the volume of assets which has multiplied in recent years. We also take a transaction fee of a few pennies or cents on derivatives that trade on the indices – for example, from every FTSE 100 futures contract that is bought or sold based on expectations of which direction the index is predicted to turn next.

Taken together, FTSE revenues and profits have risen sharply. In 2019, FTSE Russell generated revenues of £649 million and the Information Services Division in which it is the largest component an operating profit of £449 million. FTSE alone accounted for just less than a third of LSE group revenues and our division contributed 42 per cent of the LSE's entire operating profit. The profits of our division have gone up by one-third from 2016 to 2019 and, because of the benefits of scale enjoyed by all of the largest index providers, they all have healthy profit margins in excess of 50 per cent.

FTSE is not alone in this market. It competes with two large American rival index providers of roughly our size, plus a wide range of smaller competitors. The big three have also been growing at or close to 10 per cent per year. MSCI, once part-owned by the investment bank Morgan Stanley, disclosed $921 million of sales at its index division in 2019, which accounted for more than half the group. That converted into an underlying earnings contribution of $670 million and made for a chunky 73 per cent divisional profit margin. S&P Dow Jones Indices is majority owned by the data business S&P Global alongside the Standard & Poor's credit ratings arm and Platts, the commodities and energy expert. It recorded $630 million of profit from sales of $918 million.

The worth of these companies can be seen on the stock market but is also reflected in analysis by Brand Finance. According to the independent brand valuation consultancy's own Brand Strength Index, FTSE Russell had a brand value of £2.56 billion at the start of 2020. Brand Finance arrived at this figure by taking into account a range of metrics including financial data, marketing efforts, product development, online presence and perceptions among customers and the general public. Notably, the figure accounts for 80 per cent of the value of the LSE's entire portfolio of brands, which underlines how important our name has become over the years. In the orbit of banks, brokers, stock exchanges, asset managers and data firms, index providers have become a valuable part of global financial markets. Taken together, over $40 trillion of investor funds are benchmarked against the largest three players.

The beating heart of the city

Compared to the nerve-shredding moments on trading floors around the world on 12 March 2020, one building in the centre of London maintained its steady calm. The location of the LSE in the heart of the Square Mile is truly where God meets Mammon. Its main entrance is on Paternoster Square where the clergy of nearby St Paul's Cathedral used to process as they recited prayers. Now it is a pedestrian plaza bustling with City workers and decorated with a bronze sculpture by Elisabeth Frink depicting a shepherd driving his sheep over the site of what was once the Newgate meat market.

Through the revolving door past the security bag check lies the atrium where FTSE comes alive. Here, an upturned cube on a central pedestal pulses with the latest value of numerous indices and the telltale colours of red or green. On the surrounding walls a bank of world indices is constantly updated next to an electronic world map. A ticker of FTSE 100 share prices and company codes threads its way between the first and ground floors, with a CNBC newsfeed conveying to waiting visitors the latest headlines one floor above that.

Up on the fourth floor is FTSE's London headquarters. It is a modern tech environment with hot desks, break-out areas, comfortable seating and probably the best coffee in London, influenced by our Italian colleagues in Milan. Glass meeting rooms are busy morning, noon and sometimes late into the evening with screens connecting the London staff to the operations and sales teams in all major financial centres around the world. Our day starts when the Australian market opens and closes when the US one closes. Analysts collect and sift through huge amounts of corporate and financial data published in numerous languages. Large data teams in Kuching in Malaysia, Taipei in Taiwan, and Charlotte and Buffalo in the USA update data to the cloud which is drawn down, vetted and updated by senior analysts around the world.

On days like this it is quite a show. But, up or down, the method by which the indices are managed varies little day to day. In the nerve centre, a bank of 10 staff are glued to computer screens. Here, flashing red doesn't mean the market is falling; it is an indicator that something has gone wrong with the real-time calculation of the indices that continues during the trading day. All the major indices are calculated in real time. Every price change from every stock market around the world is checked by our systems with an algorithm ensuring any suspicious price which may influence an index is highlighted and checked by an analyst. Rogue prices are discarded and true prices are released. If an index opens too high or too low, the operations staff are alerted. If an index stops publishing for any reason, an alert goes out worldwide.

FTSE's computer systems are designed to be fully resilient, available 99.9 per cent of a trading day. Hardware and software upgrades are constantly required, with changes implemented most weekends. These systems ingest the details of every trade, churning the numbers and updating index values every time a stock price changes. On a normal day you can watch the indices tick over two or three times a second when the markets are active. When markets crash, the index updates are too frequent for the human eye and can only be read by the many computers attached to our electronic feeds. The screens only show the index changes the eye can read, constantly ticking over and skipping ahead when required. It is a non-stop system that needs non-stop monitoring. All three centres have to operate in sync. Taipei passes the baton to London when Asia closes. After the European markets close, London passes the baton to Fort Mill, a small town in South Carolina famous for its local peach orchards. After the American markets close, Asia is already beginning to open so the baton then gets passed to Taipei before returning to London again. Each time, our data experts must make sure that the indices tick over, as well as inputting any changes – such as new market entrants, stock offers, takeovers – anything that will affect the weighting of a stock and the behaviour of indices overall.

FTSE Russell has almost 1,000 staff in over 20 offices around the world. They are involved in client support, research, IT, operations, sales, marketing, and all the functions required to support a modern global company. What they don't get involved in is making investment decisions.

Each of our family of indices is governed by a set of rules that have been adapted over time. These rules are mechanical, instructing the system to screen stocks in a certain way, rank them on a particular measure, update them at a specific frequency. The human input, as seen by our round-the-world index management teams, is there to make sure the machines work, but as far as possible we aim to keep it to a minimum.

Of course, there are prior decisions made as to what index construction should look like. There are historic standards, such as the Industry Classification Benchmark (ICB) which is widely used to identify to which sector stocks should belong. And there is an expert advisory committee made up of index users including asset managers and representatives from investment banks that oversees each family and the decisions FTSE takes about how it is operated. Then the machine is set running with daily monitoring and quarterly or half yearly reviews which could include the criteria for eligibility or a change in the test for liquidity, which ensures that index members have enough shares freely trading to satisfy demand. Most stock indices are not owned by stock exchanges. FTSE's ownership among the big three index providers is unique in that respect. Nevertheless, it does not mean that share listing guarantees index membership.

Decision making is disclosed wherever possible. For example, minutes carried on FTSE's website from a policy advisory board meeting on 26 June 2019 noted discussions around new industry classifications for financial data providers, professional business support services and marijuana producers and the best timing for future category changes. It also disclosed FTSE Russell was exploring whether it could create a benchmark for digital assets working in partnership with Digital Asset Research, a start-up that gathers data in this space. What is kept confidential are the names of most committee members, to frustrate efforts to lobby for a particular policy decision.

New indices go through a rigorous process before they can be launched. Such is demand for new ways of tracking equities, fixed income, commodities and even privately held assets that managing the new product pipeline is one of FTSE's great challenges, in particular for Chris Woods, FTSE's managing director for governance and index policy.

Whether new indices are proposed internally or at the request of a client, Chris's policy team undertakes several stages of assessment. First of all, *technical criteria*: does this idea make sense? Then, *operational*: can FTSE run this index in practice without manual intervention? Does it have enough timely data? And finally, *methodological*: are the proposed rules clear and fair? If it is judged to have passed all three, the index is passed to FTSE's product team for construction. The last thing we want to do is create a product that we can't run, doesn't make technical sense or suffers from poorly written rules. The name of the game is accuracy and reliability.

Index construction has become more complicated over the years. To begin with, the only thing we needed to know was the number of shares a company had issued and the price of those shares. Then investors wanted greater accuracy and liquidity so we added what is called 'investability weighting', which is what proportion of those shares make up the free float that can be easily traded. And then investors have sought to replicate investment strategies and to create more tailored indices that meet their policy or investment strategy requirements. These demands will only get greater and the challenge for index providers will be to create data collection and research capabilities able to meet these needs. New data collection methods using digital technologies and new AI algorithms to cleanse and create further derived data for the investment community will all lead to new and innovative forms of indices.

Weathering the storms

The spread of coronavirus was not the first crisis to be measured through the prism of the FTSE 100. Since its launch in 1984, the index has tracked economic ups and downs, exuberance and despair and great shocks to the financial system. In every case, the index is aligned to the stock market but distinct from it, providing investors with a front-row seat to observe what is really going on.

The largest single day loss remains 20 October 1987, the day after Black Monday, as fears of a repeat of the US Great Depression swept markets. The FTSE 100 dropped 12.2 per cent, following a 10.8 per cent fall the day before. The previous Friday, trading had closed at lunchtime. The Great Storm that wrought havoc across Kent and much of the south-east of London the night before meant that few market makers made it into the City that day. Traders joked that the Kentish town of Sevenoaks which suffered badly in the storms and lost many of its ancient trees should be renamed Oneoak.

In comparison, the FTSE 100 fell 10.9 per cent on 12 March 2020, the day after Trump's coronavirus address. However, it rallied in the following days as the President attempted to take a tighter grip of the situation.

The largest single-day gain for the FTSE 100 was 24 November 2008 during the 2007–8 financial crisis. The world was in a precarious place. That autumn Lehman Brothers had filed for Chapter 11 bankruptcy protection and the UK banks Lloyds and Royal Bank of Scotland required government rescue. The 9.8 per cent bounce came off the back of tax cuts announced in the Chancellor Alistair Darling's pre-Budget report and the bailout of the ailing Wall Street bank Citigroup. A similar rally took place on 24 March 2020, when Boris Johnson's UK lockdown of homes and businesses combined with the approval of a $2 trillion bond-buying programme in the USA to cheer investors. The FTSE 100 closed up 9.1 per cent higher, marking its second-largest one-day gain.

These major market-moving events were watched by us at FTSE, but our role was to ensure that the FTSE 100 and our other major indices were being calculated accurately and disseminated around the world so that investors had the information that they required to continue to make informed investment decisions.

When the planes crashed into the World Trade Center on 9 September 2001, I was standing in FTSE's operations centre at our first office, St Alphage House, in central London watching on television. As the second plane went into the South Tower 16 minutes after the first entered the North Tower, the markets began to react. Stocks went into freefall, and the indices followed them down. Even in a moment of great tragedy, we knew that our job is to be a bystander and make sure we accurately capture those trades and their impact. For the index to stop collating prices would only feed the sense of panic that terrorists would welcome.

Anthony Cloke, who headed our operations at that time and who had joined our team straight from school shortly before FTSE was set up, had called me over to the operations centre. The first thing I told Anthony to do was to take off all the automated price checks and controls which are in-built to detect rogue price movements. The market was moving fast, so prices were hugely volatile and moving at incredible speeds, but each trade tended to be a small increment. Usually, if a share price moves more than a certain percentage in short order, it is because someone is trying to game the system. We can hold and check a price before releasing it. But in moments of high drama we do not employ the same circuit breakers favoured by the S&P 500 in New York. Better to let the index find its own value, whatever that may be.

Trading volumes that day were a multiple of those we had experienced before, but our systems were built for high volumes and were coping well. And then the phone rang. It was the LSE's deputy chief executive, Martin Wheatley. Wheatley and I had worked together at the LSE for some years and we knew each other well. When I left to set up FTSE, he ran the gilt markets for the exchange. Wheatley was bright and ambitious and quickly rose up through the ranks encouraged by Giles Vardey, who played a key role in FTSE's creation.

Wheatley had the Bank of England on the other line. Both wanted to know my view on whether we were going to be able to sustain the index calculation given the spike in trading volumes. The alternative was to switch to an indicative measure, the kind of estimate that is used before trading opens each day. My view was simple. 'I'll keep the index going as long as you keep the market open,' I said. Wheatley was minded to keep the market open, and I agreed.

It was a huge test of the resilience of FTSE and our systems. The company was only six years old at this point. The way we designed the system, if it became overwhelmed, it would calculate the index from as many prices as it could cope with and the rest would be ignored. I'm pleased to say we never got to that point that day. The screens were red, but accurate from our point of view.

I felt much more confident about the day after the Brexit referendum. Unlike the bolt from the blue that was 9/11, there was always a chance that the British people would vote to take the UK out of the European Union after 43 years of membership. At the time, the City and global investors had convinced themselves that, although the vote would be tight, the British people would not vote to leave. That evening on the way home from the office I went to vote. Then I waited for the polling stations to close and hear the early predictions. The closing polls predicted a narrow victory for the remain vote but some were questioning this. I waited to hear the first results. It was soon clear that outside of London the rest of England wanted change.

It was probably 2am UK time when it was clear to me that we would face disruption in the market. Talking to the FTSE team in Hong Kong I could see the pound was falling fast. Earlier I had texted Cloke to check who in the operations team would be in. After two hours' sleep, I rose, headed for the train station and was in the office before 7am. It was going to be a long day.

Despite my confidence, we only just managed to open the FTSE 100 on time. The stock market in the UK starts with a market auction where all the buy and sell orders are matched off against each other. This creates the opening price for each stock. Where there are no buy or sell orders to match, the closing price from the previous day is used. Once prices become available we calculate the index. This process normally takes a few seconds and the index has automated controls in place to ensure we have prices for all constituents before it will open. That day there was so much trading activity that all stocks were taking much longer to come out of the auction.

I was standing in the operations centre as we counted down to the open of the UK market. The pound had collapsed, and we had debated where we thought the market would open. Paul Terry was in charge of the operations team that morning. He is a big unflappable guy, who sometimes doubled as a bouncer at clubs in his hometown in Essex. We thought all the indices would open sharply lower but that the FTSE 100 should recover as sterling had plummeted. Most FTSE 100 constituents were global companies whose revenues were mainly in dollars and so benefited from weaker sterling. The FTSE 250 would be sharply down as this index was a more accurate reflection of the UK economy and these companies would be most impacted by a withdrawal from the EU. Paul called out how many of the FTSE 100 stocks were open. The first 60 or so opened quickly but then it started to slow down. After two minutes we were still waiting for a handful of stocks to open. I spoke with Paul and we forced open the index with two stocks still waiting for their opening prices. We were late but we were now live.

As we expected, it was the FTSE 250 – the index for the next largest 250 listed companies and a close proxy for the UK economy – that bore the brunt of investors' fears. There were a dozen stocks not priced when we decided to go ahead distributing our opening value. It was as if the world was looking at the UK with alarm and holding its breath.

Everything we did was to make sure that investors could have a view at the earliest possible time of how bad it was. My team spent their time fielding calls from clients around the world about what the market reaction meant. The FTSE 100 fell 7 per cent in early trading to just over 5,800 points but ended the day 3.15 per cent lower at 6,138. It was sterling and the second-line stocks that suffered. Sterling plunged, falling more than 8 per cent against the dollar and 6 per cent against the euro. The FTSE 250 shed 7.2 per cent to close at 16,088 points. Europe and Wall Street also reacted badly to the Brexit decision, with the Dow plunging more than 600 points, or 3.4 per cent, to close at 17,400 points.

Indices have become the way through which triumph and tragedy are communicated. Billions of dollars follow their path. How this happened is a remarkable story that stretches over decades and embraces not just finance, but academia, politics and the media. In Chapter 3 of this book, I explain how our company FTSE International was formed in 1995 to capitalize on the increasing usage of indices in the investment industry. I describe in Chapter 4 the flurry of takeovers – and several failed attempts – that have shaped our sector today. Chapter 5 looks at how FTSE 100 grew to become the club that leading companies crossed the world to join and the rules we employ that firms often argue over. Then in Chapter 6 I explore the rapid flow of funds from active to passive investment made possible by indexation that has built industry giants such as Vanguard. Chapter 7 tells the story of global expansion and tense negotiations with rulers and policymakers in territories such as China, South Korea and Saudi Arabia that were seeking acceptance from the international investment community. And in Chapter 8 I detail the creation of FTSE4Good and its impact on companies rethinking their social and environmental responsibilities. Finally, in Chapter 9 I consider the future of financial indexation, the technological opportunity ahead as well as the competitive and regulatory threats. But first of all I have to go back to the start of FTSE in 1984 and trace the roots of a brand that took its initials from two great City of London institutions: the *Financial Times* and the London Stock Exchange.

2
Starting out

Laid out on the front page of the *Financial Times* newspaper on 14 February 1984 was the usual diet of international affairs, corporate cut-and-thrust and – perhaps the biggest surprise – a rare burst of society news.

As the new leader of the Soviet Union, Konstantin Chernenko promised a continuation of the work of his late predecessor, Yuri Andropov. News of his selection jostled for attention with the rejection by London Brick of an improved £247 million takeover offer from industrial conglomerate Hanson Trust – to which the housebuilding supplier would eventually fall. There was also the announcement that the Prince and Princess of Wales were expecting their second child in September. But it was a fourth story, halfway down the page, that had the Square Mile chattering that chilly morning.

Beginnings

'Index based on 100 top companies begins,' read the headline just above the fold. It detailed the birth of a new partnership between two great City of London institutions: the *Financial Times* (*FT*) and the London Stock Exchange (LSE).

'An index based on the minute-by-minute share price movements of 100 leading companies listed on the Stock Exchange was launched yesterday in London,' ran the first paragraph. Traders, bankers and the broader financial community could have had little idea of what this alliance would come to represent across the globe. And, on the day, most will have had no idea either of what it had taken to arrive at this point. But reading between the lines printed on the famous salmon-pink pages, it was impossible to miss the tension that was bubbling.

'The indicator is expected to be known as the FT-SE index once details have been finalised between the *Financial Times* and the Stock Exchange,' the *FT* read. The quotes from the two parties that followed mixed warm praise with a dash of defensiveness. The Stock Exchange's chief executive, Jeffery Knight, insisted: 'We are expecting that the index will be called the FT-SE index. We have been talking to the *FT* for some time. We recognise the value of having the *FT* associated with the new index.' Further down, Richard McClean, the *FT*'s deputy chief executive, said there was 'no question of the FT 30 share index disappearing'.

For such a high-profile partnership, it seemed much was still up in the air. Even stranger, this breakthrough 100-member index was not strictly new that day. It had been quietly operating for six weeks but given scant coverage by the *FT* until this point. Now the index was officially live and available to all subscribers of the Stock Exchange's electronic information system, Topic. Now, suddenly, it had a new sponsor eager to spread the word.

The SE 100 – as it started life – was the exchange's response to investors' clamour for faster, more accurate information about the performance of equities markets. It was also an index that would be continuously updated and built with booming derivatives trading in mind. More controversially, it had been put together without any knowledge or involvement of the *FT*. Since 1935 the newspaper and its antecedent had compiled the FT 30, the City's flagship stock market barometer, and promoted it assiduously in its pages.

The trouble was that a new world was dawning and the *FT* risked being left behind. Updated hourly from a basket of 30 industrial stocks, the old index could satisfy neither the demand for speed, the range of companies that traded in London, nor the subtlety required for options and futures contracts. It was a useful measure, but even its biggest fans admitted it was no sophisticated benchmark to trade against.

The influential Lex comment column declared in that day's *FT* that the new index 'answers an obvious need for a market measurement which is both comprehensive and up-to-the-minute'. But could the old and the new indices rub along together as McClean suggested? It didn't help that on the first day of trading as this great fanfare was sounded the new rivals set off in opposite directions. The SE 100 closed up 0.3 points at 1018.3 while the FT 30 fell 2.4 points to 803.

The Daily Telegraph had shed more light on the situation on 12 February. The day before the launch press conference held at the Stock Exchange Tower and presided over by the exchange chairman, Sir Nicholas Goodison, it ran a story with the headline: 'Now it will be the FT-SE index', explaining that the coming together was happening 'not before a lot of heated wrangling'. There weren't just bragging rights at stake; there were commercial opportunities, too. Because the exchange developed the 100 on its own, *The Daily Telegraph* also wrote that 'there have been many in the Exchange who have argued for retaining sole control of the new index and for collecting any revenues arising from selling it around the world'.

Anyone tuned into a *Channel 4 News* report on 13 February would be more clued in. The FT 30 was in 'severe danger of being knocked off its perch by the Stock Exchange's own new index: bigger, faster and, it seems, better', explained the young reporter Damian Green. As a Conservative politician he would later ascend to the post of First Secretary of State – de facto deputy prime minister – in Theresa May's government. Back in 1984, his report carried images of traders milling around hexagonal jobbers' pitches that covered the exchange's floor and a kind of automated flip chart that updated the FT 30 value during the day. Tellingly, there was also a shot of a computer screen featuring various market indicators that relegated the FT 30 to unfamiliar second billing.

'With the SE 100 index symbolically placed above the FT index on brokers' screens, the Financial Times wants a deal,' Green reported. 'It seems the traditional FT index could soon be replaced in public affection by a more accurate FT-SE index.'

The *FT* got the deal it wanted. In fact, as it was explained to those that attended the press conference, the exchange simply hadn't had time to update its computer systems to reflect the new name. But it was not that straightforward. A week later, *The Times* reported that the two sides 'have not yet agreed what the 100-share index should be called. Stock Exchange sources said the exchange wanted financial recognition of the benefits to the *Financial Times* from the newspaper marketing the index around the world.'

What was clear is that a bitter row was giving way to an eleventh-hour rapprochement between the two famous institutions. The *FT* was close to seeing off an emerging threat by appending its name to it. But why was the newspaper group frozen out in the first place? Why did the exchange capitulate? And what prompted the development of the FT-SE 100 even before Big Bang transformed the UK's finance industry in 1986? Hedging its bets on 27 October 1983, a Times article declared that, 'The index could be run by the Stock Exchange, the London International Financial Futures Exchange, or the *Financial Times* or all three.' As I explain in this chapter, this trio all had a hand in the creation of what soon settled down to be named the FT-SE 100.

The power of print

The *FT* is instantly familiar, as much a status symbol folded underneath a businessperson's arm as a source of scrolling news and information on a smartphone. In 1984, the year the FT-SE

100 index launched, it had reached a milestone of its own: 100 years had passed since the foundation of the first of two publications that went on to create the modern *FT.*

The *Financial News*, begun in 1884 by journalist Harry Marks, found stiff competition in the *Financial Times*, a four-page title introduced four years later by James Sheridan and Horatio Bottomley. The *FT* set its stall out as 'The friend of the honest financier, the bona fide investor, the respectable broker, the genuine director, the legitimate speculator.' It also demonstrated its marketing smarts early on. Within a few years the *FT* was being printed on salmon-pink pages, which not only helped it stand out on the newsstand, but also made it cheaper to print, as the paper was unbleached.

The pair were united in 1945 under the *FT* banner, the ownership of the Crosthwaite-Eyre family and the leadership of Brendan Bracken, a well-connected Irish businessman who had been Winston Churchill's minister of information during the Second World War. The title prospered as the voice of the City, acquired in 1957 by Pearson, originally a Yorkshire engineering firm that was fast diversifying.

By the 1980s, with Geoffrey Owen as editor, circulation passed the 250,000 mark and the *FT* was working hard to expand its reach. In 1979, the first *FT* edition to be printed outside the UK was launched in Frankfurt. The famous 'No *FT*, no comment' slogan was created in 1982 by advertising agency Ogilvy & Mather along with a largely black-and-white TV ad in which a woman carries a stack of *FT*s into an office lift to enlighten a clutch of grey businessmen.

The newspaper's physical presence in the City was just as imposing as its editorial stance could be. Until 1989, the *FT* inhabited Bracken House, a red-brick and pink-stone edifice with two classical wings sandwiched around a more industrial heart that afforded great views of St Paul's Cathedral.

As the presses rolled deep in the belly of the building each night, pedestrians on the pavement outside could easily mistake the creation of tomorrow's news with a passing underground train.

Taking the temperature of the markets

For all its association with news, the *FT* also had a long association with information and the tools required to take the temperature of what was going on in financial markets. Every day, it filled six pages with the prices of stocks, government bonds – also known as gilts – and indices. The prices it compiled might be technically the preserve of the Stock Exchange, but the indices were all its own work. There were two sources of record for the UK stock market; the Daily Official List of price quotations published by the exchange, or the more widely circulated *FT* prices pages. The *FT*'s team of backroom unionized workers, who put the prices pages together every night, also calculated a wide range of indices. These comprised chiefly the flagship FT 30 and the FT All-Share that tracked the wider market, although indices for gold, fixed interest and gilts were also calculated.

It was a profitable activity. For a long time, companies were required to list their prices in the *FT* as a matter of record and were charged for the privilege. And because they knew that readers would spend a long time poring over those tables every day, advertisers flocked to the pages, too.

Yet their compilation was far from sophisticated. Computers were coming to the City, but price collection and index calculation remained a manual affair. In the early 1980s, the *FT*'s dozen-strong prices team dealt in prices but never went onto the Stock Exchange floor themselves. The young men started the week taping sheets still warm from the dot-matrix printer onto 40 boards that by late morning were whizzing over by motorbike to the exchange half a mile away.

At the other end, the boards were handed out to the *FT*'s own price collectors, a team of 15 whose job was to roam the floor talking to jobbers, who made the market in shares. In truth, this process was ad hoc. Some boards, which carried a list of every equity by industrial category, were passed around to let those on the frontline jot down the closing prices. Alternatively, the collectors copied down what they could hear.

By the end of the week, the boards had been back and forward from Bracken House to the Stock Exchange Tower on Old Broad Street five times. By Friday, they might be torn and tatty. Once in a while, they were carried into the *FT* sporting tyre tracks when they had tumbled off the motorbike into the street in transit. When they did arrive back in the late afternoon, the call went up: 'Boards are in!'

There followed a frantic half hour as the team threw the boards across the room like frisbees in the race to compile that day's closing prices ready for putting onto the newspaper pages. These tables, or 'dupes', were passed to the printers, who copied them across again for typesetting. It was a time when the print union was all-powerful. Journalists – or their close colleagues – were not allowed anywhere near the printing process. In 1983, right through the general election period, the *FT* was off the streets because of a damaging printers' strike that cost the title millions – and some of its cachet. Until that point it had seemed indispensable at the exchange, where a free copy was a daily perk.

From the prices, the final value of the FT 30 and the All-Share could be calculated with the help of books of logarithm tables. Mistakes were not tolerated and often stopped people leaving the office, when many nights of the week they congregated in the pub. Later *FT* editions captured alterations and Wall Street closing prices.

The intra-day was done more simply. The *FT* calculated the FT 30 hourly during the day on the basis of prices it received via a stock ticker tape run by the news wire Extel. The machine had for decades spewed out strips of paper carrying stock symbols, their latest price and details of trading volumes. It also carried its own news reports as well as the Company News Service (CNS) – later Regulatory News Service (RNS) – on which companies had to keep the market informed of their latest financial performance. In the days before email and social media, the so-called 'tapes' were part of a newspaper reporter's holy trinity of sources for their own stories, along with whoever they could reach on the phone that afternoon and whoever they happened to be lunching with.

Remarkably, much of this price-gathering process was replicated by the LSE, which had its own team of collectors roaming the trading floor. Their sole job was to keep a running tally of the prices of around 1,500 traded stocks while the market was open. Any changes were inputted into the exchange's Epic (Exchange Price Information Computer) system that later fed into Topic (Teletext Online Price Information Computer), a new and improved televised share information service.

In fact, there had been three teams doing precisely the same thing not so long ago, which often threw up a wide variety of prices and rows over who was correct. This activity was largely unregulated. Extel was the main provider of newspaper-ready formatted prices. It would produce lists of tables of specific stocks for inclusion in daily and evening newspapers around the country. In the late 1970s, it merged collection with the exchange's Daily Official List and Epic was later developed in 1978 to smooth out deficiencies. The *FT* remained apart, probably because the print union wouldn't support a combination that would have seen jobs lost.

Although there was no contractual relationship between the two, the *FT* supplied the exchange with its latest FT 30 calculation by phone to the exchange's price team five times a day, so that traders could see whether the market was up or down. It was the only index to change during the trading day. A value first appeared a little after 10am – more than half an hour after the market opened at 9.30am and therefore missing what was often the busiest period of daily trade. It was updated a further four times, ending with the 3pm index value which preceded the then-official market close of 3.30pm.

The price teams took pride in their work but these were cheerfully relaxed times. Market users knew that indices were frequently wrong and it was not hard to game the system. On one occasion, an exchange man called up the *FT* to chase that morning's FT 30 value.

'It's unchanged,' mumbled a voice at the end of the line.

'Are you f★★★ing joking? Everything's up here,' the man from the exchange replied.

It transpired that the person responsible for calculating the FT 30 that day had spent the morning at the dentist. He caught up with events by the time the market closed.

Enter the FT 30

The FT 30 began life on 1 July 1935, the brainchild of two journalists who, according to the future *FT* editor Richard Lambert writing on the index's 50th anniversary in 1985, 'were to be seen talking earnestly together in the old *Financial News* building on London's Bishopsgate and in nearby pubs'.

They were Maurice Green, the newspaper's editor, and Richard 'Otto' Clarke, then his chief leader writer who would go on to be knighted for a distinguished career in the civil service.

There was much to discuss at that time. The UK was bouncing back from an economic slump which in the years following 1929 had seen coal production drop by a fifth. There had been a flurry of flotations as firms in new industries such as rayon and electricals had flourished since the First World War and now they sought capital to expand. Green and Clarke wondered if there was a modern way to demonstrate the health of British industry and track the economic cycle as well as investors' fluctuating moods.

Explaining the creation of the 30 Share Index in the pages of *Financial News* in 1935, Clarke noted that indices had not been used to the same extent as the USA, 'but even in this country, where exact knowledge is not sought with such religious zeal, it is definitely useful for the operator, both professional and amateur, to have a simple daily indicator of the way in which the market is moving.' He went on to detail its construction, which was essentially the revision of an index that *Financial News* began supplying in early 1930. The new product would concentrate on the 30 most actively traded shares, with a focus on the manufacturing and mining sectors.

Clarke went on: 'For obvious practical reasons, companies which make a habit of distributing capital bonuses are not included. Nor are companies whose management is unreliable, and whose prospects (within their own industrial group) are uncertain.' The FN 30 Share Index became the FT 30 Share Index in January 1947 following the merger of the two newspapers.

The FT 30 told a tale of its times. When it was first compiled, textile companies were well represented, long before that industry went into sharp decline. Oil shares did not arrive in the index until 1977, and National Westminster Bank became the first financial services entry in 1984. Only two companies – the sugar-refining business Tate & Lyle and engineering firm GKN – remain since inception. Today, the FT 30 – which has also been known as the FT Ordinary Index – is the oldest continuous index compiled in the UK and one of the oldest in the world. But longevity is no substitute for versatility. Even now, it is a subjective basket of stocks. When a vacancy emerges *FT* editors choose the replacement.

Back in 1984, the FT 30 was already showing its age. Its constituents were not changed unless a company was taken over or failed. It was a geometrically priced index, which meant the 30 prices were multiplied together and the 30th root of the product became the index value. Therefore, each member had equal weighting and no account was taken of the size of the individual stocks. A collapsing stock such as the jet engine maker Rolls-Royce had been in 1971 could badly distort the index, even though it was far from being the basket's largest constituent. There was clearly room for improvement.

The art of the actuary

To better understand the major role that indices played in 20th-century investment decisions, it is worth exploring the development of the actuarial profession. Alongside the *FT*'s price collectors and calculators operated a different class of professional number cruncher. For the actuaries that oversaw the indices compilation, it was a matter of pride ensuring these indicators remained beyond reproach. Their administration was managed on a virtually voluntary basis by figures such as John Brumwell, an immensely dedicated index fund portfolio manager who served on the investment committee which oversaw the governance of the indices. He worked at the Prudential but spent most of his time as index auditor tinkering with the make-up of the indices to account for various share adjustments such as scrip issues – the creation of new shares which are issued free of charge to existing shareholders - mergers, takeovers, and the promotions and relegations.

Brumwell's involvement went back years, but it was his forebears that established the template for these calculations even further back in time. When they emerged in the late 17th century, their discipline used mathematics and statistics to measure the probability of future events and, in particular, their financial impact. Early analysis of age-at-death statistics allowed the British government to sell appropriately priced life insurance.

Similar methods were later applied in non-life and commercial settings, such as farmers insuring against crop failure. By the early 20th century, insurance companies had grown strongly on this widespread appetite to offset risk. Their receipts – from which policyholders would be paid out – had to be invested to generate a return. Consequently, insurance companies were big asset holders with portfolios that consisted of government stock issued to fund state works, property mortgages and company debentures, a form of debt. Company ownership was limited to railway or telegraph companies that tapped investors for building projects, but the idea of selling equities rose to prominence during the industrial expansion of the 1920s.

One of the first research papers to cover the subject of equity investment was by C. M. Douglas, an assistant actuary at the Scottish Life Assurance Company in Edinburgh. Concerned by asset depreciation in the first two decades of the century – largely caused by the onset of the First World War – he wrote in 'The Statistical Groundwork of Investment Policy' that: 'If we are to avoid a recurrence in the future, an enquiry into the foundations of our investment policy will prove to be valuable.' The paper was presented on 4 March 1929 to the Faculty of Actuaries, the body set up to represent the profession in Scotland.

The USA was ahead of the curve, as the *Financial News*'s Otto Clarke noted. In 1882, a journalist called Charles Dow went into business with a statistician named Edward Jones, taking space in a Wall Street basement. They published financial pamphlets that were known as 'flimsies' by the traders on the New York Stock Exchange who received them. What followed was a publication called the *Customers' Afternoon Letter*: a two-page summary of the latest financial news. As well as news reports, there were the latest stock prices, and, to aid understanding of the current state of markets, from 1884 an indicator was published based on the average price of a few major stocks in shipping and railroads. In 1896, Dow created a new index, purely to track industrial stocks, which began with 12 firms including the biggest oil, sugar, tobacco and electricity providers of the day. The Dow Jones Industrial Average was published in what had become *The Wall Street Journal* in 1889. It was expanded to 30 stocks in 1928 as the US economy boomed.

Back in the UK, Douglas's work led to the creation of a joint committee by the Faculty of Actuaries and the Institute of Actuaries, the organization's counterpart in England and Wales. The committee's mission was to investigate the question of investment research, and it quickly led to the creation of a new index. The Actuaries' Investment Index of prices and average yields of stocks and shares began with a base date of 31 December 1928. Its aim was to assess markets against the economic cycle and research investments for its members, who paid a subscription fee.

The decision had been taken to compile the index as an unweighted geometric mean of the price relatives – which at that time the experts said was fine as long as markets were not overly volatile. Unfortunately the Wall Street Crash followed in November 1929, international currencies swung sharply and some governments struggled to service their debt, 'and this almost certainly caused early dropping of the foreign bonds indices in 1935', as Richard Pain, chairman of the actuaries Investment Committee, wrote years later. Much else changed, including the indices initiative moving to London in the late 1930s where the lead for their monthly calculation done by hand using logarithms and manual calculators was for many years taken by Bert Haycocks, head of the Actuarial Tuition Service, who co-opted students to the task.

The 1960s brought expansion into new sectors, and the actuaries – still operating their index through two trade bodies and calculating values monthly – struggled to keep up with investor demand. Again, the USA led the way. In 1957, Standard & Poor's had introduced the S&P 500, a huge basket of 500 corporations that attempted to reflect the health of the US economy as a whole, not just a few choice sectors. It does so to this day. Rather than each member having equal weighting, each stock's importance could be adjusted as the economy altered. S&P had been building up to this point. In 1923, Standard Statistics began its first stock market indicator that featured 233 stocks, updated weekly, as it started rating mortgage debt. This was revolutionary because it was the first index to be cap-weighted. Within three years, a smaller index that was updated daily had been introduced. Standard's 1941 merger with Poor's Publishing – which compiled financial information on railroad companies – increased its coverage.

In a paper submitted to the Institute of Actuaries on 23 March 1964 – entitled 'The Design, Application and Future Development of the Financial Times-Actuaries Index' – Haycocks and Jack Plymen, a thoughtful actuary at City stockbroker W. Greenwell & Co. who had become a prime mover at the institute, explained how technology had impacted their work: 'The limitations, formerly imposed by manual calculation, on the size, the scope of the averaging procedures and the weighting methods, and the frequency of computation are no longer important.'

A joint project

The index process was due for a complete recasting, with daily calculation now required by investors and computers able to lend a hand. But the task of collecting prices for a large index on a daily basis was beyond the resource of the Actuarial Tuition Service staff. The Institute of Actuaries also had to review how it distributed its results. By post was good enough for its monthly service, but not daily. What it needed was a newspaper partner which could help with staffing and distribution. The *FT* was ideal.

'It was fortunate that at the same time as the Investment Research Committee was considering this problem the statistical staff of the *Financial Times* were also contemplating an extension of their daily index facilities,' Haycocks and Plymen wrote.

> The logical development was for the Actuarial organizations and the leading financial newspaper to enter into a joint index project, the design and averaging methods, etc., being the responsibility of the actuaries with the newspaper staff doing all the pricing, collecting the statistics and using the computer facilities of the National Cash Register Company. The selection of constituents and groups was a joint undertaking of the actuaries and the *Financial Times* statistical staff.

Their collaboration created the FT–Actuaries Share Indices that would survey the London market in its broadest sense. It was a convenient marriage, but some say an uneasy one. The actuaries, led by Brumwell, wanted an index to cover the whole market; the *FT* welcomed their expertise but had its flagship FT 30 to protect. More than two decades before the 100 index made its debut, here was another clash over what should be measured and by whom.

Despite beginning a new index together on 10 April 1962, it was not published in the *FT* initially. Apparently, some of the company's executives did not think indices sold newspapers. A young actuarial student, Peter Jones – more on him later – recalls going into Bracken House once a week to copy out the relevant numbers from the *FT*'s file so the calculations could be made using log tables. Investor demand eventually persuaded the *FT* to find column space. Starting on 26 November 1962, the FT-Actuaries Share Indices were published in the *FT* every day for the next 30 years and became best known for the FT All-Share. For some investment analysts, this is the moment the FT 30 began to lose its status as the top benchmark for measuring investor performance. But, once bedded down, the two sides enjoyed an enduring relationship. It is also worth pointing out how much of the modern company classification system can be traced back to this time. As Brumwell wrote in a paper with his colleague Eric Short in 1973, a subcommittee of the Faculty of Actuaries and the Institute of Actuaries 'undertook the mammoth task of classifying all quoted companies on what was then the LSE, publishing their findings at the end of 1969'.

Choosing options

The Niagara Falls lies less than a two-hour drive from Toronto around the edge of Lake Ontario, making it an ideal day-trip destination for tourists. In September 1983, three UK businessmen attending a conference on traded options in the city found they had Friday free before flying back to London, UK.

They needn't have bothered going to visit the famous trio of waterfalls, the longest of which tumbles noisily 2,600 feet into the river below. The rain was so heavy and visibility so poor that day they could barely see a thing. At least, they had plenty to talk about to pass the time.

In conversation were Dan Sheridan, head of the Stock Exchange's markets division, Mick Newman, the exchange's director of information technology, and the expedition's leader, David Steen of the jobbing firm Pinchin Denny, who was also chairman of the exchange's options committee. While Steen dozed, Sheridan and Newman discussed a radical plan: to create and run the exchange's first index in its 182-year history.

The trip was one of many fact-finding missions that Stock Exchange executives conducted in those years. Almost always flying first class, they jetted around the world to explore emerging technology and trading techniques to bring back the best ideas to London. In Toronto, the three wanted to understand the practical challenges involved in developing a successful traded options market.

Options fall into two categories: put and call. They give the holder the right – but not the obligation – to buy (call) or sell (put) a fixed parcel of shares at a set price within a set time frame. Rather than trading the actual shares, traders seek to make money on that right before it expires and typically for a fraction of the outlay. Options are one class of derivative – in other words, value derived from an asset class but not actually the asset class itself – that can be used as an insurance policy taken out against other investment decisions.

An options market had existed in London for many years. Indeed, they were banned for a time in the 19th century for fear they could trigger financial collapse if market participants did not honour their trades. These so-called traditional options did not operate a secondary market. The only person the contract could be sold back to was the principal who issued it in the first place.

For the modern iteration of traded options that were far easier to buy and sell, interested parties had to visit Chicago. The Chicago Board Options Exchange (CBOE) was founded in 1973 by the Chicago Board of Trade as the first marketplace for trading listed options. Its index, the CBOE 100 of leading US stocks, was the most popular stock option trading product in the world. Newman had visited a few years earlier to get some insights into the exchange's computer systems. It might have been making early advances with electronic trading, but Newman's abiding memory is of a trading floor like a bear pit. Traders handed in their guns before each trading day and there were fines for every punch thrown. Everyone on the floor wore colourful nylon jackets. The colours denoted who they worked for, but it was the nylon that was more important. The silky sheen meant it was easier to slide by one another in the crush.

The LSE had danced around the subject of options during the 1970s. It was interested – but not to the extent that it would operate a market open to non-members, which many thought would be crucial to its success. Amsterdam's European Options Exchange stole a march on London, opening in early 1977. Fearful that cash equities would also travel across the North Sea, the London Traded Options Market (LTOM) was launched defensively a year later with little fanfare. Since then, business had been slow. The exchange had similarly fumbled the arrival of futures, another derivative. In September 1982, the London International Financial Futures and Options Exchange (LIFFE) had opened its doors with much razzmatazz. Council members knew they could not keep ceding new innovations to rivals.

To get major investment funds interested in its traded options, Steen's trio realized they needed to take a leaf out of CBOE's book and create a contract based around an index, not just a handful of individual stocks. The conclusion they had come to was that that meant creating a new index, a significant development in the exchange's long history.

Toffs and tykes

London stock trading was in evidence as soon as there were assets to trade in the late 17th century. Traders met informally in coffee houses such as Jonathan's, in Change Alley, from where the entrepreneurial John Castaing began issuing a detailed list of market prices called 'The Course of the Exchange and other things' in 1698. From there, it tried various venues including the Royal Exchange beside the Bank of England, but it was not until 1801 that the club became an exchange, effectively turning an open market into a closed one, with subscription fees for members and rules to protect them.

The beginning of the modern era can be traced to 1972, when Queen Elizabeth II opened the 26-floor Stock Exchange Tower at the heart of the City on Old Broad Street on 8 November that year. Just up the street from the Bank of England, here was a new emblem of London's financial might, the Stock Exchange of Great Britain and Ireland. In reality, it was a domestic institution with little international pull. Its world would remain a closed shop for many years to come, protecting members' interests before any desire to embrace modernity. The exchange had a decision-making council made up of representatives of member firms and then a series of committees also chaired by members such as David Steen. In Chapter 3 I discuss the exchange's resistance to change that eventually led to the Big Bang deregulation I was closely involved in.

It was no stereotype to say that in those days there were two types of men that populated the exchange. The toffs had been educated at Eton or Harrow and pitched up in the City wearing top hats. The tykes were lower class, the East End barrow boys, wearing perhaps bowler hats, with an umbrella or copy of the *FT* stuffed under their arm. They were more likely to start out as 'blue buttons', the nickname for unauthorized clerks marked out as such by what they wore on their lapels. They were engaged in much running around for the dealers who were stock exchange members, such as enquiring about stock prices at one of many jobbers' pitches that filled the trading floor.

Both of these tribes had new technology to contend with. In the same year as the tower was officially opened, the exchange introduced the Market Price Display Service (MPDS) with 18 pages of market prices and initially two pages of company news summaries that could be flicked through on a black-and-white TV monitor. It was revolutionary: for many years, floor traders worked off instinct or remembered prices in their heads. The mainframe computer that powered the service was a Ferranti Argus that took up an entire basement floor.

The tower's opening followed on smartly from the closure of regional stock exchanges in Manchester, Liverpool and beyond, once used to raise funds for local railways and utilities. The idea was that London would offer improved technical support for regional clients left with nowhere to trade. That was where Newman's team came in.

The magic number 100

Newman and Sheridan returned from Toronto eager to see if a new index could be created. A small team was set to work at limited cost. Newman estimates that six people developed the index in just eight weeks that autumn and embedded it into the Epic computer system.

Why not just base an options contract on the FT 30, the best-known index at the time? It was quickly deemed to track too small a spread of companies to reflect the broader market. Sure, the *FT* gathered prices but it knew nothing about real-time information and nor was it subject to the same regulation as the exchange, which was monitored by the Bank of England. Similarly, the FT All-Share, which tracked around 700 stocks and was calculated daily, was too broad to mount regular updates, and besides, many of those didn't even trade every day. A new index was an opportunity to drag the exchange into the modern world. Speed was essential. That meant creating an indicator that could be worked out minute by minute – and dramatically improving traders' computer interface.

Initially, the work was kept below the radar, with the *FT* not informed of the exchange's plans. There was nothing sinister about that. The index was not deemed as likely to be some great commercial breakthrough, simply one of a number of work streams the technology department had under way. It wasn't worth publicizing if it was not going to go anywhere. Nonetheless, the newspaper that a generation earlier had been the saviour of the actuaries when they faced being overwhelmed by new technological demands now faced an uncertain future as London's index leader.

Newman's team had to design a system because there was nothing that any of the IT suppliers at that time did that met their requirements. But they were used to doing everything for themselves. When the price display terminal Topic was launched in 1979, Newman even had to check with Mars that the exchange could use the same name as one of its chocolate bars, advertised with the slogan 'A Hazelnut in Every Bite'.

On the Topic system, users had to tap through screen after screen to get a single stock price. Newman thought he could adapt it to create a display page that would show many prices at once. On this Teletext-like system, there was room to support 80 stock prices on one screen together with the index value itself. Later on, they thought they could squeeze 100 stocks onto the page. Not only would that exactly mirror the CBOE 100, it was a more attractive round number.

This page used the innovation of colour to flash up instant changes to individual stocks using red or green to show the trends on the day. This use of colour was at that time unprecedented around the world on a trading floors where green monochrome was ubiquitous.

Better data was also needed to create a new index. The exchange's price collection team was asked to prioritize the prices of 80 or 100 leading stocks to ensure that an index running in real time would be valid. Clearly, if any prices got delayed before inputting, then the index value would not be credible. A computer program ran every minute, calculating a value based on applying a formula to the latest 100 prices.

Progress was brisk, but trouble was brewing. Many at the exchange were fixated on the impending Big Bang which had just been approved by government and didn't welcome another, indulgent, distraction. Some of the council members were horrified when they discovered what Newman's team was doing. 'We mustn't do anything to upset the *FT*,' one told Newman. 'We do joint art exhibitions with them.'

Brighter futures

As soon as the London International Financial Futures and Options Exchange (LIFFE) threw open its doors on 30 September 1982, it was clear this new market was everything the Stock Exchange was not. Sure, it had an establishment air, with Gordon Richardson, the Governor of the Bank of England, cutting a white ribbon at a brief opening ceremony. But as the loud chatter of trading began amid the crush of orange-, red- and blue-jacketed young men it felt as if the City of London had undergone an exciting, full-colour upgrade compared to the drab, gentlemanly greyness of the exchange's business carried on a few hundred yards away in the Stock Exchange Tower.

LIFFE was bright, noisy, international, risky – even dangerous, some thought. It met the demand for new, exotic financial instruments that had been growing strongly overseas. It welcomed the world to London. It did not discriminate between the businesses that were kept functionally separate by the old Stock Exchange rules. In this new world, those members who had always followed a rigid formula of trading commissions were invited to negotiate their cut.

LIFFE had also set up shop in the Royal Exchange, an ornate trading place looking out at right angles to the Bank of England on the Square Mile's busiest interchange. The location was steeped in history because it was where London's original securities market had been sited some 300 years earlier. No wonder the *London Evening Standard*'s press boards declared 'New Liffe at Royal Exchange' as the capital's newspaper went on sale that afternoon. Its relaxed yet competitive outlook would point the way forward for Big Bang four years later.

Futures trading had an estimable past, but in London it had been limited to the London Metal Exchange and a handful of other commodities. Unlike options, a futures contract requires a buyer to purchase shares or another asset class at a specific future date unless their position has been closed before the contract expiry. For a history lesson, it is best to turn once again to Chicago, the mecca for derivatives.

Until the 1970s, futures trading was concerned almost exclusively with commodities – such as grain, sugar, pork bellies and metals, specifically the buying and selling of contracts for the future delivery of these goods. The actions of US president Richard Nixon in 1971 changed all that. Under pressure to fund the ongoing Vietnam War, he ordered the dismantling of the gold standard, the Bretton Woods system of fixed exchange rates that pegged all other currencies to the US dollar via the gold price. Suddenly, exchange rates fluctuated, risk entered the market, hedging to protect against adverse price movements was required by investors – and there was money to be made.

Leo Melamed, the chairman of the Chicago Mercantile Exchange, saw immediately the potential in free-floating currencies and announced the setting up of the International Monetary Market, a new exchange where contracts for major world currencies could be traded against the US dollar.

The rise of a new index

It took years for the City of London to sit up and take notice of this burgeoning new market. And then, it was the International

Commodities Clearing House that threw down the gauntlet. This body fulfilled all of London's commodities futures contracts. Freshly passed into the hands of a consortium of banks, it was touting for more business. Who could it entice to set up a similar market for financial futures? The man who answered the call was John Barkshire, an impeccably well-connected financier who ran his own business, Mercantile House. In spring 1980, he gathered together a working party of bankers, jobbers, brokers and traders to see if London could forge a future for futures.

They were hugely encouraged by one of the early acts of the new Thatcher government the previous October. For holiday-makers, the surprise abolition of exchange controls meant there were no longer limits on how much foreign money they could pack in their suitcase, but for global financiers it meant a far bigger opportunity.

The Stock Exchange might have been a partner in any new venture, or possibly housed it in the Stock Exchange Tower. But because of their experience with traded options, council members doubted that futures would take off either – and once again they were not prepared to let non-members take part. That left Barkshire and colleagues to convince the doubtful Bank of England this was a good idea on their own. With reassurances that futures were not overly risky if policed properly, LIFFE won support to launch with two contracts – a three-month euro-dollar and sterling. Barkshire was the market's first chairman.

It was a triumphant, colourful opening, but in less than a year LIFFE's lustre was fading. The market had to devise new products to excite its existing traders and bring in new ones. LIFFE's bosses alighted on stock index futures – contracts based on which way traders thought the market would go next – which were flying in the USA. All they had to do was figure out which index to use. Jack Wigglesworth was one of the seven secondees that set up LIFFE. He asked a colleague at his firm, the stockbroker Greenwells, to assess the options.

I should explain the important role Greenwells played in City life back then. Pip Greenwell, the Winchester public school-educated senior partner was an old-school City gent whose family firm had been set up in 1868. The people he employed were encouraged to think laterally and problem solve. Broking was just the start of it. One of his team was Gordon Pepper, who virtually invented the role of City economist by publishing research on government bonds that was required reading and readily criticized the function of the Bank of England. Jack Plymen, who had worked on the FT-Actuaries Index, was another notable Greenwells alumnus.

So, too, was Peter Jones, the young actuary who had jotted down numbers in the *FT*'s office two decades earlier. Jones was one of 12 actuaries at Greenwells when LIFFE was being established. His verdict was contained in a paper submitted to the Institute of Actuaries: 'All other things being equal, we should opt for the FT-Actuaries All-Share Index. It is clearly the "correct" portfolio hedge. But it is less well known than the FT 30 and liquidity is an essential ingredient of a successful contract.'

Once again, the two leading indices fell short, so Wigglesworth asked Jones to design something new. One sunny afternoon in August 1983 at Greenwells' office in Bow Bells House in the City of London, he tested an index of 80, 100 and 120 stocks to find the best correlation against the All-Share. One hundred was the stand-out solution for a basket of stocks: not so many they could not be tracked but accounting for 70 per cent of reported trades so as to replicate the market as a whole. Despite having gone to the trouble of setting up its own market, LIFFE was a not-for-profit organization that never had the aspirations or resource to create and run its own index. For that it needed the help of its older cousin down the road: the Stock Exchange, which had a ready supply of price information. Another Greenwells partner, Richard Lawson, was deputy chairman of the exchange and Jones took the idea to him.

Meanwhile, LIFFE knew it needed to apply some academic rigour to its plan. Jones commissioned two faculty members from London Business School (LBS), Elroy Dimson and Paul Marsh, to firstly assess the feasibility of using the FT 30 as the basis for trading index derivatives, and secondly to advise on construction of the proposed 100-company index. The pair taught classes on investment at LBS and were well known to Greenwells.

Dimson and Marsh assessed alternative designs for the new index including the number of constituents, their weightings and the frequency of rebalancing. They gave the 100-company model a clean bill of health, writing: 'We believe that there will be few problems in using a contract based on this index for hedging fluctuations in the UK equity market.'

The pair also constructed a back history of the 100 index to see how it would have behaved over the six prior years. For traders thinking of taking the plunge with these new futures contracts, it was vital intelligence.

The switch-on

Few returning to work in the City of London on 3 January 1984 could have known it would be a year when new technology came to the fore, whether that was a man flying over the Olympic Stadium in Los Angeles wearing a rocket pack or the first Apple Mac computer appearing in shops. It would be nice to think the handful of executives who convened in the Stock Exchange Tower that morning hoped their new innovation would capture the spirit of the age. In reality, the event to mark the switch-on of the SE 100 after several months' preparation was notable for its brevity. The five-minute gathering lasted just long enough for some or all of the exchange – chairman Sir Nicholas Goodison, Mick Newman, his boss George Hayter,

Dan Sheridan, David Steen and perhaps Peter Jones – to check the computer program was functioning properly and breathe easy when the index began edging upwards.

Purists in the options market, including Steen, were in favour of starting the index with a value of 100, just as Chicago's index had. However, so the daily movements would create more interest among traders it was agreed that the SE 100 would begin life at 1,000 points. Only one of the 100 largest companies by market value was excluded: BL, the holding company for the faltering car producer British Leyland, on account of being 99.7 per cent owned by the government.

Somewhere along the way, efforts to create an index to serve the options and futures markets had united. Precisely how is lost in the mists of time. Both projects might even have operated in parallel for a while, given that the exchange employed 3,500 staff at this time and much of their work was siloed by committee until it percolated up to council level. But all parties do agree on two details about that January day: the *FT* was nowhere to be seen – and senior figures at the newspaper were livid about it.

From rivals to collaborators

David Palmer, the *FT*'s general manager, was the first executive to get wind that a rival index was being launched. A formal announcement was made by the Stock Exchange council on 17 November 1983, by which time a steering committee, including Peter Jones, had also been set up. In the following day's *Times*, the writing was on the wall.

'The move was initially designed to meet the needs of the London International Financial Futures Exchange and the Stock Exchange's traded options market,' a news-in-brief item read. 'But the FT 30 share index has long been considered unrepresentative of the market's price movements, so the new index could quickly replace it. The *Financial Times* had no comment to make last night.'

Richard Lambert, who would go on to edit the *FT* from 1991, was apoplectic. That summer of 1983 Lambert had just returned from 18 months spent in the *FT*'s New York bureau. On visits to the Chicago exchanges he understood the potential impact of futures trading and how the role of indices was becoming more important. What enraged Lambert even more was that the Stock Exchange had brought in the Institute and Faculty of Actuaries to validate the SE 100. They had worked closely with the *FT* on its indices since 1962 and not breathed a word of the new project. Lambert, at that time deputy editor, checked to see whether the actuaries could get involved under the terms of their long-standing agreement with the newspaper. He unearthed a letter written in 1963 by A. W. Shillady, the boss of the *FT* share price department and creator of the All-Share, to discover that their arrangement was completely informal.

It was too late to stop the SE 100, but over several frantic weeks the *FT* tried everything from lobbying to threats to get involved in the new venture. It pledged to run the FT 30 in real time and in direct competition to the SE 100, even though it was well aware of the shortcomings of its index and that the *FT* had no way of collecting share price data with the frequency that that would require. At a string of meetings with anyone that would listen, Lambert attempted to hammer home the *FT*'s importance for the credibility of any index because of its long track record. What gained traction in the press was a story that the *FT* had been approached by one of the Chicago exchanges to trade a futures contract based on the FT 30, but this seems to have been an elaborate bluff.

It was clear to the *FT* that the exchange and its partners were deadly serious. That January, a notice on pale-green paper and with no mention of the FT 30 was circulated to interested parties. Under the Stock Exchange crest featuring the motto 'Dictum meum pactum' (My word is my bond), it explained the launch in a series of questions and answers.

The SE 100 went down well. Traders liked the fact that market sentiment had been distilled into a single indicator so they didn't have to buy and sell off instinct. And they loved the fact they had a screen that displayed 100 prices at once. But, behind the scenes, tensions remained.

An internal note written by the LIFFE chief executive Michael Jenkins in November 1983 set out his concerns should a coming together not be engineered. It expressed his preference that the index carry an 'FT' prefix.

'There is a close association between the *FT* and Stock Exchange indices,' Jenkins wrote. 'It will be easier to market an index which retains that association. Put in another way it may be difficult to explain convincingly why the Stock Exchange has not followed precedent and involved the *FT*. Since the *FT* is likely to be hostile to a Stock Exchange 100 index, it may not be above impugning lack of objectivity to the new index.'

He added: 'The *FT* will be very upset if they are not involved. I do not believe that it is in the Stock Exchange's interests or in LIFFE's to fall out with the *FT*. They have been particularly supportive of LIFFE and we need that support to continue.'

Many in the exchange disagreed with this view, but it seems that the chairman, Nicholas Goodison, saw the upside of collaboration even though the *FT* had contributed nothing to the SE 100's development. He was fully supportive of the index launch but summoned Sheridan and Newman to his office to see if they might find a way of working with the *FT*. In the end, after much briefing and counter briefing, Frank Barlow, the *FT*'s chief executive, a no-nonsense Lancastrian and a tough negotiator, came to an arrangement with Goodison: they would publish and support the 100 index, but only if it changed its name. Even though it had no stake in the venture, Barlow was able to repel efforts to call it the Stock Exchange FT Index, or SEFT. Only putting the *FT* name first would do. Those conversations marked the beginnings of a brand that would eventually resonate the world over.

Following January's low-key launch and February's confusing press conference, FT-SE's effective birth was 3 May 1984 when both the first options and futures contracts based on the index were first offered for sale. Sir Nicholas Goodison had a busy morning, launching index options at the exchange before racing over to the LIFFE floor in the Royal Exchange where efforts to say a few words using a megaphone were comprehensively drowned out by rowdy traders. The media was sceptical about the fuss.

'It is hard to escape the conclusion that the launch of these contracts and of the FT-SE 100 today owes more to the need of the Stock Exchange to refurbish its image and of LIFFE to revive its fortunes than to providing new instruments of financial and economy value,' Kenneth Fleet wrote in that day's *Times*. 'Imitating the fecund inventiveness of the American commodity markets does not necessarily serve the needs of London nationally or internationally.'

The FT-SE 100 as a derivatives tool first and foremost might have gone over the head of the man and woman on the street. But its creators had not reckoned with the speed with which its make-up and responsiveness turned it into a widely quoted symbol of market confidence. In no time at all, it assumed leadership from the FT 30, which did not disappear – as Richard McClean had vowed – but became little more than a curiosity.

A new world

One of the biggest events in the life of the nascent FT-SE 100 had been set in train long before its birth was decided upon. On 19 July 1982, the government announced plans to sell just over half of its stake in British Telecommunications (BT). This was not exactly a surprise. Margaret Thatcher had been swept into Downing Street in 1979 promising greater competition and deregulation for British industry and ultimately that meant privatization. In readiness, British Telecom was split from its parent company, the Post Office, in 1981.

But the decision to sell shares in the company was seismic nonetheless. The issue was more than three times oversubscribed. The government was keen on establishing a model of wide ownership for such a national asset, so two-fifths of the 3 million shares on offer were allocated to 2.1 million members of the public. Many of them had never owned a share in their lives.

Much hung on its success. The Thatcher government was not just selling shares in Britain's phone company, it was selling the dream of share ownership and the model of privatization that others had dismissed.

Great excitement surrounded the first day of trading for BT shares, on 3 December 1984 – and even more so when the stock rose. Better still, BT was given special dispensation for direct entry into the FT-SE 100. It was immediately the largest stock, accounting for 8 per cent of the index.

Privatization became a hallmark of Thatcher's premiership. Before she was ushered from office in 1990, dozens of companies were transferred from the state to the public markets, supplying water, energy, coal and transportation to the nation. These giant share sales powered the go-go 1980s, on the back of which the FT-SE 100 grew famous.

Two final points. On the day of the *FT*'s front-page announcement of 14 February 1984, the 'Lex' column informally christened the new index as 'footsy to its friends'. It is an urban myth that the name was chosen by Martin Taylor, who would go on to become chief executive of Courtaulds Textiles, Barclays Bank and an external member of the Bank of England's Financial Policy Committee. He stayed in touch with 'Lex' writers but had actually left the *FT* – and editing the 'Lex' column – for Courtaulds in 1982.

And while the *FT* may have muscled its way into the SE 100, it did not want to be caught out again. Soon afterwards, and under Lambert's guidance, it created an index of world stocks in 1987 – of which more in Chapter 7. Pointedly, the Stock Exchange was not involved. The creation of the FT-SE 100 was a pivotal moment for the Square Mile – but the story of indexation still had a long way to run.

3
Coming together

St Alphage House had loomed over the Square Mile in one direction and the Barbican Estate in the other ever since it had been built during the 1960s redevelopment of London Wall. The unwelcome addition to the capital's skyline was named after Saint Alphege, a hermit monk who rose to become Bishop of Winchester, and his eponymous church ruins that stood before the 18-storey tower block.

When I began working there in the spring of 1996, the property's Brutalist concrete and steel was beginning to show its age. I didn't care – and nor did I read much into Alphege's story of triumph despite humble beginnings. After a decade working at the Stock Exchange, this dilapidated base just along the road from *The Daily Telegraph* City office and Salters' Hall – home of the Worshipful Company of Salters - was exactly what I had campaigned for.

St Alphage House was the first home of FTSE, or more correctly FT-SE International, the company that had been set up to create a global indices powerhouse from the tentative joint venture hashed out in 1984. Or at least that was the lofty idea I had in mind as discussions between the exchange and the *FT* waxed and waned for months. The venture I had been appointed to run had to move out of the Stock Exchange Tower half a mile away on Old Broad Street to show independence from both parties. The question was where to go.

The exchange had occupied St Alphage House for many years, with a long-term lease, and, understandably, no one was willing to rent this outdated and unattractive office space.

It used to house banks of typists who kept a record of every stock trade completed. More recently, it had been home to Taurus, the exchange's doomed IT project, of which more later. Now it was lying empty.

On first inspection, I was not surprised. The kindest thing I could say is that it was functional but hardly welcoming. We were given the podium floor, a vast open space upstairs from where the surly security guard sat. Gaining entry was like going into a bank vault because the door was small, heavy and bolted. Once inside, there were stained carpet tiles and trailing wires that constituted a health-and-safety hazard. Staff snagged their clothes on the edges of the second-hand furniture.

The walls were dark and depressing. The heating was poor and there was no ventilation to speak of. Because we had glass on most sides we were either sweltering or shivering depending on the season. Even worse, because our windows looked out onto an elevated walkway designed to separate pedestrians from traffic at street level, anyone could stare in at what we were doing. That included bankers from neighbouring Lazard who could often be spotted making their way to the nearby Podium pub. Despite all its drawbacks, St Alphage House became a decent base. For less than £50,000 we fitted out the place and in time installed computer servers at the back of the building to calculate end-of-day stock prices.

On that first morning, I surveyed the room. There were nine members of staff, most from the exchange and one sent by the *FT*. Anthony Cloke, the youngest member of the team who had joined us a few years earlier on a youth training scheme but who was fast becoming indispensable and an expert on UK indices, piped up: 'So what's the strategy, Mark?' Immediately I shot back: 'Global domination!' There were some smiles, but I could tell no one was convinced. To be honest, neither was I, despite my usually unfailing optimism. Growing an international business from here could not have been harder to imagine. Our shareholders' expectations were not particularly high, either. But whatever our surroundings, I knew the opportunity was large.

To spread the word about FT-SE International we launched a quarterly newsletter to trumpet developments. The first edition of *Taking Stock* from winter 1995 bore the headline 'New company now operational' over a picture of my youthful team and both shareholder logos. It wasn't all youth; we had experience, too. I was gratified that John Brumwell, the veteran Prudential actuary who had overseen the domestic indices for years, joined us as company secretary. It gave us a sense of continuity as we headed into the new world.

That edition of *Taking Stock* was prescient, too. In reference to changes being made to the listing classification of brewers, which tended to make most of their money from operating pubs and restaurants, one headline on page two ran: 'Change is brewing.' It certainly was. My plan was to commercialize the handful of indices we had been granted by the exchange and the *FT* and then replicate the model in market after market overseas.

Global domination had never been part of the original business plan. I had argued that the indices and services required by investors in the UK were largely the same as those required by investors in the rest of the world. With the backing of our two parents, we should aim to be the leader in the UK, providing the market with the best set of domestic and international indices in the world. The investment required to do this would be significant but we could offset this by offering the same set of indices to investors worldwide at marginal additional cost. Outside the UK, we would be the alternative index supplier providing these investors with greater choice. Like any start-up, before we could do that we had to make sure we kept the lights on. On one occasion early on, there was a loud pounding on the door late at night. It was a man from the electricity company, who had come to cut off supply because the exchange had omitted to pay the bill. My finance director, Paul Grimes, handed over his credit card to prove we were good for the debt. Our handful of customers wouldn't have taken it too kindly if the indices suddenly ground to a halt. Here was a new dawn with new responsibilities I could scarcely have imagined when I first entered the exchange for the first time just over a decade before.

From Dagenham to the City

I was careful to take in the scene at the LSE that morning in June 1985. It was 17 months since the FT-SE 100 Index had started life, but it hadn't really impacted on me. Like most people, it was the huge British Telecom share listing that took place in the previous December that brought awareness of the City into my world – even though I hadn't bought any of the stock.

The ground floor of the exchange opened out into a trading area where jobbers would stand shouting out prices as if they were manning a market stall. They quoted the prices of shares and bought and sold during the day, working with brokers who acted on behalf of investors including the public. The government broker, who sold debt on behalf of the state and lent an air of gravitas to proceedings, paraded around in top hat and tails. Off to the side there were two bar rooms, which seemed to be open all hours. It was an enclosed community that had hardly changed over the years. Little did I know that within a matter of months this would all be swept away by reforms that would dominate my working life. But I had become used to great change. This grand institution was a handful of miles from my modest upbringing but it could have been a world away. At the age of 24, I had already travelled a long way.

I was born in Upminster in East London, the middle of three boys. Our sister arrived 10 years later. My dad had started his working life as a milkman but after his military service in the post-war years he became a manager of a butcher's shop and we lived in the flat upstairs. We were happy but never had much money so Mum had two jobs: she pressed records at the Poly-Gram factory in Walthamstow and at night she was a door-to-door insurance agent. Later, we moved to Dagenham, a town dominated by the local Ford car plant. I got a paper round at the age of nine and began opening up the shop for the news-agent from the age of 11. I have always enjoyed working and I have always been an optimist, which is just as well. Our tight family finances meant I left school at 16 but carried on study-ing at night classes.

I joined Lambeth Council in 1980, as a clerk supporting the housing and town planning committees. Lambeth Town Hall was a Grade II-listed building, constructed at the start of the century in red brick and Portland stone, and stood over a busy junction in Brixton town centre which was renowned for its vibrant African-Caribbean community. Its tall clock tower made it unmissable but the surrounding area was more down-at-heel, having been blighted by race riots.

My job was to prepare policy papers and town planning applications for consideration by the local politicians who made up the committees. It was in the days when reports were typed onto stencils and corrections made using Tipex. Reports had to be printed in a centralized print room and collated by hand, with a group of us walking around a long table putting one paper behind another. The other, and more interesting, part of my job was to oversee the running of five housing tenant committees, trying to put right the many housing issues tenants faced on the run-down public housing estates throughout the borough of Lambeth. I chose to run the committee for Brixton, the most deprived and difficult area. During the summer of 1981, I cycled to work through areas where police had been dispatched to keep the peace but it was still a tinderbox where hostilities were never far from the surface. Many council meetings took place at night, and I remember gazing out from the town hall windows at a sky flashed red from burning buildings.

Lambeth Council was led by 'Red' Ted Knight, a socialist firebrand who was an early influence on Ken Livingstone. As the leader of the Greater London Council at the time – before Margaret Thatcher scrapped it in 1986 – Livingstone always seemed to be in the building, no doubt fomenting rebellion. The leaders' politics could not have been further from those prevalent at the Stock Exchange, which I was shortly to join.

With council cuts on the way, my wife took a keen interest in my career, encouraging me to send off my CV for one job after another advertised in the *London Evening Standard*. The first I knew about the opportunity to become a clerk at the LSE was when I was called for interview. They wanted someone to assist the secretary of the projects committee who also headed the exchange's new Information Services Division management support team.

I was organized and proficient, still young and keen to learn. I knew nothing about the City, but this role offered more pay and more security. Here was another committee with projects to deliver on. I doubt anyone else saw parallels between the exchange and Lambeth Council, but I could. Only later did I discover I had been recruited to a role where I would be deeply involved in the biggest change the City had ever seen: Big Bang.

Big Bang

Big Bang stemmed from a build-up in tensions between the City and government during the 1970s. It was devised as the solution to an Office of Fair Trading probe into the exchange that was opened just before Thatcher was swept to power in 1979 and had led to a case due to be heard by the Restrictive Practices Court (RPC) beginning in October 1983. The case focused on the rulebook that had been preserved by the exchange for decades: the fixed minimum commissions on share trading, the enforced separation of brokers and jobbers under a 'single capacity' system and the exclusion of foreign member firms. Momentum was building to break open what was seen as a cosy club, although many of the features that the case raised doubts over were exactly what its participants thought made it special.

The council of members that controlled the exchange had done all it could to preserve its reliable income stream despite investors grumbling that its high prices were hampering competitiveness. Overseas exchanges had opened up to foreign members but in London progress was glacial – women had only been finally admitted as members in 1973. However, the abolition of exchange controls in 1979 had seen a flurry of international firms open in the Square Mile, and improving technology meant prices that were once the preserve of those present on the trading floor could be accessed by numerous non-members. Still the council of members dug in, clinging to self-regulation under the general umbrella of the Bank of England. It was remarkable, given that as far back as September 1974 the exchange received a letter from the government's Board of Trade suggesting that it would have to register the rules it followed with the Office of Fair Trading.

Sir Nicholas Goodison, head of the stockbroker Quilter Goodison, had marked himself out as one of the exchange's rare reforming members during the 1970s. Sir Nicholas was quick minded with an uncompromising sharp intellect, raising an eyebrow to indicate he begged to disagree. He listened first but had usually reached his conclusion long before I, or anyone else, had finished speaking. As the exchange's energetic chairman, he was concerned about the rising cost of the impending RPC case and the remedies that might be imposed if it was lost. If the rule-book was thrown out by the RPC in its entirety, the exchange risked descending into chaos. He appealed for compromise.

Sir Nicholas's pleas initially fell on deaf ears. It was only after the Conservatives were returned for a second term with an increased majority in the June 1983 general election that Nigel Lawson and Cecil Parkinson – newly installed as Chancellor and Trade and Industry Secretary, respectively – persuaded Thatcher that Sir Nicholas's plan was workable. The Bank of England was supportive, too.

That plan was momentous, focusing on scrapping fixed min-imum commissions that had sustained City firms for decades. It soon became clear that one reform would lead to another. What became known as 'Big Bang' – symbolizing an overnight change rather than a phased approach to new pricing – her-alded overdue investment in an electronic trading system that made the historic divide between brokers and jobbers negligi-ble. And for smaller firms to survive on lower fees, fresh capital was required. That necessitated a flurry of takeovers. So much for modest changes which the exchange could control: the genie was truly out of the bottle.

While Peter Jones, Mick Newman, Elroy Dimson and the cast of characters described in Chapter 2 worked away on cre-ating the 100 index, the countdown to something even big-ger was on. The exchange was given until the end of 1986 to implement fundamental changes. A target date was set that gave Sir Nicholas several weeks' wiggle room: 27 October 1986.

In charge of delivering Big Bang was the chairman of the exchange's projects committee, Patrick Mitford-Slade. He was a man of impeccable breeding who after serving in the King's Royal

Rifle Corps – later the Royal Green Jackets – joined Cazenove, the family stockbroking firm. In those committee meetings we always seemed to sit in a line, with Mitford-Slade next to my boss, then his number two and me on the end. I felt like the Ronnie Corbett character in the *Frost Report*'s famous comedy sketch about the English class system. All I could do was look up.

But within a few months, as it became clear that progress towards Big Bang was not fast enough, I found my feet. Most of the exchange's departments were sending two or three people to the projects committee by this point. The room was crammed. Mitford-Slade declared he needed fewer people in attendance and those on the committee needed to take greater accountability rather than passing work around. He proceeded to go around the room, selecting who he wanted to be there next time and insisting they step up to the plate. When he got to our group, he said that I should be the project's secretary – and then he strode out.

Chief among my responsibilities was overseeing the installation of the new quote-driven trading system, Stock Exchange Automated Quotations (SEAQ), which was fast became a symbol of Big Bang's leap into the future. Very early the morning of 27 October, we ran through all our pre-market checks. Everything seemed to be working. The clock ticked down to 8am, and we switched on in time. We were live, up and running, and the new buy and sell prices of the UK's largest companies started to appear on the screens. But before my coffee could go cold, at 8.27am the screens suddenly went blank as demand exceeded all our internal forecasts. 'It's like the M25,' I gamely offered as an excuse to Sir Nicholas as the team scrambled to work out what was going wrong. 'We have underestimated capacity and there is just too much traffic.' The exchange chairman looked at me with a raised eyebrow and stalked off to face the press.

Brave new world

Once Big Bang happened, I was in search of a new role. Those first-day glitches did not weigh on my prospects. Hitting the deadline agreed with the government and the Bank of England was our number-one priority and we made it.

But the changes that Big Bang promised were only just the beginning of a transformation that swept through the Square Mile. One decision led to another. There was a flurry of take-overs as broking and jobbing firms fell to UK merchant banks and American, Swiss and French lenders, while international members such as the Japanese bank Nomura were welcomed to the once inward-looking exchange. The membership changed dramatically following a merger with the International Securities Regulatory Organization, an overseas grouping based in London that might otherwise have become a competitor for world trade. Now the exchange catered for overseas and domestic securities.

Still, the embrace of this brave new world only made the exchange question its future even more. People thought its structure of mutual ownership was fast becoming a relic of the past. And simply serving its members in the traditional way was no longer enough. What should the Stock Exchange look like? Did it really need a physical trading floor? The hustle and bustle I first encountered in June 1985 became a mausoleum in a matter of weeks after Big Bang. At first, the UK stockbroking houses including Smith New Court wanted to remain on the Stock Exchange floor but they soon got used to the convenience of staring at monitors in their own office.

In its review of the Big Bang reforms, the Bank of England admitted the speed with which the trading floor declined in importance was unexpected. Before Big Bang, 28 of the firms intending to make a market in equities and gilts decided to maintain a presence on the floor, compared with 19 jobbers there previously. But within the first few weeks of trading, as much as 75 per cent of exchange business, other than traded options, was being conducted off the floor. That rose to 95 per cent by December 1986. The American firms that were increasingly setting the pace couldn't think of anything worse than standing around all day, so they built their own high-tech dealing rooms from where they worked the phones. And they drank less, too. Soon all that was left in one corner of the old floor was the London Traded Options Market (LTOM). Brokers that used to be tightly packed into offices within the tower with a back office around the corner in Finsbury Circus decided they could fan out across the Square Mile.

Fearing it had become the architect of its own demise, the exchange knew it needed to remain useful. And that use came down to the pricing information it had so jealously guarded in the past. There was a drive to provide services at a commercial rate beyond the membership. As the realization dawned that there was money in data – or at least there could be – I was in precisely the right place. A long-running project begun by my previous boss that had been lost in the slipstream of Big Bang landed on my desk. What would a business plan for the exchange's information services division look like? The task suited the mood, but I elicited mixed interest when I presented my thoughts to the exchange's executive committee in the summer of 1987. I argued that in future the value was not in the Topic information terminals it was selling but in the information content itself. For simplicity, I used the music industry as an analogy. We owned the words of important songs, we wanted those songs to be popular and widely played, but we should receive royalty payments from those who played them and benefitted from them commercially. The only point made by the exchange's chief executive,

Jeffrey Knight, was to pull me up on a split infinitive in the document I had prepared.

Nevertheless, a few tasks came my way in those years, such as how the exchange and LIFFE should develop our handful of indices to respond to 1999's introduction of the euro into the European Monetary Union. Index futures trading on LIFFE on the FT-SE 100 had begun to take off, and we knew that the introduction of the euro would create demand for new tradable indices. Robert ('Bob') Steele, head of the US investment bank Goldman Sachs in Europe at that time and someone who we all felt was headed for greater things (he eventually went on to become Under Secretary of the Treasury for Domestic Finance (2006–8) and Deputy Mayor for Economic Development in the administration of New York City mayor Michael Bloomberg) agreed to chair a committee of leading international banks and fund managers in London. This led us to create the FT-SE Eurotrack 100, a basket of the largest European companies outside the UK. It mirrored the FT-SE 100, enabling traders and investors to trade all of Europe with just two indices. LIFFE launched futures on the FT-SE Eurotrack 100 in June 1991 but after several years trying we just could not build the trading volumes to support the new futures contracts.

What really propelled me forward into the world of indices was when I strayed into policy regulation to help resolve a spat that epitomized the struggle between the old and new City.

Every three months, the FT-SE 100 is subjected to what is known as 'triple witching'. This is the short time during the market when all outstanding index futures, index options and stock options contracts are settled and the payment price is set. The final index value at the end of this expiry period determines the price for all contracts. Millions of dollars can be made or lost during this time by trading houses. In 1989, there were record levels of contracts to be settled at expiry, and two houses with very different trading positions and philosophies were responsible for many of them. Goldman Sachs, led by Steele and backed by his highly educated computer-driven traders, moved the market in one direction, and De Zoete Wedd, the jobbers' firm which had just been merged into Barclays, took a different view and stubbornly tried to move the market in the other direction. For half an hour, the FT-SE 100 swung like a pendulum in one direction and then the other. Goldman Sachs, the technically savvy newcomer to the London market, may have proved itself the match for any of London's older houses but the press and investors cried foul.

Together with Peter Jones, the architect of the FT-SE 100 who had been elevated to become the first chairman of the committee overseeing the index, I was despatched to investigate this volatility and come up with a solution. Both Goldman Sachs and De Zoete Wedd were called in to explain their behaviour. Neither had broken any rules, but we could not allow such behaviour to go unchallenged. The two houses were 'power trading' – a form of masculine showing off to which the City was no stranger – so Jones and I drew up a series of recommendations to improve monitoring of traders' positions ahead of expiry and to reduce their ability to influence the market during this particularly sensitive time. Our recommendations were well received by the market, and so we began to turn our attention to the governance around the FT-SE 100 itself. Jones's committee – made up of representatives of the exchange, LIFFE, the *FT* and various City trade bodies – held meetings to approve the quarterly reshuffle of FT-SE 100 constituents depending on the movement in market capitalizations, but there wasn't much infrastructure beneath that. Years had passed, but I noted that, in addition to this flagship index being inadequately policed, no one was exploiting its potential.

Crown jewels

Responsibility for the FT-SE 100 was spread across several departments and nobody could claim ownership or take the decisions to make improvements. Peter Wells led an impressive research department, but the governance, operation and development of the FT-SE 100 was of little interest to him. Similarly, the IT department had other priorities, and the FT-SE 100 sat on old standalone technology. John Stolworthy and Peter Sterlini, who had served as runners on the market floor pre–Big Bang, ran the operation of the index making all the constituent changes but sat unloved alone in the company news department of the exchange. Will Oulton, a young talented floor official in the FT-SE 100 options pit, wanted to develop more indices. Encouraged by Jones and his committee, I decided to bring these people together and, without changing any management reporting lines, started to get everyone working together. We all need to pull in the same direction, I said.

The exchange appreciated the running of the FT-SE 100 which fulfilled an important role as a headline index. But its focus was on trading and futures had been grabbed by LIFFE, a separate organization, so there was a limited benefit to doing more. Over at the *FT* there was a huge amount of data, but I felt its operation was run really to support the journalists and the core newspaper rather than as an independent business. However, the *FT* had a hand in what I saw as two crown jewels.

The FT Actuaries All-Share that since 1962 had been the broad benchmark for the UK market that the vast majority of index funds had gravitated towards. It represented the total UK market, and the FT-SE 100 was its smaller and tradable sister. If the FT-SE 100 was to be an effective index for futures trading, it needed to be aligned to and follow the same rules as the All-Share over which the actuarial double act of Richard

Pain and John Brumwell still held sway. And then there was the FT Actuaries World Indices, published daily in the *FT* since 1987, covering 23 countries at inception and winning a strong international following. Illustrating just how labyrinthine this world was, the same actuaries, Richard and John, performed the same roles for the World Indices as they did for the All-Share. And just like the All-Share, the World Indices had no exchange involvement. Even the *FT*, which lent it its name, only owned one-third of it. Because the *FT* didn't have the overseas capability, Goldman Sachs calculated prices for the Americas, and Wood Mackenzie, the Edinburgh broker, contributed the international numbers. As well as disparate ownership, there was no consistency with methodology or the classification of companies that read across to the other indices. It meant that brokers could lobby the actuaries ahead of us and game the system. What was fast becoming clear to me was that for FT-SE to grow it needed to bring all the parties – the *FT*, the actuaries and the exchange – together and pulling in one direction. It needed to become a single unit, one company, with just one globally recognized brand.

A step forward

It wasn't clear at the start of 1992 what a big year it would be – for me and for the UK indices that I was spending an increasing portion of my time on. I joined many of the committees that oversaw these indices and encouraged them to broaden their membership. I reasoned that, if we could produce something that all City stakeholders wanted, it would make for a better business. That meant bringing on board fund managers for whom the indices were crucial tools. What I needed was something new around which all of these disparate stakeholders could gather.

My Trojan horse was the FT-SE 250. The summer the previous year, Standard & Poor's had launched a mid-cap index
for the US market, citing evidence of a 'mid-cap effect' in
which middle-sized companies often outperformed their larger
peers. Most investors at that time differentiated between large-
cap stocks – the largest companies that usually operated on
an international basis – and small-cap stocks – the smaller and
less liquid companies that were more domestically focused.
The problem this created was that stocks that lay somewhere
in between these two were in no-man's land, overlooked and
unloved. The recognized small-cap index in the USA was the
Russell 2000, and the recognized large-cap index was the S&P
500. In the gap between the bottom of the S&P 500 and top
of the Russell 2000 the S&P MidCap 400 fitted nicely. It was
immediately popular.

I saw this as an opportunity. But the UK market is consid-
erably smaller than the US market, and there was very little,
if any, evidence of a mid-cap effect in the UK. To add to the
challenge, the FT Actuaries All-Share had been shrinking and
was only just over 500 stocks in size. What would we do with
the rump of the All-Share immediately below what we determined to be the mid-cap? We would need to convince the *FT*
and the actuaries to extend the All-Share to create a new small
cap section if we were going to make this work. We would also
need to combine the governing committees and align the different industry classification systems used by the exchange and
the *FT* and actuaries. This was beginning to look like a big and
complex project, and I would need the enthusiastic support of
all three parties if I was to stand any chance of making it work.

Unsurprisingly, it took some time to get all parties to agree.
The *FT* was standing on the sidelines, unsure whether this was
a good idea or not. The actuaries who had steered so many
of the early indices were resistant, too, because this would put

the UK indices outside of their control. What changed this time was that I brought the City's biggest fund managers into the conversation. Previously, the actuaries had determined the direction of travel without broader industry input. It was a like a retailer launching a new range without first sending samples to a focus group.

There were also unforeseen issues which had remained unresolved for some time which needed to be tackled. No total return indices – which include the investment of dividends back into the index – were publicly calculated in the UK because two rival actuarial firms which measured pension fund performance – the WM Company and Combined Actuarial Performance Services (CAPS) – had taken different calculation approaches. I gave the actuaries two options: to resolve their differences and provide us with a single, approved approach, or we would ask the broader industry group I had now established to take on this challenge.

Gordon Bagot, head of the actuarial team at WM and an astute Scot, took the lead on this and, with the backing of Nick Fitzpatrick, chairman of CAPS, created a new measurement standard.

We also had to agree a minimum size for companies joining a new enlarged All-Share, and so sought the opinion of all the major fund managers in the UK. This would have the result of increasing the number of stocks in the All-Share to over 700, covering 98 per cent of the market by value, and boosting the following of some 200 small-cap stocks.

One of the last discussion points was how many stocks the new mid-cap index should comprise. The committee I assembled was split between 200 and 250 companies. In the spirit of a new consensus, I went around the room. The last person to speak on the matter was Tim Breedon, who led Legal & General's investment team at that time and would later become chief executive of Legal & General itself. He argued for 250 not 200, saying the market should expand not contract. We agreed 250 it would be.

Having agreed all the design features, I had to ensure all parties had a role and an interest in the new integrated set of indices. The exchange took ownership of the large- and mid-cap indices, which it was to calculate in real time, namely the FT-SE 100 and FT-SE 250, and the *FT* took ownership of the new small-cap index and enlarged All-Share, which it was to calculate at the end of each day. The industry classification systems were combined to form one system, and Nick Fitzpatrick became chairman of the committee overseeing it.

The FT-SE 250 and the new relationship between the three parties was launched on 12 October 1992. The extension of the All-Share took place at the year end. The new indices had an immediate effect and mid-cap stocks in the UK first outperformed the rest of the market in 1992. It was an auspicious start but we were still a long way short of forming a single company and uniting the UK indices with the FT Actuaries World indices.

FT-SE and HSBC: tricky negotiations

I can't remember when I started calling myself the exchange's head of indices. It was a joke at first, but it stuck the more I got involved in projects like the FT-SE 250. One day late in 1992, the phone rang. It was Christine Dann, the head of information services and my boss, calling from her office to tell me the executive committee was appointing me to the newly created role of head of indices. Given what I had already dealt with, perhaps I should have been careful what I wished for.

On 17 March 1992, my 31 birthday, the Hongkong & Shanghai Banking Corporation (HSBC) launched a multibillion-pound bid for Midland Bank, one of the UK's largest lenders. It was not altogether surprising, given that HSBC had taken a 15 per cent stake in the Midland five years earlier. But the political row was huge. People within the Bank of England opposed the deal because they thought that, if anything went wrong in Hong Kong, the bank would withdraw all the deposits from the Midland to plug the gap. I used to be able to read about these corporate manoeuvrings in the pages of the *FT*, but like a ton of bricks dropping on my in-tray, I was immediately involved. This was the first time to my knowledge that an index would play a role in such a major global transaction. HSBC needed FT-SE's acceptance to get the deal done as it envisaged it.

The bank, led by the gruff Scot Sir Willie Purves, already had a listing in London as a foreign company. When it approached us, our starting point was that it would take over Midland Bank, Midland would be taken out of the FT-SE 100 and HSBC would increase its weighting in Hong Kong, where it had a primary listing and was part of the local Hang Seng Index. Global investors seemed happy enough with that solution.

But that wouldn't do. In the storm over headquarters and jobs, HSBC wanted to show it would look after this new UK interest. Delisting might not have perturbed investors, but it would not have gone down well politically. There was a second element, too. HSBC wanted the global recognition that entry into the FT-SE 100 would have afforded them. The bank was also conscious that indexation was taking off in the UK in a way it had not yet in Asia. FT-SE inclusion was a way of attracting a whole new set of shareholders who would have to buy their stock for the first time.

This debate was an acute reminder that the way in which the indices were being run up to this point was totally fragmented. HSBC had a phalanx of well-paid bankers, lawyers and accountants at its disposal. I ran a nascent department buried in the exchange which – albeit with good intentions – had been making it up as it went along. This technical discussion, under the radar of the media storm of a significant foreign takeover, meant I had to convene actuaries, the *FT* and the exchange with regulators, the Treasury and the Bank of England looking on.

The crux of the matter was that the FT-SE 100 gave you status, but the passive funds only had to follow a stock if it was in the FT Actuaries All-Share. I wanted to avoid a distortion between the two because it would have caused havoc on the futures market. We needed a straightforward agreement. HSBC toyed with the idea of taking a primary UK listing. It committed to moving its head office and chief executive to the UK. But to meet our rules, HSBC needed to give up its Hong Kong listing and status. That was very unpopular with HSBC. It wanted to remain a constituent of Hong Kong's Hang Seng Index while at the same time be a member of the UK's FT-SE 100. In the end, a compromise was reached in which the enlarged company would issue two share classes stapled together, each share class having a UK and a Hong Kong registration. The UK share class would represent the Midland Bank weighting, and over time HSBC would bring these share classes together creating a single stock listed and traded on two separate exchanges.

HSBC exposed the governance shortfall of having the actuaries' Investment Committee determining rules and the treatment of stocks independently of the exchange's FT-SE 100 committee. Richard Pain and his committee, encouraged by HSBC's bankers, were leaning in one direction, and the more robust FT-SE 100 committee led by Peter Jones was leaning in another. I pulled the two committees together for a joint meeting with bankers. We faced a problem. In London, the market makers on the exchange would only make firm prices in the London registered stock, the old Midland.

The joint committee, with Richard needing some encouragement, decided that, unless we could receive guarantees from the London-based market makers that they would also cover the Hong Kong registered stock, only the London-registered Midland shares would be included in the FT-SE 100. HSBC's bankers were distraught. We adjourned the meeting and gave them an hour, no more. Come back with at least three committed market makers or only the Midland line goes in, we told them. An hour later, and no doubt many favours called in, we had our three market makers.

The accord was agreed only after the final offer document for Midland shareholders had been produced. In its stock market announcement on 11 June 1992 to notify investors that the paperwork for the £3.9 billion deal was being posted out, HSBC disclosed that, 'Since the Final Offer Document went to press, the FT-SE 100 Index Steering Committee has announced that all shares of HSBC Holdings will be eligible for inclusion in the FT-SE 100 Index from the date on which the Final Offer becomes unconditional in all respects.'

On the back of this matter, I served on the Hang Seng steering committee for several years which gave me some vital international perspective. Its concern was that HSBC had become so big that it dominated the Hong Kong index. Sharing ideas was vital as our industry grew. But I knew FT-SE couldn't face another negotiation like that one.

A tougher line

The creation of the FT-SE 250, the extension of the FT Actuaries All-Share and the merger of HSBC with Midland gave me the impetus to get the FT, Actuaries, and Stock Exchange aligned to upgrade the governance and various committees overseeing their UK indices. Straight away, a new FT-SE Advisory Steering

Committee was formed to oversee rule changes and decisions on stock selection. The steering committee would sit above the other practitioner committees with its membership made up of the most senior fund managers in the industry. It would be global in its perspective and would set standards for the rest of the industry to follow. Committees had been the lifeblood of the exchange and certainly of the indices that I was trying to nurture. This one had to be different, though, with sharper teeth and one or two sharper members. I needed a strong chairman, and I sought guidance again from Peter Jones. He advised me to meet someone called Donald Brydon.

Donald was CEO of Barclays' fund management business. He was a large, intimidating Scotsman with a no-nonsense reputation and direct disarming style. He was the perfect chairman to pull the disparate stakeholders together.

One of its early tests came from Richemont, the South African conglomerate. Advisers to the business had suggested that if they reorganized their assets it would boost shareholder value. The idea was to separate the tobacco operation, including Rothmans cigarettes, from its luxury goods interests, such as Montblanc fountain pens and Chloé fashion, into two listed groups that would each have a dual holding company structure, one split between London and the Netherlands, the other between London and Luxembourg.

It was an elaborate reorganization, generating upwards of £50 million for the investment bankers who had dreamed it up. But I warned Richemont's brokers that the plan meant they would drop out of the FT-SE 100. On the day the split took place, the shares duly tumbled as they were ejected from the index. The team at Richemont, which was controlled by the group chairman Johann Rupert, were irate and appealed to Brydon's committee. In those days, any other regulator was nowhere to be seen. We were judge and jury, and, just like in the HSBC case, we needed to be credible. In a landmark decision for us, the committee heard both sides of the argument and rejected the Richemont's call to be reinstated. I admit the system had been hard to police before, but we were starting to show we would not be a pushover.

That left the ownership structure. The FT-SE 100, which had become hugely important to its member firms and the fund managers who tracked its progress, remained a gentlemen's agreement between the *FT* and exchange. It was clearly inadequate. The growing family of indices required a company structure around them to invest in the product set, manage risk and act on the opportunities arising from international expansion. How could I get two shareholders with very different priorities to pull in the same direction?

Time to talk

Giles Vardey's first board meeting at the exchange was one of Peter Rawlins's last as chief executive. The former Arthur Andersen partner and managing director of one of the largest Lloyd's of London insurers appeared to have met his match. After four years at the helm, he took complete responsibility for the failure of Taurus, a long-running IT project that had engulfed the exchange. The Transfer and Automated Registration of Uncertified Stock (Taurus) programme was finally abandoned in March 1993 after years of delay and overspending. It was supposed to replace paper share certificates with computerized share settlement and promised savings for the exchange's member firms. Such a system was also intended to extend London's primacy over Paris or Frankfurt as Europe's top financial centre, just as the launch of the FT-SE 100 had done almost a decade earlier. Instead, Taurus ran up exchange costs of £80 million and even more for member firms which had spent heavily in anticipation of its introduction.

Rawlins was hired as a bright spark, but from what I saw of him my impression was he was too abrasive and was alienating the exchange board. He always thought the force of his intellectual argument would win the day. Actually, what this conservative bunch wanted was to feel comfortable with their decision making. The failure of Taurus also meant that a number of clearing functions were shifted from the exchange to the remit of the Bank of England. Not only was the exchange's reputation being called into question, but it was losing a chunk of its business as well.

Without a full-time boss, Vardey was left to pick up the pieces. The newly arrived head of markets came in as a practitioner, rather than a bureaucrat, having worked his way through investment banking jobs at Salomon Brothers, County NatWest and Swiss Bank Corporation in London and New York over the previous decade. I liked him: he was someone who was going to get things done. And I knew I needed a sponsor higher up the organization to put my plan into action.

After Taurus, Vardey was heavily involved in the introduction of a new electronic trading system, the Stock Exchange Trading Service (SETS). It represented another battle with member firms but this time the exchange was determined to do things properly. An expensive array of consultants from Andersen Consulting were brought in to clear up after Taurus and implement SETS. The plan was to introduce an order-driven, not quote-driven, system where market makers posted offers to buy and sell on an electronic bulletin board.

Big Bang might have redrawn the City but the exchange's lagging technology remained static. It was claimed that the best price was always displayed on the trading screen which featured a distinctive yellow strip on it. However, market makers regularly undercut that price on the phone, where much of the trading still took place.

For this reason, the big trading firms – Smith New Court, Kleinwort Benson and Barclays de Zoete Wedd – thought the market making system was fine, even though retail involvement was getting lower and no one was making money from making markets in the FT-SE 100 stocks. Market share was an obsession for these firms, not enlarging the cake. In 1993, 30,000 trades – or bargains – a day was considered busy. Thanks to the advent of electronic trading that improved the efficiency of the market, today 2 million trades can be completed without batting an eye.

The old jobbers were proving to be more entrepreneurial than the exchange. They could see that international equities were growing fast and began taking positions in French and Germany stocks and charging commissions at both ends of the trade. Pretty soon there was greater liquidity in those companies in London than anywhere else, which pointed the way for the growth of indices. The world was coming to London, even if not all of the old guard welcomed it. Vardey helped banks and brokers bring more international listings to the capital with 'The London Story', some marketing materials that highlighted our strengths.

Fresh ideas

In autumn 1993, there was an interregnum at the top of the exchange and the atmosphere was febrile. The chairman, Andrew Hugh Smith, was minding the shop while the search for a new leader to replace Rawlins continued. Like most of those that sat around the boardroom table, Hugh Smith had done well out of Big Bang, selling his firm Capel-Cure Myers to Grindlays only for the enlarged company to be promptly gobbled up by the Australia & New Zealand Banking Group afterwards.

It meant there was an opportunity to strike out with new ideas. Fortunately, the reforming Vardey liked mine. He could see the growth opportunity ahead for indices and the only way FT-SE could capitalize on it was to become a fully fledged company with ground rules, good governance and a profit and loss account. Vardey resolved to raise it with the *FT*.

An early conversation between Vardey and John Makinson about such a combination did not go well. One day in early 1994, just after the FT-SE 100 marked its 10th anniversary, Vardey went over to the *FT*'s offices, which by this time had crossed the Thames to Southwark Bridge Road. The bookish and thoughtful Makinson was newly installed as managing director of the *FT*, having spent eight years away, first working for advertising group Saatchi & Saatchi in the USA and then founding his own investor relations firm, Makinson Cowell.

I sensed the *FT* was wary of anything the Stock Exchange did technology-wise. That was unsurprising given the collapse of Taurus was fresh in the memory. In fact, Makinson's opening gambit was that he wasn't sure if the *FT* wanted to strike a commercial arrangement with an organization whose brand was so poor and its reputation so clearly tarnished.

Vardey got angry. Although still an exchange newcomer, he was determined to defend the institution, talking up its 150 years of heritage and the fact the *FT* had had its fair share of problems over the years. 'If you're going to take that attitude then there is no point having this conversation,' Vardey said, getting up to leave. The following day the phone rang at the exchange and talks resumed.

In common with the exchange's motivations, the *FT* agreed to consider a tie-up as it experienced its own fair share of anxiety. As trading went more and more electronic, the newspaper's executives could see a decline in the value of the stock price quotes that companies paid to list in their pages every day. And with that, the classified advertising that ran alongside the prices pages was also under threat. Pushing ahead with a commercial indices business made eminent sense. It also fitted with two other prongs of the *FT*'s expansion at that time: to be more digital and more international. In May 1995, the website FT.com was launched. Two years later, a US print edition was added to the fold.

But despite its willingness to engage, the *FT* appeared to be hedging its bets. After all, of the two companies, it was the one that had the long-term association with the actuary profession. Frank Barlow, the chief executive of the *FT*'s parent company, Pearson, thought that a bigger index business could spin off a lot of data and anchor a larger information business.

Two strategic moves made by the *FT* became a bone of contention at the Stock Exchange Tower. The first came in late 1993 before talks began. Pearson acquired Extel for a knockdown £74 million from United Newspapers, publisher of the *Daily Express*. The deal brought all manner of new information assets into the company: analysis of stock prices, corporate actions and reference materials. It shifted the *FT* further into the world of financial data and pitted it against suppliers such as Reuters, Knight Ridder and Dow Jones.

Then, in early 1995, just as merger talks with the exchange intensified, the ownership of its attractive FT–Actuaries World Indices was rejigged. In its opinion, the exchange insisted that a bank should not be involved in the calculation of the indices because it deterred other banks from using the indices and created unnecessary conflicts of interest. The *FT* responded. Out went Wood Mackenzie, the Edinburgh broker and a founding partner in the indices. In came Standard & Poor's alongside Goldman Sachs, which retained its interest. The exchange reacted badly to the introduction of what it saw as a direct competitor into its orbit. Why would the *FT* do such a thing if it was serious about building FT-SE? It would be another four years until S&P agreed to be bought out.

There was further opposition at the *FT* that I later found out about. Stuart Clarke, a strong operator who had built a career in data running Extel and took over the *FT*'s data products division when his business was acquired, lobbied hard to scupper the combination with the exchange. He wanted the *FT*'s index interests to be moved to his division so he could strike out on his own. A flurry of emails to Barlow and others fell on deaf ears. When Makinson found out about the plot during a lunch that Clarke attended, he blew his top.

Clarke had a reasonable case to make, but unless the *FT* merged with the exchange it ran the risk of having to compete with it. Worse, if the two sides did not partner up, the *FT* could have its brand taken off the FT-SE 100, which by this time was London's leading benchmark. Closer ties seemed like a fait accompli, but it didn't mean it was easy.

There were plenty of senior staffers in the exchange who regarded the *FT* with the same suspicion they reserved for Reuters. The news agency had taken the exchange to the competition authorities in protest at having to pay for the market data we supplied to them. Some people even suspected it had designs on developing its own exchange business because it already owned a broker, Instinet. Reuters' chief executive, Peter Job, assured Vardey over lunch that nothing could be further from the truth.

A deal, at last

By this time, the exchange had a new chief executive. In November 1993, Michael Lawrence had arrived from the Prudential where he had been finance director. Like Rawlins, he was smart and determined to drag the exchange's technology into the 20th century. He might have lacked the human touch but he did enjoy the finer things in life, splashing out on a red Aston Martin, bought from the comedian Rowan Atkinson, to celebrate his new role. But, back in the boardroom, he expressed doubts about the exchange losing control of the FT-SE 100, regarding a pooling of resources as an unnecessary retreat. The independent directors on the board, however, led by Donald Brydon, were supportive of bringing together the major index players in the UK. They could see the benefits for the industry.

Nevertheless, the majority of negotiations were business-like and respectful, if not warm. Neither side tried to gain the upper hand. It was always a 50/50 joint venture under discussion. The creation of the company was broadly agreed by spring 1995 subject to legal hold-ups and the approval at board level of both companies. Who would run it was not. I made my case, with support from Vardey and Dann, who thought I had the right commercial skills rather than someone with an editorial background. Some at the *FT* were not keen on what they saw as an exchange man taking control and tried to drum up their own candidate, Andrew Hughes, who ran the newspaper's financial statistics operation. However, he did not apply, so any campaigning for him soon petered out.

It meant there was just one man left to convince: Sir John Kemp-Welch, the exchange chairman. Just like Patrick Mitford-Slade ahead of Big Bang, I had to prove my worth to another Cazenove lifer.

It was a long journey up in the lift to his rooms on the 23rd floor that day. The room was brightly lit with low, comfortable chairs it was impossible not to sink back into, almost as if Sir John was trying to put his guests off guard. He was a curious character: he was very statesmanlike but took a long time to get to the point. Members longing for an extrovert appointment, akin to Dick Grasso who began championing the New York Stock Exchange so competently that year, were disappointed.

Sir John shirked the limelight and at one point called in corporate investigators from Kroll to try to uncover who was responsible for a string of boardroom leaks to the media. Before the year was out, he would be hauled before the Treasury Select Committee to address politicians' concerns at the exchange's rapid managerial changes. It was not his natural habitat.

Sir John offered me tea and then launched into small talk. Like so many of the executives I had sold this idea to, he was intrigued to know how I was going to the grow the business. And then he asked what I thought was a very old-fashioned question: 'How would FT-SE benefit the members?' I was momentarily stumped but answered how I had done to others: we could drive down the price of doing business if we offered our service in more markets. And what about making a joint venture between two very different organizations work? Sir John seemed satisfied I could manage the politics. My appointment was confirmed soon afterwards.

The *FT* didn't manage to supply the new venture's leader, but it did chip in a finance director in the shape of Paul Grimes, heavily recommended by Makinson. He had been working on the *FT*'s Great Leap Forward project to digitize and internationalize the company. It spoke volumes about the mistrust that still existed between both sides because Grimes was expressly told to keep an eye on the exchange people by Alan Miller, the *FT*'s finance director. He was also advised he was going into a part-time role, and would he like to become finance director of another *FT* joint venture, the Newspaper Licensing Authority, at the same time? It was soon clear I would keep him fully occupied.

A low-key start

There was meant to be a party to celebrate the birth of our new company. With no sense of irony that we had been standing still while our shareholders thrashed out an accord, we had booked Madame Tussauds. At the time, the famous waxworks museum off Baker Street was still owned by Pearson, the *FT*'s parent company, so our night out wasn't going to break the bank. But Makinson, who was the first chairman of FT-SE International, as we were christened, put paid to the plan. The newspaper man didn't think it would create the right sort of headlines. Both sides saw the signing off of a deal as a formality given they had been working together for so long. It all contributed to the feeling that this was a low-key start. Expectations were low, and I was worried that morale was at the same level.

Neither side put money into the venture. There was a loan facility instead. It was clear that after stating the cost of going global was marginal they were going to take me at my word. FT-SE International began trading on 16 November 1995 when contracts in the name of the two parent companies were assigned to us. They were worth an annual £2.85 million, which gave us a reasonable starting point, but we had barely cut the apron strings. Fees for rent, accounting support, consultancy, facilities management and data services were still flowing back to both shareholders. We never needed the loan facility, in fact. To bring in cashflow I changed the commercial arrangements with clients so that fees were paid annually in advance.

In our first set of accounts, covering the 15 months to the end of 1996, we reported a profit after tax of a princely £430,000 on turnover of £4.4 million. I recall about £1 million a year was coming from 'real-time' revenues – the early subscription fees from the FT-SE 100 and FT-SE 250. A chunk of the remainder came from the resolutely low-tech sale of monthly handbooks for each index at £150 a time.

It was small beer, particularly when I had mapped out a business plan that suggested we could target annual sales of £50 million within five years. In those first accounts, we set out our stall as follows: 'The principal activities of the company are the design, calculation and management of financial indices, and the granting of licences to the users of the company's registered trademarks.'

Asserting our authority was vital. Our sales team started out scouring advertising panels in the *FT* for any firm comparing their performance against any of our indices. That gave us a reason to put in a call. Did they realize they had to pay for the privilege of using our information? Did they want to hear about the range of other data services we could offer them? With some users we had huge fallings out. For a time the BBC took down FT-SE 100 prices from its Ceefax teletext service when we asked them to pay. The next thing we knew, they had launched their own major companies index in partnership with HSBC. Was the state broadcaster and the UK's biggest bank trying to put us out of business? Fortunately, no one used it, and it only served to remind people of the growing value of our brand.

The licensing had worried me. I had already travelled 4,000 miles to resolve a little local difficulty. In 1993, I went to Chicago with the Lord Mayor of London, a historic role filled each year by a City grandee charged with raising the profile of London as a global financial centre on his travels. Sir Francis McWilliams was a jovial Scot who trained as a civil engineer but turned to arbitration later in his career. On that trip with him I granted a licence to the Chicago Mercantile Exchange and the Chicago Board of Trade to trade the FT-SE 100.

It was early days for international expansion – and ironic that my first overseas deal should be with the markets that inspired the creation of FT-SE – but I had an ulterior motive. Back at home, LIFFE, whose demand for something to measure a new futures contract against had led to the creation of the FT-SE 100, had become part of the problem. Because it predated every other customer, it was trading the index without what I thought was an adequate licence and certainly without paying up. Its executives brandished an old document which they claimed gave them the right to continue. Never mind that the FT-SE 100 would not have existed if Jack Wigglesworth and colleagues had not planted the idea in the exchange's mind in 1983 – I was determined that everything had to operate on a proper commercial footing.

Because of the Chicago agreement, LIFFE eventually took out a licence of its own. For the first time, it was being formally recognized that FT-SE International actually owned the FT-SE 100. If I was going to build a business from this and other indices, it was a crucial step. Another strategy, no more popular, was to unbundle our service from that of the exchange. Every user of the Reuters, Bloomberg or another data vendor's terminals that by now populated trading desks across the City paid about £90 a month for a supply of prices and information from the exchange. That included our indices, until we stripped them out of the package and began charging £4.60 a month ourselves. The exchange could have reduced its prices to compensate but instead, to general grumbling, it put them up.

What's in a hyphen?

But I am getting ahead of myself. I should point out that some vital details were not ironed out until after the company was incorporated. I had managed to bring the *FT* and the exchange to the table, but there was still a final push to unite two of the City of London's great institutions.

Eleven years on from the birth of the FT-SE 100, I was amazed that the creation of the company that would house it was just as eleventh-hour. On the day we made the announcement to the world at a briefing in Stock Exchange Tower, I went down in the lift to greet the *FT* retinue led by Makinson; Vardey joined me in the welcoming committee.

Speeding up in the lift to the 23rd-floor meeting room where most committee meetings were held, it was clear all was not well. The awaiting media never knew that the two sides had got this far but had still not signed the shareholders' agreement. At least 18 months had passed since Makinson raised concerns over the exchange's reputation, and the sole sticking point was what to call ourselves. It was agreed we put on a united front that day and kick the decision into the long grass of the first board meeting.

That is why we began life with the name FT-SE International, which I didn't like at all. The hyphen symbolized a disjointedness I had to eradicate. It was typical of the hodgepodge of the last decade. In many places overseas the 'FT-SE 100' (with the hyphen), our flagship product, was routinely called the FT 100, or FT-SE or FTSE. The exchange hadn't been bothered to correct anybody, and as you can imagine, the *FT*, which was itself trying to expand globally, didn't mind the confusion. Even an amateur branding consultant like me knew we would benefit from some unity and consistency before we began to grow – as long as both sides could agree.

Makinson was not chairman of FT-SE for long. In December 1995, he was promoted to become finance director of Pearson towards the end of Barlow's time in charge. It was agreed that the chairmanship would rotate annually between a representative from the *FT* and the exchange so Makinson was quickly replaced by Miller, the *FT*'s suspicious finance director.

Before he departed – and before we had even had chance to move into St Alphage House – Makinson opened one of our first board meetings that autumn declaring the company name had to be addressed. Who would break the impasse? Makinson suggested that both shareholders should listen carefully to the views of FT-SE's sole independent director. He was referring to Keith Percy, who was at the time the chief executive of asset manager Morgan Grenfell. Percy had replaced Brydon on the FT-SE steering committee and carried his role through to our incorporation.

Makinson knew Percy well. When he had been a writer for the *FT*'s 'Lex' column, he often called Percy, who was then an analyst at the fund manager Philips and Drew, for his opinion on various City matters. They had discussed this pressing matter several weeks before. In the hope of encouraging Percy to side with him in the board meeting, Makinson made sure his view was clear: the *FT* had the stronger brand and the business would thrive if all of its products and services were simply rebranded under the *FT* banner, regardless of the shared ownership. It could not have been planned as such, but what revenge that would have been on the exchange, which had attempted to go its own way all those years ago?

What the chairman didn't know is that I had breakfast with Percy on the day of the board meeting in the hope of guiding his thinking. Percy was a good check on my early ambition, always asking whether I was sure we weren't attempting to do too much too quickly – the classic downfall of a start-up. It is one of the reasons I asked him to stay on as a consultant when he felt he had to resign from the board a year later, after an investment fraud centring on the fund manager Peter Young had enveloped Morgan Grenfell and Percy was forced to defend himself.

I conceded to Percy that 'SE' on its own could have referred to any exchange around the world because it didn't have a geographical handle on it. But I knew the exchange brand resonated more the further you went from London. *FT* was undoubtedly the stronger brand, but my view was that by dropping the exchange from the title it would be very difficult to maintain the collaborative relationship going forward. Given how long it had taken us to create a new company, relations were fragile and I knew I needed both sides on board if this new venture was going to fulfil its potential. Keith didn't need persuading at all. He strongly preferred the joint name, suggesting to his fellow directors that day: 'For God's sake, can we just drop the hyphen?'

The board, including Makinson, eventually agreed. It took a special resolution the following July before we could formally change the name, but as of September 1996 the hyphen was finally banished for ever. FT-SE became FTSE. Now we had a name I felt sure could take on the world.

4
Going global

For four brief months in 2011, it looked as though the LSE would finally take the plunge. In the previous decade or so, since it converted from a member-owned organization to a public limited company, the famous City institution had seen off a United Nations of takeover overtures from Deutsche Börse, Sweden's OM, Australia's Macquarie Bank, and Nasdaq. In 2007, it acquired Borsa Italiana for £1.1 billion, but the deal was viewed as a consolation prize as consolidation swept the sector. Clara Furse, the exchange's chief executive until 2009, had performed the peculiar trick of preserving the company's independence while leaving it decidedly on the back foot. With the deep-pocketed Borse Dubai and Qatar Investment Authority taking significant equity stakes, more than ever it felt as though the exchange was not in charge of its own destiny.

The proposed merger with the owner of the Toronto Stock Exchange (TMX) was certainly a transformational deal – if not necessarily the right one. Announced on 9 February 2011, it promised to create a company with all the uneasy compromise that typically comes from sensitive cross-border negotiations. And it was a surprise pairing, given that most analysts thought that all roads led to Wall Street for anyone wanting to forge a lead in the exchanges world.

The enlarged group would be led by Xavier Rolet, the adventurous and debonair Frenchman who replaced Furse at the helm of the LSE in May 2009. Under his guidance, London would remain home to the group's international listings and technology. However, Toronto would house its primary listings service – a key activity for multinational companies that were some of the exchange's biggest clients. And the group's chairman, Wayne Fox, a retired vice chairman of the Canadian Imperial Bank of Commerce, would sit in Toronto rather than the top floor of Paternoster Square in the heart of London's Square Mile. As Rolet put it in the official statement: 'We are aiming at nothing less than becoming a true powerhouse in the global exchange business.' For an industry with roots in local communities that bought and sold based on trusted relationships, now the ambition was to be an 'international gateway' for clients. The address no longer mattered.

Global mergers and tie-ins

Toronto and London were not the only ones attempting to pair off. The year 2011 marked a deal frenzy as the exchanges and indices companies that powered global markets tried to build scale and cut costs as competition grew from alternative trading platforms run by banks and other third parties permitted after a relaxation of the rules. The deal frenzy that threatened to redraw the landscape was given added piquancy that summer as the weakening US economy turned trading screens red day after day. It served as a reminder that investors craved data that tracked rises and falls on which to make their investment decisions. More important than location was powerful technology to power split-second trading and the deepest pools of capital.

Just a day after London and Toronto announced they would combine – to much bemusement and hand wringing – Deutsche Börse, the LSE's long-time suitor, revealed it was merging with NYSE Euronext, two years after earlier talks over a combination had ended. Seven weeks later, a partnership of IntercontinentalExchange (ICE) and Nasdaq attempted to break up that union, tabling a $11.3 billion bid for NYSE Euronext, which was rejected, sweetened, rejected again and withdrawn after failing to win regulatory support. In the end, the combination of Deutsche and NYSE was also scuppered by regulators. When the European Commission eventually prohibited the proposed merger on 1 February 2012, all parties had moved on. Later that year, ICE scooped up NYSE Euronext on its own.

A dizzying array of combinations was possible. There were bumper bonuses for the investment bankers, which led those chief executives who did not want to be left behind into multibillion dollar tie-ups. However, the creation of global players was repeatedly constrained by local concerns. On 8 April 2011, Singapore Exchange killed its $8 billion bid for its Australian rival, ASX, when the Australian government rejected the offer, even though it had been cleared by the competition watchdog four months earlier. Politicians said the deal would have reduced the country's economic and regulatory sovereignty and posed risks because of ASX's dominance over clearing and settlement. Singapore was immediately talked of as a suiter for the LSE whose Toronto adventure had quickly turned sour.

In the end, Rolet's dream was defeated by the Canadian establishment. A quartet of national banks who look out at each other at the intersection of Bay Street – Canada's Wall Street – with King Street in downtown Toronto did not want an international interloper threatening their cosy club. The Bank of Montreal, Scotiabank, the Canadian Imperial Bank of Commerce and Toronto-Dominion Bank had survived the financial crash in good shape because they had not dabbled with exotic financial instruments such as credit default swaps. They viewed as the thin end of the wedge the erosion of TMX's sovereignty, reasoning that, if the LSE was let in, then the international investment banks – Barclays, Goldman Sachs, Deutsche Bank, Morgan Stanley and JPMorgan, which had limited presence in

Canada – would not be far behind. Many in the Royal Bank of Canada were thought not to like it either, but they stayed quiet because they were advising the LSE on the deal.

Alongside Canadian pension funds the quartet formed a consortium, the Maple Group, which in May had its £2.3 billion counterbid for TMX rejected. It was a momentary setback. Patriotic lobbying went into overdrive, and after the banks went hostile the LSE formally threw in the towel on 29 June, knowing that it had not secured sufficient shareholder support for its plan. By October, the Maple Group's proposal was accepted by the TMX board, ensuring that international consolidation would not reach Toronto any time soon.

A different duo

What very few people knew is that while the LSE struggled to find a partner, FTSE had, too. By 2011, my consolidation efforts were dead in the water. While a number of suitors had courted the exchange, my efforts had focused on just one potential partner: Dow Jones Indices.

We had spent the best part of three years in on-off merger talks. Compared to the frenzy of multibillion-dollar deals that were sweeping the exchange sector, this was relatively modest. But its impact on FTSE's future would have been huge. Every reason why the exchanges were scaling up applied to indices, too. Technology, speed, accuracy, geographic coverage and a grab for clients: ever since I drew up the business plan for FTSE in 1995 to convince its two shareholders to formalize their arrangement, I knew that in time a very small handful of index companies would lead the industry. Sixteen years on, I still puzzled over how to bring both of my investors around to my way of thinking. The truth was that the LSE and *FT* were increasingly strange bedfellows.

The *FT* had been a great supporter, particularly when Rona Fairhead, Pearson's finance director, moved to become chief executive of the FT Group in 2006. Pearson believed in data businesses. Both FTSE and International Data Corporation (IDC), another venture it part-owned, ended up being very successful from quite basic beginnings. It turned out that Stuart Clarke, the former Extel boss who tried to scupper our FT-SE merger, did not have long to lick his wounds. Soon after blessing that merger with the exchange, the *FT* bought IDC and Clarke was sent to the USA to run it having combined it with the old Extel business. It mushroomed in a matter of years from understanding the power of equities and bond pricing data embedded inside the plumbing of every bank and fund manager around the world. In the financial world, data was becoming the new oil. Stock-picking active investment managers were just starting to go out of fashion, and the forward-thinking firms were investing in data analysts and quantitative investment approaches that relied on huge volumes of data. Indexation and passive management was still in an embryonic state, and little did any of us know how that would mushroom to dominate investment and markets around the world.

FTSE took a little longer to take off than IDC. Fairhead was keenly interested, sometimes attending key client meetings with me. She helped brush up our image by encouraging us to move to smarter premises in Canary Wharf, the Docklands district to which many of the City's biggest firms were relocating. It was all very well attacking the market with the mindset of a start-up but we needed to invest in ourselves if we were to step up and serve the financial markets worldwide. We needed a makeover to demonstrate we were a serious player. It was time to upgrade. In New York we did the self-same thing as in London when we relocated to the Rockefeller Center, a business landmark. And in Hong Kong, we moved to the prestigious One International

Finance Centre (IFC) with its 88 floors looking out from the business area in Central across the receding harbour to Kowloon. The journey on the Star Ferry was taking less time every visit I made to Hong Kong, as land was reclaimed and buildings were thrown up on both sides of the water.

The property upgrades really elevated us in how we viewed ourselves and, just as important, how our biggest clients viewed us. Of course, we continued to publish our data in the pages of the *FT*. It still lent us the imprimatur of authenticity, but I knew that fewer and fewer people were poring over our numbers in those salmon-pink pages. This was a real-time business now. The synergies we had with the *FT* were weakening, especially because Pearson's chief executive, Dame Marjorie Scardino, had made driving into the business of education her number-one priority. In 2002, she made clear she would sell the *FT* 'over my dead body', but I wondered if that applied to FTSE, too.

In contrast, the LSE was far less settled. It was less used to dealing with joint ventures, and our meetings were more scatter-gun. Clara Furse, the former Crédit Lyonnais and UBS investment banker, had arrived as chief executive in February 2001 as the company was preparing to list its own shares that summer. The flotation, which came after the LSE demutualized a year earlier, provided options to expand but in reality it opened the exchange up to further takeover overtures.

Within a few years, Furse was facing fresh competition ushered in by the European Union's Markets in Financial Instruments Directive (MiFID). Enacted in November 2007, the legislation was designed to expand choice and drive down the price of share trading. Furse, who led the futures and options business at UBS, should have understood our business but she made it clear she didn't see much value in FTSE even though for a time we were the biggest contributor of LSE cash flow. Furse was unwilling to explore how we could scale up the business. It meant that meetings with Dame Marjorie and Fairhead could appear fractious.

Recruiting

Irrespective of the attention I drew from each shareholder, I knew it was my responsibility to strengthen FTSE from top to bottom: our people, our technology and our strategy. I had started with the sales and marketing teams. In July 1999, when we totalled just 30 people across the whole business, I recruited Donald Keith, a tall and engaging Scotsman with a flair for sales and a mischievous sense of fun. He grew up in the Highlands and won a scholarship to Fettes College in Edinburgh where he was one year behind Tony Blair, though, whereas Blair went to Oxford, Donald won a scholarship to Cambridge University where he studied law. He had run a large division within the big American health insurance company, Sigma, and was our first big hire.

Donald initially focused on Europe, strengthening the sales teams and opening offices in Paris, Frankfurt and Madrid. He developed partnerships with many of the leading exchanges across Europe. In 2001, I asked him to recruit his own successor and promoted him to be my deputy. He recruited three big hitters: Imogen Dillon-Hatcher to run Europe, Paul Hoff in Asia and Jerry Moskowitz in the USA. All three were personalities and set out to grow the business around the world, knocking on doors and building partnerships in countless cities in countless countries. Sales were now growing in double digits every year, and we were beginning to attract the biggest fund managers and banks as our clients.

I knew I also had to strengthen the other teams to keep up with the increase in sales. As in many small businesses, Paul Grimes, our finance director, doubled up as chief operating officer, running the technology and data operations as well as all finance and administration. Paul was the heartbeat of FTSE in the early years, looking after almost everything to do with the running of the business while Donald and I spent our time building out the client base around the world. We relied, trusted and depended on him totally. And he was the staff champion, ensuring their views were heard and involving them in decisions which affected work practices and their environment. But in 2007 I decided that I had to split the roles to enable us to continue to grow, and Paul took this as an opportunity to move on. It was a huge change for us, but I kept telling myself that we had to keep moving forward, constantly building momentum.

We brought in a new finance director, Nick Teunon, and a new COO, Guy Warren. Nick was another Cambridge University graduate, very bright and quick minded. He joined us from the Press Association where he held a similar role and quickly bonded with Donald and myself. Rona and the board liked him, and, with their encouragement, he quickly upgraded the governance and finance functions. Guy came from Misys where he had ran the banking technology division. He also made an immediate impact, improving the quality of our technology and operations and upgrading the teams. Finally, I needed to strengthen our research capabilities. Here, I got lucky.

The collapse of Lehman Brothers in 2008 would have unexpected consequences for us. We had for many years been working with the research team at Nomura International, the London outpost of the Japanese bank. They had the research capabilities we did not, and I had made a deal with them whereby they undertook calculations and research we were not set up to do. The team was headed by Reza Ghassemieh, an Iranian by birth, who was sent to Edinburgh by his parents to gain his degree. Not speaking much English and unaccustomed to the harsh Scottish winters, he had a steep learning curve ahead of him. But he prospered and eventually found his way to the City and worked his way up to heading the Nomura research function in London that supported their international trading activities. When Lehman collapsed, Nomura acquired its European equities and banking operations. The bank now had two world-class research teams, so Reza and I approached the management of Nomura and convinced them to let the existing Nomura research team in London join FTSE. We now had top-class research skills.

My original tongue-in-cheek strategy of 'global domination' had filled out to become 'One global team, operational excellence, understanding and solving our clients needs'. We began to focus on serving the largest asset owners, those that had their own chief investment officer and teams and who were capable of making their own decisions rather than following the crowd or the advice of financial consultants. The USA and China were by far the biggest markets so that is where we focused our attention and resources. I recall a dinner we hosted where Sir Alex Ferguson, the legendary Manchester United manager, shared his tips on leadership. He emphasized the importance of loyalty to the club – or company – above all else. I couldn't agree more.

Stalemate

Yet no matter how I grew and professionalized FTSE, there were some things I could not achieve without shareholder backing. It was a great shame that Clara Furse and I clashed repeatedly. Early in her reign at the LSE, she blocked my plan for FTSE to take ownership of the CAC-40, France's leading share index. The idea was for Euronext, which had been created in 2000 from the merger of the Paris, Amsterdam and Brussels bourses, to take a stake in FTSE in exchange for handing over the running of their indices. It would have pushed us deep into

Europe, which was just what the LSE was trying to do with its business. But it seemed to me that Furse could not countenance ceding further control of FTSE to create a bigger entity.

We reached a similar stalemate with Dow Jones Indices (DJI). Led by the world-famous Dow Jones Industrial Average, which had been created in 1896, these 130,000 equity indices had been entwined with *The Wall Street Journal* since the days of Charles Dow and Edward Jones's partnership. They were still held in high regard by the Bancroft family that controlled the business, but also viewed as something that could be split off without impacting the core newspaper and news wires franchise.

The *FT* in particular wanted to merge us with DJI. Here was an irony. The *FT* and *The Wall Street Journal* had circled each other nervously for years, trying to become the global leader in the provision of business news from opposite sides of the Atlantic. And yet they knew index consolidation was coming, there was nothing to lose, and the opportunity to take out duplicate cost was huge. At a dinner in New York, I brought together Fairhead and Jonathan Howell, the LSE's finance director, with Mike Petronella, my opposite number at DJI. It was a good-natured conversation, although I recall Petronella turned up with a car wrench concealed in his overcoat. He wasn't threatening us – just on his way to tinker with a motor with his son later that night.

Furse took a long time to decide whether or not she would engage. Dow Jones was slightly smaller than FTSE at the time so we were considering a 55/45 split in the enlarged venture. Eventually, I was surprised to hear that Furse backed the deal – as long as the LSE could maintain control without paying any money in. It was a totally unworkable stance.

News Corporation was no less willing a seller. After the media mogul Rupert Murdoch acquired Dow Jones in 2007, his lieutenants quickly set to work to see how they could recoup some of the $5 billion outlay. The *FT* had not cooled on the idea, either. In fact, the FTSE/DJI projected savings had been injected into the mix when the *FT* and *The Wall Street Journal* briefly discussed a merger that would have seen off the Murdoch takeover interest.

My last attempt at a deal came in 2009, when Furse had been succeeded by Rolet, one of the few senior bankers to emerge from the wreckage of the collapse of Lehman Brothers the previous year with his reputation intact. He was a bundle of pent-up energy, insightful and challenging, who loved nothing better than setting far-reaching goals to drive his management team forward. It started immediately he joined the LSE. First, he wanted to get the banks and brokers back on board after Furse had alienated them, and then, with the backing of Chris Gibson-Smith, the LSE's thoughtful chairman, drive growth in shareholder value through acquisitions and increased sales. I felt sure he would see the logic of DJI.

The deal terms had moved on a little by this time. The plan was for us to pay News Corp $110 million to inject DJI into FTSE, finally giving us critical mass in the USA. Then, the three equal shareholders would have had the option to withdraw in three to five years' time when we listed the business on the London stock market. We even agreed the name: FTSE Dow Jones. A combination would have put us on a par with MSCI, our closest competitor, which had gained a useful currency for more deals when it listed on the New York Stock Exchange on 14 November 2007.

The personnel had changed at the LSE but my frustrations with them had not. The LSE's finance director, Doug Webb, thought the multiples we were discussing were too high. More broadly, the board couldn't make up its mind what to do with FTSE. At first, I thought Rolet was employing delaying tactics in the hope of negotiating for better terms. But in some meetings he would say he loved the business and he wanted to build it. Then in the next meeting he would declare the exchange needed cash, that we were not core to his plans and should be sold. At this point, Les Hinton, a lifelong newspaper man and one of Murdoch's right-hand men, started talking to us about how they would pay to buy both shareholders out.

The *FT* was happy either way, as long as its brand name was protected. By this point it wasn't holding us back but equally it wasn't contributing very much to our future. Rolet was keen to sell, aggressively so. That was until Dow Jones submitted a low-ball offer after doing some due diligence. An angry Rolet named his price for FTSE as £900 million, far more than either side valued us in their books, 'and not a cent less'.

We reverted back to merger talks. In the end, I was told the exchange could not commit the $55 million required. I suspected it didn't like the idea of a third investor around the table and wouldn't have supported an initial public offering either because it did not like the idea of losing control of FTSE. The Dow Jones deal was dead and it was a terrible blow.

Within two months of that final rejection in late 2009, I was frustrated but not surprised when 90 per cent of DJI was sold to the Chicago Mercantile Exchange (CME), the world's largest derivatives exchange operator. It was a defensive move for CME, which wanted to secure exclusive rights to offer futures on the DJIA and related indices which otherwise would have expired in 2014. Dow Jones kept a 10 per cent stake in the new venture and received $608 million.

That was not the end of it. Late in 2011, the same year that Rolet had been frustrated by the Canadians over TMX, CME announced it was rolling the DJI business I had coveted together with S&P, another key index player. The resulting S&P Dow Jones Indices, which brought the flagship Dow Jones Industrial Average under the same roof as the S&P500, counted $6 trillion of assets following its benchmarks.

It was a big boost for McGraw-Hill, S&P's parent company, which had announced a few months prior it would demerge its education business to focus on financial data. It was also an early victory for Alex Matturri, who had joined the S&P team in 2007 and was made chief executive of the enlarged business. I had a lot of time for Alex, who had previously worked on the other side of the fence, as senior vice president and director of global equity index management at Northern Trust Global Investments (NTGI), where he oversaw a $185 billion passive investment business for the world's third-largest quantitative manager.

But it relegated the Dow Jones brand to a bit-part player in the index industry. I would have kept using it more widely in the USA, alongside FTSE in Europe, and FTSE Dow Jones would have become a powerful global brand. Now all I could do was rue missing our chance and falling further behind MSCI. But there was still one more deal to be done before 2011 was out – and it filled me with dread.

The competition

I should explain more about MSCI. Despite S&P's success in gaining control of DJI, I have never regarded it as FTSE's closest competitor. I reserve that accolade for MSCI.

I have a huge amount of respect for Henry Fernandez, MSCI's chairman and chief executive. He is a pugnacious autocrat who has built a world-leading business over several decades. He is fiercely competitive but has also on occasions put aside those instincts to collaborate where he believes it is in the best interests of the industry as a whole. Our approach towards the indices world has much in common, but our starting points were very different.

Fernandez was born in Mexico but grew up in Nicaragua. His father was an intelligence officer in the Nicaraguan army, which goes some way to explaining why Fernandez is a great patriot. Even when he went to study economics in the USA he took a job at the Nicaraguan Embassy. The country's Sandinista Revolution of 1979 meant he could not return home so after qualifying as a legal immigrant he was hired by Morgan Stanley on Wall Street. Keen to be an entrepreneur, he quit to set up private equity firms first in Mexico City and then Miami. It was John Mack, Morgan Stanley's legendary chief executive, who brought him back to the bank as a managing director in 1994 after three years away. It didn't take him long to discover MSCI, at that time a fairly unloved asset within Morgan Stanley, and recognize it had all the tools required for an investment revolution. Fernandez moved to Geneva, and the rest is history.

Rewind a decade. Morgan Stanley was incredibly prescient when in September 1985 it purchased the rights to the publications and stock market indices of Capital International Perspective from the Capital Group, an asset manager based in Los Angeles. Capital International had been publishing indices since 1969 and covered more than 1,600 companies in Europe. The deal was masterminded by Barton Biggs, Morgan Stanley's long-time chief investment strategist who was early to spot the appeal of emerging markets as well as indices. He reasoned that, if investment was going global, investment managers needed someone to provide the tools to help them do the job.

Based in Geneva, at that time Capital International's flagship product was a monthly publication that compared companies' stock price performance, cash earnings, book value, yield and reported profits, adjusted to take into account differences from market to market. Think about the timing. In London, we were still a year away from Big Bang. FTSE International wasn't even a glimmer in my eye. Yet the deal puzzled many. Some doubters thought that investors would not elect to buy statistical information from an investment bank, which could be prone to conflicts of interest. How wrong could they be.

And now fast-forward to another acquisition. MSCI's purchase of Barra in April 2004 was a wake-up call for me and the rest of the industry. It confirmed what was possible in our world and precipitated my move to New York because I knew FTSE had to crack North America. Paying $816 million for Barra – which had itself been spun out from a Wall Street bank, JPMorgan Chase, six years earlier – rounded out MSCI's already impressive portfolio. Its risk analysis tools were already used by many of the same clients who followed MSCI's stock and bond indices. In addition, the deal gave Fernandez the critical mass that set his firm on a path to the public markets.

By November 2007, when there were already rumblings that financial markets were overstretched, MSCI brushed aside concerns to record a triumphant market debut. Its initial public offering of shares on the New York Stock Exchange was priced at the top of expectations, raising $252 million, with the stock soaring 52 per cent during its first trading day. At that time, MSCI was managing more than 100,000 equity, real estate investment trust and hedge fund indices.

The listing offered a route for Morgan Stanley to sell down its remaining stake at great profit over several years. By 2009, MSCI had formally broken free of its parent. It could focus on growing faster, and, because of the listing, now had the currency to carry out more deals. I admit I was envious, because Fernandez had the freedom to set his priorities and there was no longer one – or two – powerful shareholders breathing down his neck.

I respect Fernandez hugely, but we never really got on despite meeting for breakfast from time to time. I felt that he always regarded himself as leading the dominant market player and thought of FTSE as the smaller business constantly running to catch up. We were David and he was Goliath – but you know how that story finishes. There were several times when I think he thought FTSE was finished. One such occasion was when we bought out Goldman Sachs from the then named FT/S&P-Actuaries World Index in 1999. Without the backing of a Wall Street bank, how could we hope to prosper?

Nevertheless, we had a knack of upsetting him, such as when we got more coverage in the pages of the *FT*, our 50 per cent shareholder. Nor was Fernandez particularly happy when FTSE acquired the Baring Emerging Markets Indices and combined them with the FTSE World Index series in 2000 creating a much stronger competitor to MSCI with an index covering 49 countries with some 2,300 constituents. We began setting standards for global markets and how emerging markets should be defined and promoted or demoted which he thought MSCI had a monopoly on (more on that in Chapter 7).

S&P has always been well known in our industry, but it is less involved in sales to the big asset owners, which is what MSCI and FTSE both do with our global benchmarks. This is where we successfully became a thorn in Fernandez's side. We went through periods when Fernandez wouldn't talk to me, in particular when we won a large piece of business from funds giant Vanguard, of which more in Chapter 6.

In a pitch, the asset owner states which benchmark they want to follow and fund managers then compete to run that business for them. Choosing between index providers has been likened to the battle between Reuters and Bloomberg to install their terminals on as many traders' desks as possible. What is clear is that the banks no more want Reuters without Bloomberg than they want FTSE without MSCI. Competition is good.

Lunchtime speeches

To understand how these businesses grew is to understand the rivalry that existed on Wall Street in the decade after FTSE was incorporated. Two key relationships I benefited from in the early years came as bitter enemies vied for supremacy in the worlds of investment banking and financial information.

Morgan Stanley and Goldman Sachs had been at each other's throats for decades, whether that be in trading, wealth management, corporate advisory or derivatives. These were boom years, and the growth in indexation was just another front opened up along a wide-ranging battleground of finance and the streams of information that underpinned it.

While Morgan Stanley had cleverly created MSCI, Goldman Sachs responded by persuading the *FT* and actuaries to create a competitive index, the FT-Actuaries World Index, which it had a third interest in. As a result, we quickly became Goldman's dog in this fight. Even before I had created the business I wanted in the UK from our humble beginnings in St Alphage House, I found myself regularly on a plane, frequently accompanied by Mark Zurack or another partner from Goldman Sachs.

Mark was a New Yorker who had joined Goldman Sachs in 1983, starting in equities derivatives research and working his way up to partnership at a young age. He was shrewd and very bright but someone who also gave his time generously to junior colleagues and someone I felt I could learn from and trust. The bank was invaluable in opening doors to me at some of the world's largest asset owners.

These trips followed a pattern. I had had to be persuasive before, in forging FTSE International and developing new indices, but I really learned how to pitch in those early days thanks to Goldman. We would do a tour of numerous funds in New York and Boston. To break up one-to-one meetings morning and afternoon with the most important managers there was always a lunch session where I suppose I was the entertainment. One of the Goldman partners would get up to introduce me and I would take to my feet. While everyone tucked into their meal I spoke until the coffee was poured about what FTSE could offer them. I must have lost about 15 pounds because every time I stood up the food was being served and by the time I sat down it was being cleared away again. This went on for 10 days or so.

People wanted to hear what I had to say. Money had begun switching regularly by this time because there was an army of consultants that kept reminding pension funds of the cost of active management. The fees could no longer be justified. Actuarial consultants published a league table of the fund managers, and no one fund was in the upper quartile for very long. Investment methods were like catwalk fashions. No sooner were they in style than they went out of style again. Those league tables reminded investors that indices really captured the market. If we tracked the midpoint, then statistically half the market should outperform the index and half should underperform. If you add in the cost of paying someone to manage that money, the cost of a passive index should always beat those active funds. It made less and less sense, unless you could find that mystical golden fund manager who always outperformed the index after taking his fees into account.

Once I convinced the lunchers of the value of passive investing, then I had to explain to them 'Why FTSE?' Just like a fund manager wins mandates from an asset owner to look after their money, I was on a mission to win more business by persuading them that our indices were more accurate in capturing a true view of the market, and that we were a better long-term partner for clients than the competition. In the USA, that generally meant explaining why they should ditch MSCI for us. These were good-natured conversations. Once when I opened my briefcase in a fund manager's office, they spied a folded-up umbrella. Everyone found it very funny – but at least it reminded them to buy British.

Our strategy at this time was to focus on the largest asset owners in the world, very large pension plans and sovereign wealth funds. These organizations had their own investment teams, and because these funds were largely passive investors, replicating the indices they were following, it meant the design and operation of the index was more important to them. They didn't have to follow everybody else. They could make their own decisions based on what was best for them. Our coverage of the global equity markets was much deeper than MSCI's, meaning that we included all the important large and mid-cap stocks and were only selective in the small-cap area where we removed the stocks too small or illiquid for large international funds to trade. We involved the largest fund managers and brokers in helping us improve the governance and running of the indices. We were ahead of MSCI and started to win business among the big asset owners. I encouraged them to hold beauty parades because we were becoming more confident in our ability to win.

The power of the pitch: CalPERS

There was one pitch in Sacramento, the state capital of California, where umbrellas were definitely not required. Goldman had introduced me to the California Public Employees Retirement System (CalPERS), one of the largest asset owners in the world. Invited to pitch for our first piece of business from them, I flew in the night before and it was still sweltering hot. Sacramento was hardly a tourism or business mecca in those days. I'm not sure it is today. We gathered in a mid-priced hotel for an ordinary meal with some very average Californian red wine. Potentially billions of dollars were at stake, but the reality was very humdrum. It was an early start, leaving the hotel at seven and beginning my two-hour presentation at eight.

The CalPERS office reminded me of a government building: spacious but ordinary. Its officers run a state fund and they are not wasteful with their money. Despite managing billions, everyone was dressed down in chinos and button-down shirts. The room I entered was full: I recall that there were 12 of them and probably eight of us, including three from Goldman, me and one of my salespeople. You could have been in a meeting in Silicon Valley, which was only a couple of hours away.

After the first five minutes, questions poured in. They changed the agenda around as they saw fit, and it became quite an interrogation. Our timing was excellent because many of the largest asset owners were looking to introduce a much more systematic approach to global investment – essentially anything outside the USA. CalPERS wanted to diversify because the larger part of its funds were invested in the US stock market. The low risk way of going global was some form of passive investment.

My pitch was that, if you were approaching global equities, we were the ideal partner. We had built a better benchmark than MSCI, which covered about 70 per cent of the market by value. This meant that MSCI had to be very selective in choosing which stocks could be included in its index. What's the point of following an index that actively selects its constituents? I argued. You might as well just give your money to an active manager. The governance processes around decisions were also much looser in those days. The management of MSCI was able to select the countries to be included with no real challenge. It was judge and jury, and if you didn't like the decision, hard luck.

I knew we could do better than this. We increased our coverage out to 85 per cent of the market by value, which at that time was about as far as you could go given our access to data and the illiquidity of many markets outside of the USA. We also put in place much stronger governance processes around how we classified countries and when to promote or demote a country and we set up advisory groups of the leading investors and banks encouraging them to challenge our decisions. Investors such as CalPERS welcomed our new approach. They wanted more professional global benchmarks which they could use to diversify their funds more cheaply and with much greater transparency.

Zurack chipped in that, if you invested with MSCI, you could lose half a percentage point or more every year because it was effectively acting as a monopoly and hedge funds could front-run the crowd of index funds all following the MSCI index at the same time. Working with FTSE reduced the market impact and would help to avoid that price inflation.

CalPERS was asking questions about certain countries: why was one included here, or what about the political issues there? My answer was that we could customize the index for them. If they had a list of countries they deemed inappropriate for them to invest in, FTSE could exclude those countries from the index. It was a huge gamble. We had never changed the rules in this way for a client before. I thought to myself as I said it that we would struggle to do so. But I didn't want their interest to peter out just yet. I threw it in to win. Customization was about to become a big part of future pitches. It wasn't easy for the guys back in the office. You can customize once and it is like creating a whole new series, but to set yourself up to do it time and again adds a whole new level of complexity. It wasn't greeted with great applause. Everyone wondered how it would be possible. But we sat down and worked it through.

Initially, CalPERS used us in a hybrid benchmark for their passive portfolio and MSCI for the active mandate. The relationship developed in stages. The big win came on 16 March 2001, when we announced that CalPERS would use a customized version of the FTSE All-World Index as its primary international equity portfolio performance benchmark. It was a major international win for us and, more importantly, gave us a foothold in the USA from where half of the world's money is run. CalPERS would adopt the FTSE benchmark for both passive and active international funds, adding up to $35 billion in total.

A few years later the relationship deepened again. CalP-ERS rationalized both its domestic and international benchmarks and made us run off against MSCI, S&P and Russell for the mandate. We won. Within a short space of time, we went from just running their small world index fund to actually running indices for all of their passive money, roughly $500 billion. All of those rounds of pitching were definitely paying off.

The networker

The second key relationship in FTSE's early years was with Reuters. We had long ago moved past the point where the news agency had complained to the competition authorities about the exchange's prices. Under the chief executive Peter Job, it had bigger battles to fight. Reuters was locked in a race with Bloomberg to supply market-sensitive news first, packaged with analysis and an array of datasets on terminals that were a familiar sight in City trading rooms.

The business was notoriously lumpy, governed by whether Wall Street was in a boom or bust. When times were good, traders might have one of each terminal on their desk so they could benefit from both feeds of news and data. In a downturn, they would have to choose which to keep, assuming the traders themselves hadn't also been junked in a wave of cuts.

Bloomberg was only launched in 1981 by Michael Bloomberg, a general partner at Salomon Brothers who used his settlement fee to begin a data business. But its terminals, costing getting on for $20,000 per year each, had earned a reputation for being simpler to use and always innovating. For example, Bloomberg added a messenger service that made its terminals more indispensable than Reuters. How could Reuters differentiate itself? That was where we came in.

One of our biggest challenges when we set up FT-SE International was how were we going to calculate and publish our indices in real time. At the time, the FT Actuaries All-Share and FT-Actuaries World Indices were all calculated at the end of the day and published in the *FT*. Only the UK FTSE 100 and FTSE 250 were calculated in real time, and this was done by the exchange using real-time prices from their own market. To be competitive, we needed to calculate all the indices from around the world in real time, 24 hours a day, initially five days a week, every working day except New Year's Day. The operational challenges were huge, and the costs were outside of our budget. This is where Reuters and a man called Herbie Skeete came to our aid.

Herbie was larger than life and well known in exchange circles worldwide. A Jamaican by birth, he travelled the world for Reuters maintaining their relationships with exchanges and data providers. We hit it off immediately. Reuters would provide the real-time prices from around the world to us and calculate and publish all of our indices, including the FTSE 100. We would manage all changes to the indices from terminals based in our offices in Hong Kong, London and New York. This meant moving the calculation of the FTSE 100 off the exchange's systems and onto Reuters. Neither the LSE, Bloomberg or any of Reuters' competitors were happy about this. But for us, we had a solution to one of our biggest challenges, and by 1999 Reuters was a key partner.

Herbie became a champion for FTSE, and Reuters took on the same task for many more index providers. It was a win-win. We were also invited to some of the City's liveliest parties, courtesy of Herbie, who seemed to know everyone. The London Dungeon was a popular venue, where the cells were filled with unsavoury characters that we joked were ex-bankers, not jobbing actors. FTSE and Reuters had become close partners. Eventually, the company adopted our company classification system, which was a shot in the arm for our international ambitions.

Finally, a deal

When Xavier Rolet returned empty-handed to London from Toronto in summer 2011, one of the first meetings in his diary was with Dame Marjorie Scardino. It appeared to me that the Frenchman had a warmer relationship with the Pearson chief executive than his predecessor, Clara Furse, had had – although their partnership still had its ups and downs.

At one point Rolet – keen to buy the *FT* out – suggested that the LSE would become a very obstructive joint-venture partner if he didn't get his way. That extended to causing problems with everything from dividend flow to licensing. Such behaviour threatened to shrink the value of FTSE, which I had built over many years. Given how important we were to the group's cashflow, it also seemed counterproductive. The Texan-born Dame Marjorie, who appears folksy and softly spoken but is actually incredibly firm when she makes her mind up, was having none of it.

By July 2011, however, they were getting on famously. In Dame Marjorie's corner office off the Strand, which had a balcony looking out over the Thames, they talked about anything and everything – including commiserating over TMX – with the exception of the venture that they had in common.

Rolet had had a setback but he still had a strategy. His target for some time had been to transform the LSE into a $10 billion business. That was quite something given its value was closer to $2 billion when he set out. In 2009, when he rejected the FTSE/DJI merger, he succeeded in acquiring MillenniumIT, a Sri Lankan software firm specializing in capital markets technology. Another deal was for Project Turquoise, which was effectively a bailout of an alternative trading platform backed by nine investment banks that had failed to live up to its billing as a major competitor to the LSE. At this time, the major clearing house LCH.Clearnet also came onto his radar. Rolet was a man in a hurry and up for more deals.

I expected Pearson to exit its FTSE investment at some point. Since Glen Moreno became chairman of Pearson in 2005, the company had accelerated its charge to become the world's top education company. The former Fidelity International chief executive was a big man, thickset, slow and deliberate, but very perceptive. He encouraged Dame Marjorie to redouble her efforts and that meant hiving off more non-core assets to pay for learning assets.

'It is not the role of a company to diversify an investor's shareholding,' he told me in one meeting. 'That's the role of the stock market.' It was rather an ironic comment, given that FTSE had been deeply involved in giving investors the precise blend of asset exposure they wanted for a decade or so.

As everything else that wasn't education-related was gradually being offloaded, I knew that FTSE's time would come. What made us even more appealing as a sale candidate was the fact that indices were trading on anything up to 14 times earnings, a higher premium than most of the assets that Pearson retained. I heard they were under pressure from the credit ratings agencies to reduce borrowings if they wanted to preserve their rating – something that a leading company would want to do at all costs.

Dame Marjorie also had half an eye on her future and the company she wanted to hand over to her successor. In October 2012, 15 months after the Rolet meeting took place, she announced she was stepping down to be replaced by John Fallon, one of her first hires when she arrived at Pearson in 1997.

So when the phone lines between the Strand and Paternoster Square began buzzing in September, it was no surprise. Ever since the original agreement was struck in 1995, the LSE had first refusal if Pearson wanted to exit. In the end, the agreement and the price were locked in very quickly in a series of conversations between Rolet and Scardino: £450 million, valuing the business I had built at a remarkable £900 million. 'And not a cent less,' as Rolet said when Dow Jones had been sniffing around.

Divorce terms

It was the details of the divorce – ongoing agreements about use of the brand and the *FT*'s exclusion from the indices market – that took a long time to thrash out. Pearson also wanted a clause that prevented the LSE from selling us on for at least two years.

After all, the exchange was taking with it the 'FT' that 16 years earlier John Makinson and colleagues thought should have been the sole brand the indices carried. Pearson wanted its use thoroughly protected. From the LSE's point of view, it needed a watertight guarantee that the *FT* could not re-enter the indices market they were leaving any time soon. Night after night, advisers from both sides were closeted away in the offices of Freshfields just off Fleet Street. It wasn't until the end of November – a week or two after the S&P and Dow Jones Indices merger was consummated – when I was let in on the secret that an announcement was imminent.

Fairhead had been in touch. At short notice, she was in New York and could we meet? Late on a Friday afternoon, we sat down in the corner conference room at our office in the Rockefeller Center, gazing down Sixth Avenue to Central Park as the sun began to set. I suspected something was up. Our ownership had been unresolved for too long.

After all the will-they-won't-they uncertainty, Fairhead explained that she was not going to tell me the *FT* was selling out anything other than face to face. She had flown out especially. I don't mind writing that it was an emotional meeting.

By that point, I had known Fairhead for 10 years since she joined Pearson as deputy finance director in 2001 and all the way through her battle with breast cancer.

She thanked me for accepting the news graciously. What choice did I have? Fairhead was clearly choked up, and perhaps even scared for us given how hot and cold Rolet had blown over the last two years. What would happen next? I immediately called Donald Keith and Nick Teunon back in the UK. We were united in our sadness over what we saw as a loss of independence. In the statement announcing the sale on 12 December 2011, Scardino paid tribute.

'FTSE is a bellwether of global financial markets and a world-class business,' her comments ran. But, alongside the plaudits, there was also a steely finality. 'We have enjoyed supporting the company's excellent and highly professional team to build the business. Proud as we are of that long association, FTSE's strategy is different from our own. We wish it every success as we continue to build our digital business information services around the *Financial Times*.'

The notice also included our latest financial details. In 2010, FTSE reported total revenues of £98.5 million and earnings of £40 million. Aside from marvelling at our very healthy profit margins, these numbers demonstrated how far we had come. Compared to what we had made in 1996 – that first year back in St Alphage House – our sales had grown more than 28 times and our profits by 84 times. Neither shareholder could complain.

Part of the family

I was worried about what came next. FTSE had fought for its independence right from the start – even if the grim reality of going our own way began with occupying the down-at-heel

St Alphage House. I was also worried about my future. It was not impossible that at my first meeting with Xavier Rolet following the LSE takeover we would agree that I should depart. What actually happened was far less severe. And when I asked Rolet to step up a couple of years later, he did not disappoint.

FTSE was brought under the wing of the LSE to some extent, which was to be excepted after they spent £450 million. We had a lease to get out of at Canary Wharf, so it was a gradual shift. First of all, I was given a desk at their headquarters in Paternoster Square and I would spend two days a week there when I wasn't travelling. Then the whole team moved in.

We took a floor which I redesigned so it felt like my FTSE still: totally open-plan, which was the complete opposite of the LSE at that time. There were some nerves internally because Rolet was not involved. But when he saw it, he loved it. In time, the rest of the exchange began to look a lot like our floor, which, I comforted myself, was our little takeover of sorts.

Rolet's style was hands-off and he credited me with being independently minded. But the exchange's influence was brought to bear in the £9 millions of synergy targets I had been set. There are two ways to hit the numbers: increase revenues as a result of the deal, or cut costs. Someone had the idea that we would generate more income from trading derivatives on the FTSE 100 at the exchange, but they were already trading on LIFFE, so it was a non-starter. Moving the trading of a derivatives contract from one market to another was not easy and rarely successful. I had to rewrite the plan. We replaced S&P in running Italy's headline index, the MIB, which became the FTSE MIB and expanded the range of domestic indices for the Italian market. We sold our data into the users of both exchanges. We also had to cut costs and that meant cutting more jobs, including almost all of our IT, finance and administrative departments. It was a painful time.

Aside from my own future, I had been concerned about the conflict of interest which was created by the takeover. I had been criticized in the past for adopting a set of rules for our indices that were designed to protect the interests of investors. Sometimes my stance wasn't the best one for attracting listings to London, but I operated at arm's length from the exchange. Not anymore. Rolet well understood the conflict of interest, and not once did he ask me to compromise in order for the exchange to win more business. I could not ask for more.

One development that made my new taskmasters uneasy was the deal I struck in March 2013. The LSE might not have had much luck in Canada, but FTSE was successful. The agreement to pool bond index businesses with TMX at a cost to us of £72 million created a significant competitor in an emerging asset class. In total, assets using our indices as benchmarks would total £640 billion. Cross-border deals were not impossible after all. There were more to come.

Best buy

It must have been 2012 when I started courting Northwestern Mutual. It was a huge financial services company ranked in the top 150 of US corporations and a member of the Fortune 500. PJ Solomon, a New York–based boutique investment bank that I had used for many years at FTSE, approached them initially on my behalf. Based in Milwaukee in the Midwestern state of Wisconsin, Northwestern was not involved in the securities trading industry but it had buried within one of its operating companies an asset I was keenly interested in. They had owned Russell, one of the largest providers of US indices, since 1998. After Dow Jones had eluded us, there were few acquisitions that made sense in the USA, the biggest securities market in the world. Russell ticked every box.

The company began life in 1936 as a small brokerage set up by Frank Russell in Tacoma, Washington, a city a short drive south of Seattle. Much of its success can be traced to Russell's grandson George, who joined in 1958 after graduating from Harvard Business School. He expanded Russell's money management arm as well as branching into consulting services for institutional investors and major US corporations with large pension plans, such as General Motors and JCPenney. In 1980, it began using its research nous to create investment funds for smaller retirement plans and individuals, managing money directly for the first time. Then, in 1984, it evolved again. The same year the FTSE 100 started life in London, Russell created the Russell 1000, Russell 2000 and Russell 3000 indices, so that investors had something against which they could measure fund managers' performance.

The Russell 2000 was the main measure of small-cap performance in the USA and the Russell 3000 was a broader benchmark quite similar to the FTSE All-Share in the UK. Retail funds tended to follow the S&P 500 because it was easier and contained fewer stocks, but the pension funds preferred the much greater diversification provided by the Russell 3000. For that reason, Russell was always on my radar. When three firms – FTSE, MSCI and S&P – set up the Index Industry Association in 2012 to represent our shared interests, I made sure it was my job to bring Russell into the fold. It was a great chance to get to know them but it was sensitive because they thought they should have been there from the start.

I went to dry, hot Milwaukee to try to persuade John Schlifske, the chairman, president and chief executive of Northwestern to sell Russell to us, or at least consider the option of merging the Russell indices into FTSE and keeping a stake in the enlarged business.

The set of products mapped well onto ours, but the amount of money tracking them also convinced me we had to act.

Russell had $6 trillion following its indices. FTSE had $8 trillion. I knew a takeover would be transformational for us. More importantly, I knew that if we failed to take over Russell our last chance to be a scale player in the USA would be gone and therefore our chance to be a truly global indices firm, too. It was hard to overestimate the importance of the USA, which accounts for half of the assets in the world.

Schlifske thought the idea was worth further consideration and we met again, this time with Len Brennan who had run Russell since 2011. Brennan in my view was a little old fashioned, having spent most of his career at Russell, leaving for six years to run another investment manager also based in Seattle. He believed in active management, and I could tell he was more than a little wary of indexation. That said, he didn't want his indices to be broken off and rolled into a larger enterprise that might make life even tougher for his fund managers. Brennan was adamant a deal would not happen. Schlifske tried to reason with him, but Brennan was having none of it. The meeting finished, and John Sheldon and Jeff Jacobs of PJ Solomon and I reluctantly got up to leave. Schlifske was mad. He summoned Brennan to his office, and as we were leaving we heard the door slam and voices raised.

Second chance

That was the end of that. But I kept close to Northwestern nonetheless, and I didn't have long to wait. In late autumn 2013, Northwestern decided to sell Russell and I was one of the first people its bankers called to drum up interest. Of course, finding the target finally willing was one thing. I knew MSCI would be in the hunt, too. We had been chipping away at MSCI for a long time, but this deal would draw us level. Otherwise, it would have taken us 10 to 15 years to get anywhere close.

Gaining the backing of our sole shareholder was another matter. Russell was a huge bite. The exchange hadn't even backed us on DJI at a marginal cost. How on earth could I get them to stump up in excess of $2 billion in what would be their biggest ever deal? The Russell takeover came with problems, too. Rather than splitting the company into its two parts, Northwestern had decided to sell it whole. We had to establish our interest not just for the index, but for the whole business, which managed assets of $266 billion. But the first round of the auction also gave us an opportunity to see how likely it was Northwestern could be persuaded to carve up the business or if it would entertain a joint bid with a fund manager to take on the asset I was not interested in.

The LSE had a central corporate finance department led by David Lester. David had joined the exchange from McKinsey, the global management consulting firm. He had run the technology division of the exchange before leading its information services division as my predecessor and then became the exchange's chief strategy officer. He had been kept extremely busy since Rolet's arrival in 2009. David and I presented jointly to the board as well as the executive committee, of which I was a member. I remember selling in the deal and what it would do for FTSE, not just in the USA but internationally. But all the questions were about the asset management side of the business.

The most material change at board level since the exchange had bought out the *FT* was the arrival of David Warren as chief financial officer in 2012. Warren was steeped in the exchange world, having spent nine years as finance chief at Nasdaq OMX. He, in particular, had little truck with the idea that the exchange should suddenly be investing in the world of asset management which he felt would create a clear conflict of interest because so many of the group's clients managed assets, too. Rolet was more measured. 'Let's focus on the first round,' he said, trying to calm the room. 'One step at a time.'

Tensions rose. Rolet stayed on the fence right to the end – just as he had when I thought we were going to buy DJI five years earlier. In the end, he was the saviour of the deal. In the last meeting before we had to decide whether to push the button on an offer, he ruled that the only way we were going to be successful was if we bid for the whole of Russell.

The final three bidders were reputed to be MSCI, FTSE and the Canadian Imperial Bank of Commerce. We suspected that MSCI had held talks with the fund manager to take that side of Russell off its hands if it was successful. In the end that theory was academic because we bid $2.7 billion for the whole business and were successful. I was elated.

After we were successful, we announced a strategic review of the asset management business. That would have been a sign to all the other fund managers we served on a daily basis that the exchange was not about to expand aggressively into the asset management business. It would give us the time to really understand the business and to determine which parts would fit with FTSE and the exchange or would need to be sold on.

For all the cut and thrust that had taken place among exchanges in recent years, this was the LSE's biggest acquisition, exceeding what it paid for Borsa Italia in 2007. What a vote of confidence in FTSE. Not only that, but some $1.6 billion would have to be raised through a rights issue. It was a significant commitment.

When the deal was announced, on 26 June 2014, Rolet made clear the importance of the move. 'The acquisition of Russell is another significant milestone for the London Stock Exchange Group,' he said in a statement. 'With this acquisition we are strongly positioned for the changing dynamics in the global indices market.' It was another way to drive the group further into North America, exactly what the TMX combination was designed to achieve three years earlier. We were now of similar size to both MSCI and S&P indices and positioned for growth.

I was confident we could overtake both. Briefly owning Russell Investments proved to be no trouble. In October 2015, TA Associates, a Boston private equity firm paid $1.15 billion for the business. A Chinese brokerage, CITIC Securities, had also been interested. I didn't mind which of them took it off our hands. My sights were trained on the future.

It had taken 30 years, but we had gone from an idea on the LSE floor to one of the biggest index providers in the world. It was a triumph for London and ensured that our brand would be known globally. I had not achieved the independence and the stock market listing I had once dreamed of – but this wasn't half bad. FTSE had emerged from the deal-making years as a leader. As the industry readied itself for a dramatic growth spurt, we were just in time.

5
In the club

It was spring 2011 and Ivan Glassenberg, chief executive of Glencore, the secretive Swiss commodities trader, was the talk of the town. After years of rumours, this figure of fascination in global business circles was finally bringing the controversial company he had led since 2002 onto the stock market.

It would be one of the biggest listings that London had ever seen, raising as much as £5 billion of new funding and aiming for a valuation of up to £40 billion. Although low profile, Glencore was vast, trading everything from coal and copper to wheat. It had also bought up mines in some of the world's most politically unstable regimes and ran an oil fleet with more ships than the Royal Navy.

At its heart was a hard-driving band of brothers who had worked together for years. Glasenberg and colleagues stood to crystallize multi-million and -billion-pound paper fortunes from going public. The phalanx of bankers and lawyers working on the transaction would also enjoy their biggest payday in a long time.

But there was a problem. Despite their untold wealth and powers of persuasion that had won lucrative supply contracts and control of assets the world over, I wasn't convinced that Glencore qualified for entry into the FTSE 100. Too few shares were being offered for sale in this listing by the 485 partners that owned Glencore. Funds that tracked the blue-chip index – buying a basket of shares to mirror the weighting of each of the 100 stocks it contained – would struggle to lay their hands on enough.

It was a stumbling block that the company that always got its way was struggling to come to terms with. Listing its shares in London was only part of the deal. To do so without accession to the blue-chip club would be simply unacceptable. The debate had raged between both sides for weeks, and now Glencore, which as it talked to us was simultaneously wooing London's largest pension funds on an extensive investor roadshow, was running out of time.

Over the years, I have dealt with many of the biggest companies in the UK and beyond – and with them come some big personalities in senior leadership positions. Tempers often fray on the way in and the way out of the FTSE 100. Later in this chapter, I will detail encounters with Paul Polman, the chief executive of grocery group Unilever, as well as an incident arising from the *Daily Mail*'s parent company and its dominant shareholder and chairman, Viscount Rothermere. After the challenge of HSBC's takeover of the Midland Bank and ever since we introduced the steering committee that was initially chaired by the fearsome Donald Brydon, we knew how to deal with changes and the inevitable challenges to what we proposed. It is just as well we did. As a small private company, we often found ourselves picking a path between the conflicting desires of vast wealth and establishment institutions. That meant we had to keep standards high – we needed to be impartial, transparent and trustworthy.

An elite club

Since the index was created on a windy January morning in 1984 it had changed to reflect something the pioneers of that first list could not have realized. Companies were lured to trade their shares in London because of the deep pools of capital the market offered. But there was something else. The

FTSE 100 – which was calculated from the total market capitalization of its constituents and changed as each individual share price fluctuated through the trading day – had developed enormous cachet. For us as guardians of its membership, the stakes had been raised.

The FTSE 100 had obviously become a byword for scale, but also a kitemark for quality. Not only did its members attract extra funds to their shares – because index trackers were forced to buy them – but it could bolster the reputation of firms. That boost counted double if the company in question, like Glencore, was based somewhat off the beaten track. Finally, that prestige was enhanced by the finite resource of membership, capped at 100. No more, no less: in the corporate world it was like gaining access to debentures at Wimbledon or being given a box at the Albert Hall.

I know chief executives who have retired from full-time executive office with one aim for the latter stages of their career: to chair a FTSE 100 company. Many have been frustrated because they never made it into that exclusive club. If you consider that some individuals juggled two or even three chairmanships concurrently, membership was even fewer than 100. And, unlike the Athenaeum Club or RAC Club or any of the other exclusive members' retreats that line Pall Mall and St James's, getting in wasn't as easy as being proposed and seconded by long-time friends or colleagues.

In most cases, the market decides. That is, shareholders need to approve whoever chairs the company they own. They need a safe pair of hands to keep the chief executive in check and make sure the strategy is delivered on. If the face doesn't fit, change it. In 2004, the former chairman and chief executive of the Bass brewing empire Sir Ian Prosser faced the ignominy of being dumped as chairman designate of Sainsbury's after a particularly vicious investor outcry.

Then there is promotion and relegation in and out of the FTSE 100, which has nothing to do with personalities and everything to do with stock performance. The FT 30 prided itself on its subjectivity – and its members are to this day selected by *FT* editors – but the FTSE 100 aspired to be totally objective. And we were – most of the time.

FTSE holds a quarterly meeting to review the constituents of the FTSE 100 and FTSE 250, which I added in 1992 to group together the next largest 250 qualifying stocks traded in London. Based on the market value at close of business the night before the meeting, a stock will be promoted into the FTSE 100 if it ranks in 90th position or above. Correspondingly, a stock will be removed if it has fallen to 111th position or below. In some quarters, there is brisk trading a day or so before our decision is taken. I suspect that some companies will do almost anything not to lose their hallowed status.

Even those chairmen who have chaired a hatful of FTSE 100 firms still crave more. The celebrated industrialist Sir John Parker had five blue-chip chairmanships to his name, including the diversified miner Anglo American, which owns De Beers diamonds. In March 2020 that became six when South West Water's parent company Pennon, where Parker served as chairman, achieved promotion after bobbing around near the top of the FTSE 250 for some time.

Sir Roger Carr is another serial FTSE 100 chairman drawn to these big jobs, I think by a sense of duty as much as for what it does to his standing in business and political circles. On his watch, Cadbury Schweppes was sold to American food group Kraft, one of the most highly charged foreign takeovers of a British company in recent memory. He moved on to chair Centrica, the owner of British Gas, and then defence contractor BAE Systems, so he is fairly fearless.

Who's in, who's out?

FTSE 100 membership has transformed over the years. The comings and goings say everything about Corporate Britain, but also London's place as a global financial hub. Some great industrial names have gone that housed a multitude of activities. Bowater (diesel engines and telephone cards), Hanson Trust (cigarettes and building aggregates) and GEC (shipbuilding and electronics) were old-style conglomerates strung together by historical quirk or the whims of all-powerful managers such as Sir Eric Bowater, Lord Hanson and Lord Weinstock.

I suspect the rise of FTSE aided their decline. Rather than spending time getting to know one company with numerous assets or learning to understand a leader's particular idiosyncratic style, shareholders wanted focus. And that meant simplicity either from buying into a company that did one thing well or a basket of shares conveniently grouped together. It meant conglomerates fell out of fashion and were broken up either voluntarily by their managers or after a period of shareholder pressure. Outliers were not welcome.

In their place have emerged technology and telecoms firms, some of which were barely imagined in 1984. One of these, Vodafone, used the currency of its FTSE 100 membership to impressive effect as it built an international mobile phone empire through deal after deal, planting flags in the USA, Germany and India. It is also a young company, only taking its name a year after FTSE 100 began life.

A quartet of others – Just Eat, Takeaway.com, Auto Trader, Rightmove and Ocado – have transformed the way we buy takeaway food, cars, homes and groceries. And because so much investor money is chasing stocks with the power to disrupt whole industries, their sky-high valuations despite often skimpy profits are enough for the average restaurant company, car dealership, estate agent and supermarket chain to go green with envy.

The other big change has been the rise of the service economy and numerous companies that don't make anything in the traditional sense. Coffee shops are always seen to epitomize the shift from production lines and factory gates – although the UK remains the world's seventh-largest manufacturing nation. Whitbread, the owner of coffee chain Costa until Coca-Cola offered them a sensational price for it, has been through more changes of corporate direction than most. But it is the out-sourcing companies that for a time had the biggest impact on the FTSE 100 numbers-wise.

The focus that shareholders demanded from conglomerates led all manner of non-essential activities to be contracted out to someone else. These specialists bid for administrative contracts, customer service work, catering, cleaning and caretaking – the tasks that someone else did not want to bother with. Capita, Serco and Compass became some of the biggest firms in their field until some – not all – found that they, too, had over-stretched themselves like the conglomerates of old.

The debt-fuelled deals that took place in the run-up to the financial crisis of 2008 saw several well-known names exit the FTSE 100. The UK has always prided itself on transparent, open markets with few vested interests or political interests. Rightly or wrongly, that meant some companies were vulnerable to takeover. In short order, ICI, Alliance Boots, the owner of Heathrow and Gatwick airports, BAA, and the mobile phone operator O2, all disappeared from the index at the hands of Dutch, Swiss and Spanish acquirers.

It was a reminder of the international nature of business and with it has come the internationalization of the FTSE 100. At the Lord Mayor's Mansion House banquet for bankers in June 2004, Mervyn King, then the Governor of the Bank of England, talked about the 'Wimbledonization' of the City, which is, as he put it, 'hosting a successful tournament where most of the winners come from overseas'. The FTSE 100 has been a magnet for all-comers. To extend the tennis analogy, Andy Murray's career success has shown that domestic talent can thrive, too. But I tend to agree with King's point that the Bank of England is not there to expressly engineer the promotion of more British financial institutions to the global top ranks. Instead, FTSE has concentrated on 'creating an environment which encourages innovation and provides first-rate infrastructure', to borrow his words delivered to guests in the Square Mile's sumptuous Egyptian Hall that night.

Since the Millennium, the path to London and to my door was beaten with increasing frequency by companies about which many UK investors knew little. In 2003, Vedanta, the Indian mining company listed in London, followed two years later by Kazakhmys, a copper extractor from Kazakhstan. Eurasian Natural Resources (ENRC) arrived in 2007, and then Fresnillo, a Mexican silver miner in 2008, and in 2010 Essar Energy, a power, oil and gas supplier that was spun out of the Indian Essar conglomerate. Because they were all resources companies, they had few if any assets in the UK. But they were riding the boom created by China's soaring consumption of raw materials. London and the FTSE had long been home to some of the world's biggest mining concerns such as BHP Billiton, Anglo American and Rio Tinto, so it was a natural place to come. They changed the complexion of the FTSE 100 for ever.

A rich seam

I was initially concerned about this. FTSE, as part of London's corporate and financial infrastructure, had to be welcoming, but we also had to maintain high standards for investors. Not anyone could be guaranteed entry just because of their scale and the corporate brokers pushing their case said so. The powers-that-be suggested I should relax a little. There was a particular incident I recall.

In the spring of 1999, I attended a seminar at the Bank of England to discuss preparations for the year 2000. It seems silly now, but there was some concern that when the date passed over from 1999 to 2000 it might cause numerous computer systems to fail. If it had caused turmoil, the so-called Millennium Bug would have been a legacy of early computer programs that used two-digit date codes instead of four. In the event, the disruption was minimal. We, like most of the financial world, had employed independent software analysts to review our coding to reassure us that we could cope with the Millennium Bug. And that is what I told attendees that day – that the index would be up and running as usual when traders returned to their screens on 2 January.

As the seminar ended I got up to leave, but Sir David Clementi asked if I had a moment to chat. Sir David was a big figure at the Bank, where he had served as Deputy Governor since 1997. In addition to his membership of the Monetary Policy Committee, which set the UK's interest rates, he oversaw day-to-day management of the Bank and had specific responsibility for the work that was done on financial stability. He was steady, dependable and a big thinker who made his name at the investment bank Kleinwort Benson where he worked for 22 years, rising to become chief executive.

The year 1999 had been busy for London listings. One country in particular was the cause of all this activity: South Africa. Ever since the mining group Billiton had listed in London and joined the FTSE 100 in 1997, other firms listed in Johannesburg had been casting envious looks in our direction. Billiton had easier access to capital to expand beyond its South African aluminium interests. Another miner, Anglo American, as well as

financial services group Old Mutual and South African Brew-
eries, owner of Castle lager, made the same journey, transferring
their primary listing to London and seeking entry to the FTSE
100. It was clear more would follow.

To some degree, this internationalization was inevitable.
The UK was already an significant equities hub, accounting
for 6 per cent of the global market compared to the nation's
3 per cent share of world gross domestic product. Bigger, global
companies were seeking larger pools of capital. But we had to
think through the changes carefully if it meant the UK's leading
index would decouple from the UK economy over time.

Institutional investors including pension funds who bought
the UK index to cover the cost of their UK liabilities were
raising concerns. Most of them invested over half their funds in
what they thought were large safe British businesses. Suddenly
they were being required to buy foreign mining companies
at what they believed were inflated prices dreamed up by the
big investment banks. The earnings of these companies were
in US dollars not sterling, and the value of their shares were
influenced by global events not the UK economy. There was
increasingly a mismatch, and the FTSE 100 was beginning to
become detached from the UK economy. These investors did
not want what they thought were emerging market companies run from outside of the UK and largely shielded from the
influence of the UK's corporate governance bodies included in
their domestic portfolios. These mining companies were much
riskier than the safe UK businesses they had previously held in
their domestic funds.

And then there was the fact that some of these new foreign
companies were controlled from overseas by a single foreign
investor holding 50 per cent or more of the company. Under
the UK listings and corporate governance practice of 'comply
or explain', UK investors argued that Russian oligarchs were

unlikely to follow UK practices if it was not in their interests. It was clear we could not have an open-door policy allowing any foreign company to choose to join the FTSE 100 club.

On the one hand, FTSE was caught between worried asset managers. On the other, the likes of Cazenove was raking in fees from companies that were keen to list in London and enter the FTSE. The Treasury and the Bank thought it good news, too, as it helped grow London's share of global trading.

Cazenove was no less powerful than it had been in the days of Patrick Mitford-Slade, who oversaw delivery of Big Bang. In fact, its reach was greater. It had made a virtue of being one of the few broking houses not to sell out to American and Swiss competitors in the latter half of the 1980s. Now it provided powerful consiglieri to a huge swathe of FTSE 100 firms, acting as eyes and ears among shareholders.

The most influential of those consiglieri was David Mayhew, tall, thin and always immaculately dressed. The year 1999 was a busy one for him. As adviser to NatWest, he made a rare misjudgement that autumn, championing the bank's combination with Legal & General to forge a bancassurance giant that would offer banking services alongside life and protection policies. Shareholders thought it was a stinker, and the fallout forced NatWest into the arms of the Royal Bank of Scotland.

That it was proposed in the first place suggests to what degree Cazenove thought it could walk on water. Mayhew seemed to be involved in almost every conversation our committees were having at that time, and he was a regular attendee because he was acting for so many companies including several of the arrivals from South Africa. He could see the way the wind was blowing and used his considerable influence to push back against our rules. I was careful around him because he had the ear of everyone.

Sir David Clementi and I walked through the Bank of England's ornate corridors to his grand office where I took a seat. I paraphrase, but the nature of what he had to say to me was: 'Look, old boy, you're not playing the game.' Now I knew what it was like to be on the receiving end of the Governor's eyebrow.

Stung by the criticism that I was not working in the best interests of the UK and the City of London, I reminded him of the impact of our decisions on British pensioners who were more than likely invested in the broad FTSE 100 portfolio whether they liked it or not. IPOs (initial public offerings) are priced by the brokers based on perceived demand. If we brought these overseas stocks into the index in the way that Cazenove and other corporate advisers would like, the passive index funds would appear to be buyers. This would create an artificial demand which the bankers could use to inflate the IPO price.

Sir David was taken back by my response. He was hearing the other side of the argument probably for the first time. I suggested he could put some of his concerns in writing or we could carry on talking. It would be a good idea if he raised these issues with one of our committees of leading fund managers. He did and, as the debate continued, subsequently came to speak at a number of our events and became a supporter of our governance approach.

The Bank adapted its stance but over time so did we. The flurry of South African arrivals ended, but other countries had their eye on what we could offer them. FTSE had set out looking for three things from companies that wanted to join the FTSE 100: the UK incorporation of the company, a premium LSE listing and a UK tax domicile. Over time, those rules were eased but we had to tread a difficult path and the right direction was not always clear to us or the large institutional fund managers that depended on our judgement.

I started the process by changing the membership of our advisory committees, bringing on US, European and Asian fund managers who invested in the UK to ensure we took a more international view. They questioned why we insisted on companies having a UK tax domicile rather than allowing them to structure their tax in the most efficient way for the benefit of shareholders. After all, many of these companies earned most of their revenues outside of the UK. Some companies incorporated in the Channel Islands or other tax havens such as the Cayman Islands to save money. Should they fall out of the index because they had made that decision? Or should we throw them out, forcing people that were invested in them and had engaged with them to sell? We decided they could stay, so our Holy Trinity was relaxed and the primary driver to admission became a premium listing on the LSE. Our changes were motivated by not losing companies from the index that people intuitively felt were UK companies. But such was the attraction of the FTSE 100 around the world that we had all sorts of companies beating a path to our door and demanding a level playing field for themselves.

Glencore: a controversial case

A decade later, the FTSE 100 reflected London's status as the world's financial capital. Glencore's ambition to join the club was no surprise. It was not a household name but its reach across global trade was breathtaking. There was suspicion among investors, but there was a fascination, too, about how this business had been built. Discretion had been its watchword, as evidenced by its headquarters that were tucked away in the small town of Baar, a few miles outside Zug in central Switzerland. Now it was finally taking the covers off its operating model. Glencore had been founded in 1974 by Marc Rich, a slick commodities trader who was indicted in the USA for tax evasion and striking oil deals with Iran during the Iran hostage crisis of 1979 but later pardoned by President Clinton. Having long ago severed ties with Rich, some likened this listing to the 1999 flotation of Goldman Sachs, when partners at Wall Street's leading investment bank became multimillion-aires overnight.

Its past meant it was a controversial flotation from the off. There was the worry that Glencore might use its public listing as currency to buy out Xstrata – a mining peer it part-owned and knew well because it had taken Glencore's coal assets and built itself up into a diversified miner. In fact, one alternative to a flotation was rumoured to involve engineering a reverse takeover of Xstrata, which was already in the FTSE 100. Either way, investors wondered what exactly they would be getting by buying this stock.

The company had been working up to a listing since 2008 and had assembled an expensive cabal of advisers. Almost every investment bank in the City seemed to be on the ticket: Credit Suisse, Morgan Stanley, Citi, you name them, they were involved, plus the blue-chip law firm Clifford Chance and pub-lic relations outfit Finsbury.

With such an army of support, it was surprising then that vital jigsaw pieces were slow to be slotted into place in the early months of 2011. One question yet to be answered was: who was going to become Glencore's non-executive chair? It was a vital role if Glencore was going to comply with UK rules of good governance and usher in the type of challenge that a strong board should offer. The former BP chief executive Lord Browne was mooted, only for his name to be swiftly struck off the list. Eventually, the company alighted on Simon Murray, a former French Legionnaire who made his name working in property, telecoms and banking, largely in Hong Kong.

Glencore was incorporated in Jersey and tax registered and headquartered in Switzerland but wanted to be in the FTSE 100. That was not impossible, as long as it incorporated here. Because of its size, the company would qualify for fast entry to the FTSE 100 on its first day of trading. This was extremely rare. Only two stocks had achieved that privilege before and both were major privatizations. There was British Gas, which had been marketed heavily with the 'Tell Sid' advertising campaign of 1986. Prior to that in 1984 there was BT, the first of the big state monopolies to be sold and the spearhead of Margaret Thatcher's policy of bringing share ownership to the masses. In both those cases, as with Glencore, from a size point of view keeping the stock out of the index would be distorting because the FTSE 100 would no longer be reflective of the wider market.

Of more pressing concern to me was the number of shares that was actually going to be listed. As a non-UK incorporated company (Jersey did not count as part of the UK for the purposes of the inclusion rules), Glencore needed 50% free float to be admitted to the FTSE 100, but it was planning only a 12% free float at the time of the IPO. Glencore fell a long way short. At the first meeting, with their advisers ranged along the table opposite us, the company put their case, we put ours, and a list of issues emerged that we asked them to resolve. I left that meeting thinking they weren't going to be able to do it. Glencore wanted all the benefits of FTSE membership without ceding any control to outside shareholders. Investors just weren't going to wear what they were suggesting.

At the next meeting, they were clearly more focused. The finance director, Seve Kalmin, was there, along with his head of investor relations, two more colleagues plus two sets of bankers. In total, there was probably a dozen of them. It was a real deposition. Glencore's executives were a tight-knit bunch. Kalmin had been in the top finance role since 2005 but joined the business six years previously as a finance general manager at Glencore's coal business that had gone on to become part of Xstrata. Glasenberg also began in coal.

Despite the strength in numbers, nothing had really changed. I told Kalmin they had to go public with their plans. There was only so much confidential information I wanted to hear, otherwise FTSE would technically be made insiders to this transaction – never a good idea. Big stocks could list in London without joining the FTSE 100 but it was not ideal.

An unexpected intervention

The problem was the restricted nature of the stock. A large number of Glencore's management held large stakes in the company. My concern was the lack of evidence that these people were free to sell. By holding their shares for longer they could limit the supply, which would have the effect of keeping the share price artificially high. I needed 100 stocks that were liquid – in other words, there needed to be sufficient numbers of buyers and sellers at any one time. They argued that enforcing that rule would deprive investors of the chance to access the flotation, which can be a good time to buy before the stock appreciates.

Glencore had begun to shift its stance slightly, offering to limit restricted stock to just key senior staff. But we needed to know what that meant, how other members would be free to sell, and how and when that stock would come onto the market.

I was flanked by Chris Woods, who just over a year earlier had become FTSE's head of governance and policy and quickly became one of FTSE's leading thinkers. Chris graduated from Cambridge in Physics, got his D.Phil in Atomic

Collision at Oxford, and his MBA at the London Business School in Finance. He was the closest thing to a rocket scientist in finance and had served on our advisory committee when he was the chief investment officer in London at State Street Global Advisors, one of the largest index investors in the world, so he knew the lie of the land. He had later moved to Man Group, the hedge fund manager, and after a meeting in Nice for EDHEC, the world-renowned French business school on whose international advisory board we both sat, I persuaded him to join us.

Maintaining standards

Our position at that point was that Glencore would not go into the index, and we would wait for a period of three or six months to review. But at the same time we were all trying to make it work. That is what made this situation so unusual. Glencore actually met the rules in every way apart from this particular issue. And there was some sympathy among the investors that we didn't want to create too many barriers for companies to come to London.

Glencore kept nudging up the portion of shares it would sell and we took soundings from the largest passive investors – BlackRock, Vanguard, Legal & General and State Street – initially one by one and then collectively. Their views varied. The biggest concern was about the FTSE 100's reputation and price distortion. They were set up to track indices so they wanted to make sure that the value of those indices – the combined value of the stocks within any given index – was fair. They also wanted reassurance that the companies that were granted access were good quality and should meet certain operating standards.

That the FTSE 100 had internationalized to such a degree did not concern investors. They could also buy the FTSE 250 if they wanted a closer proxy to the health of the UK economy. What perturbed some of the trackers was that, after the influx of mining stocks, the FTSE mix had changed. By this point some 40 per cent of the index weighting came from resources stocks, including oil and gas. Some were long-standing members and big dividend payers, such as BP and Royal Dutch Shell. That was fine. But because the index had hitched its wagons to basic commodities in this way, trading was going to be more volatile than it had been a generation ago.

My number-one job had always been to uphold the reputation of the index, but I was also mindful of political concerns. Around that time in 2011, there was some renewed pressure to keep London ahead of the pack as the premium location for share listings and fund raisings. There was always competition from New York, but Hong Kong had also stepped up efforts to woo new mandates. It had made particular strides in the luxury goods sector, with fashion house Prada exploring a listing there that year.

Before approaching us about inclusion, any company seeks clearance from the UK Listings Authority (UKLA), which is part of the Financial Conduct Authority (FCA). At the time of the Glencore transaction, it was housed within the Financial Services Authority (FSA). The UKLA is a global centre for the issuance of securities, which means it oversees every tradable financial instrument including shares and bonds. It also monitors market disclosures, reviews prospectuses in which companies must set out their offer for prospective shareholders, and ensures the listing rules are obeyed.

After that, a firm seeks access to a regulated platform, in this instance the main market of the LSE. And then, if admissible, they can apply to become a member of any of the FTSE indices. It wasn't a perfect system because one of these institutions could put pressure on another to act. Most stocks, Glencore included, did not want one approval without another. The banks pushed for more liberal rules which would increase access to

London listings, and the fund managers sought higher stand-ards to restrict the inflow of riskier companies to the index. We chose to listen to the concerns of investors rather than the banks, as these were the ultimate users of the indices who we were serving. Xavier Rolet, the LSE's chief executive, knew it was best that the exchange boss had no influence over the index, but that didn't always ease his frustration.

In the end, there was a breakthrough. Glencore would release enough staff from restrictions so as to create a minimum free float of 50% of the company within 12 months after the IPO date. The ultimate decision comes from consensus building between the company, major investors and their financial advisors. We hosted a final meeting in our Canary Wharf headquarters with all the investors and interested parties in the same room. We don't quite take a vote, but we do go around the room and gauge approvals, yes or no. The view of major investors was that, although Glencore had come in lower than our threshold at the time of the IPO, inclusion into FTSE 100 should be permitted given the company would have 50% free float within a year's time, and in the meantime the founders would retain sufficient 'skin in the game' to assure investors. The company that always seems to get what it wants did so once again but there would be consequences for the UK market.

On 14 December 2011, seven months after Glencore made its stock market debut, we conducted a wide public consultation and announced changes to increase the minimum free float required for entry into the FTSE UK indices by UK-incorporated compa-nies from 15 per cent to 25 per cent with no exceptions, even if the UKLA approved a premium listing with a lower free float. The decision firmed up what had been guidance up until now. For the five overseas miners that did not meet the threshold at that point – ENRC, Essar Energy, Ferrexpo, Evraz and Fresnillo – there would be a two-year grace period for them to comply or they would face an embarrassing eviction.

As soon as the listing day itself, it was clear Glencore's stock was not liquid enough for everyone that needed to buy. I knew that something had to change. We consulted widely through autumn and our amendments were endorsed by 83 per cent of City investment managers we talked to. However, I was still caught in the middle of another row.

In the newspapers I was criticized by Ian Hannam, the banker at JP Morgan Cazenove who had brought many of these exotic mining stocks to London, for taking a 'Little Britain' stance that would hit the UK economy. He labelled FTSE's decision as a 'death knell for London IPOs (initial public offerings),' just as the market had become more difficult.

Yet corporate governance experts said I had not gone far enough. The powerful National Association of Pension Funds wanted greater protection for shareholder rights, calling for a clear timetable to review the 25 per cent minimum and an eventual move towards 50 per cent.

It illustrated to me just how much FTSE 100 membership matters. Trillions of pounds track these chosen 100 companies and the wealth of millions of people depends on their performance. It is the club that everyone in the corporate landscape wants to join. And when they do make it, they realize the scrutiny of them and of us is intense. That is exactly as it should be.

Read all about it

All the while I was trying to ensure that standards were kept high by the new entrants to our indices, there were parallel efforts to nudge long-standing members of the FTSE 100 and FTSE 250 to be more transparent and easier to trade. Such efforts are typically welcomed in the pages of the *Daily Mail*, the voice of Middle England whose business pages try to champion the interests of small shareholders. The drive for better corporate governance is a regular topic of its news and commentary – except when the subject happens to be its own parent company.

Daily Mail and General Trust (DMGT) was listed on the LSE in 1932, a decade after it was established to manage the Harmsworth family's interests that had expanded since brothers Alfred and Harold began publishing the *Daily Mail* in 1896. Over the years, the company has diversified into trade conferences, websites and information companies and was large enough to move in and out of the FTSE 100 on occasion. What the company was surprised to hear from us in 2010 was that, unless it made changes, it would be dropped as a member of the FTSE 250 – and in fact from all of FTSE's UK indices – in June 2012 as part of a shake-up.

DMGT stuck out because it had a dual listing. One class of shares carried the voting rights kept by the family and was very illiquid. There was a second – ordinary – class for everyone else. They were easier to buy and sell but exerted very little power over the direction of the business.

Our changes were prompted by the UKLA, which replaced its regime of primary and secondary listings with premium and standard listings in 2010 and decided to exclude non-voting shares from its regime. FTSE followed suit.

In the old way of running indices, approximation used to be good enough. Now you have better data flows and the investors want much greater accuracy because costs matter. Therefore, we have to represent how the portfolio deals with things in a much more exact way. Problems arise from the lack of liquidity and stocks that can't easily be bought. As standards get higher, every so often anomalous companies become affected.

The announcement started a two-year countdown; none of these changes was meant to be a surprise. I knew DMGT's finance director, Stephen Daintith, from his time at Dow Jones, with whom we had negotiated – ultimately unsuccessfully – to

acquire the group's indices division. We had two or three meetings, where he came back with a number of questions. The situation was very awkward for him and in one particularly tense
encounter he left seemingly in tears.

DMGT clearly didn't want to be cast out, but I don't think
it was going to fight tooth and nail like Glencore – and it
clearly wasn't going to restructure or append voting rights to
the second class of stock. Its concern was that this would be
dressed up as an issue for the *Daily Mail* – and it hated to make
it into the headlines itself. There was a list of five stocks the
changes affected and all the rest fell into line, including the
blue-blooded asset manager Schroders which had a very small
portion of non-voting shares that it continued with.

On 18 April, FTSE announced that DMGT's A ordinary
non-voting shares would leave its UK index series on 18
June following the next quarterly index review. We explained
why they had fallen foul – because they had no voting rights
attached. DMGT issued a statement of its own to clarify the
situation after confusion among its shareholder base.

In the stock exchange statement, Daintith said: 'We explained
in our 2010 and 2011 Annual Reports that FTSE's adoption of
the FSA's new listing classifications for determining the weighting of share classes in their indices would mean that DMGT's
weighting in the UK Index Series would fall from 75% to 0%
once our "A" shares are re-designated by the FSA as having a
standard listing.' He added: 'This change will have no impact on
the approach DMGT takes to its obligations as a listed company.
It will continue to adopt the obligations and practices of the UK
Listing Rules as they have applied to DMGT historically, maintaining the highest standard of governance and disclosure including the application of the UK Corporate Governance Code.'

Further changes several years later mean that DMGT may be
ejected from FTSE's global indices, too. In a way, it was collateral
damage. When Snap, the company behind social media service

Snapchat, listed shares in March 2018 it did so with no voting rights attached at all. This was the apotheosis for Silicon Valley founders who wanted to retain as much control over their companies as possible. I felt it was unacceptable and set a dangerous precedent. Not only did we exclude Snap from all FTSE indices, we also added a new requirement for developed market companies to have more than 5 per cent of voting rights in the hands of independent shareholders by September 2022. If anything, DMGT has moved in the opposite direction because in 2013 Viscount Rothermere's family trusts bought all of the company's voting shares.

A Marmite stock

So many companies have clamoured to get into the FTSE 100 over the years I have lost count. On occasion, firms tried to leave, too. But that was not usually such a popular decision with their shareholders.

It is not our role to encourage or dissuade companies from seeking to join or leave the FTSE 100 or another of our indices. We are impartial. But it is important that companies understand our rules and can factor them into their decision making. This reduces unnecessary friction. In 2018, I got wind that something was happening at Unilever. A couple of big investors mentioned to me a plan the company was formulating that threatened its inclusion in the FTSE 100. Currently, the Anglo-Dutch consumer goods group had a dual structure, with shares listed in London and Amsterdam, but its incorporation and primary listing in London ensured its FTSE membership.

If that changed, it would be a blow, and not just for investors. Unilever was embedded in the UK. Its Dove soap, Magnum ice cream, Hellmann's mayonnaise, Marmite spread and Persil washing powder lined supermarket aisles. It invested heavily. Despite its global outlook, two of its six research and development sites were based in the UK. And it was forward-looking. Its founding father, Lord Leverhulme, built homes for his soap factory workers at Port Sunlight on the Wirral in the north-west of England more than a century ago. Of course, that presence does not disappear just because of where its primary listing is located, but it can affect the focus on a market over time.

Unilever's chief executive, Paul Polman, was something of legend in British business by this point. He didn't just lead one of its largest companies, he was outspoken on doing business better, whether that was helping small farmers in developing markets link to his group's vast supply chain or cutting down on global water consumption. But sometimes the tall, patrician Dutchman was caught out, as happened in early 2017 when Unilever attracted an unwanted £100 billion takeover approach from the ruthlessly run Kraft Heinz that threw fresh attention on his campaigning ways. That offer was ultimately unsuccessful, but it forced Polman to take a fresh look at sharpening up performance, including offloading Unilever's spreads division which included the Flora margarine brand. I was convinced that that this new-found defensiveness was where this latest move came from. The Dutch listing rules were more helpful when it came to fending off takeovers.

Polman and I were both speakers at a Stock Exchange event on 2 February 2018, almost a year after Kraft dropped its audacious attempt. The market was opened that day by Brenda Trenowden, the global chair of the 30% Club, which campaigns to get more women on FTSE 350 boards and in senior management roles. FTSE launched a new gender diversity index that morning to support the 30% Club and there was a roundtable discussion about how companies and investors engaged on the issue that featured Polman and Hiro Mizuno, the chief investment officer of Japan's government pension investment fund.

As soon as the programme ended, I took Polman aside for a quick word. I wasn't looking for confirmation of what Unilever was up to, 'but if you are thinking about this, here are some of the issues you may want to bear in mind,' I said. I also informed him that any switch was going to be unpopular with UK institutions for whom Unilever was a big FTSE 100 constituent. Polman didn't want them to sell, but I explained the passive funds would have to if it dropped out. As we parted, I recommended that Unilever's investment banking advisers got in touch to talk further.

Sure enough, Unilever declared in March 2018 that it was replacing its twin headquarters with one base, a single legal entity incorporated in Rotterdam. It positioned the decision as a historical tidying-up. Its two listed holding companies went back to the merger of Lever Brothers with Margarine Unie of the Netherlands in 1930. The company had designs on remaining in the FTSE 100, but our rules say that if you incorporate, list your shares and offer sufficient liquidity in another country then that's where you belong. Unilever thought that keeping its listing in London as well as its operations would have given it some leeway. But by June the company admitted it would be 'extremely unlikely' it would remain in the FTSE 100 after the restructuring even though it would maintain its premium listing. It would instead take up membership of the Dutch Euronext index. By September, the stage was set for a battle with shareholders who didn't want it to exit the blue-chip club.

Polman is very charismatic and used to getting his way. In the beginning, we talked directly but when I explained again the issues he was going to face, he lost interest. He pushed forward his finance director, Graeme Pitkethly, to take the problem away. We went through the numbers with Unilever to show them how much money followed the UK and how much followed the European Union indices. It seemed illogical to us. We just didn't think they were seeing the issues clearly. Pitkethly and his team were in our office constantly. I think Polman doubted what I was saying because he thought I had a vested interest in Unilever staying put.

The departure of one of the original members of the FTSE 100 and the third-largest by market value was a blow to the UK government which was still trying to work through what a post-Brexit world would look like. Decisions like this made me think London was no longer the global centre that it used to be even though the FTSE 100 retained prestige. But we had to remain impartial. As stapled units – where two different share types are legally bound and traded together – fell out of fashion, two more Anglo-Dutch firms, Royal Dutch Shell and the professional publisher and data business Relx, had consolidated in London. By moving in the opposite direction, Unilever was the odd one out, and it raised the question of why. There was Brexit, of course, which could be taking the sheen off the attraction of a UK listing for global entities. But in London's favour was that the other markets in Europe were too small for these companies and drew far less interest from the hugely powerful passive funds.

Unilever pointed out that its Dutch arm was valued at a fifth more than the UK arm and that more of its shares were traded in the Netherlands. The UK investors retorted that they were not being compensated adequately for what they were giving up, including the dividend stream. The passive funds were not incentivized either. Worse still, foreign investors in the Netherlands pay a 15 per cent withholding tax. Unilever was trying to drag people along, not getting them on board. From meeting after meeting, Pitkethly came back with the same issues.

Nevertheless, the company took it to the wire. And what we told them would happen did indeed play out. Pitkethly knew they were going to lose, but Polman was determined to push this through as his swan song. There were scheduled meetings on 25 and 26 October to vote on the plan, with the new shares due to begin trading on Christmas Eve 2018. They never got that far.

Unilever needed support from 75 per cent of UK investors to make the proposed changes but, despite more than 200 meetings with investors and taking out full-page newspaper advertisements to press its case, it never got close. Numerous UK investors sounded off about the plan, including Legal & General Investment Management, Aviva Investors and Royal London Asset Management. Less than two months after admitting defeat, Polman announced his retirement.

And then, a postscript. Eighteen months after Polman had left the building, Unilever performed a remarkable U-turn. On 11 June 2020, the company announced it would unify its legal structure under a single UK parent company, retaining its membership in the FTSE UK series with the expected inclusion in the AEX index as well. The new chairman of Unilever, Nils Andersen, said: 'Unilever's Board believes that unifying the company's legal structure will create greater strategic flexibility, remove complexity and further improve governance.' It was a fascinating battle. As has been the case so often, FTSE had a front-row seat. I seek to do two things in those situations. First of all, uphold our rules so that investors get a fair deal. And where our rules do not adequately cover the circumstances, I mediate to find a solution which the majority of investors will support. The FTSE 100 has become such as powerful brand because so many vested interests come together. It means, as in the case of Unilever, that sometimes one entity, however powerful, cannot call the shots.

Reputation matters

I should mention finally NMC Health, another FTSE 100 company that was caught out – with far more damaging consequences. On 27 February 2020, in a very rare event, it became the first member of the blue-chip club to have its shares suspended from trading for many years.

NMC – which stands for National Medical Centre – became the first Abu Dhabi-based company to list in London when it arrived in 2012. It had a fascinating backstory. The founder, Bavaguthu Raghuram Shetty, came to the oil-rich UAE from India in 1973 with $8 in his pocket and the debt from his sister's wedding to pay off. He set up as a drugs salesman and then opened a pharmacy shop and clinic into which he used to carry patients on his shoulders in lieu of an ambulance. The group grew to operate numerous private hospitals, day care centres and fertility clinics across the region. Its shares appreciated strongly and entered the FTSE 100 in September 2017.

NMC got into trouble less than three years later, attracting the attention of short seller Muddy Waters, which published an annihilation of its finances alleging doubts over asset values, cash levels, profits and debt. The company rebutted the lot, only to disclose later inaccuracies in the share register, including Shetty's stake, part of which may have been pledged as collateral elsewhere, and a series of off-balance sheet loans. The FCA investigation is still ongoing.

What a mess. FTSE takes seriously anything that poses a threat to investors or the reputation of the flagship FTSE 100 index. In all instances relating to corporate behaviour, we are reliant on the domestic regulator. In this case, that is the UKLA which has been subsumed into the FCA, the UK's securities regulator. The FCA monitors market disclosures, reviews and approves prospectuses and operates the listing regime which requires issuers to comply with the listing rules. We need to know the companies we admit are of a certain quality, which is why we go beyond the listing rules employing minimum standards around the free float of shares and who holds voting rights. However, we cannot have standards so high they significantly reduce the number of companies if we are to continue to be an accurate measure of the whole market. Nor is it for us to vet or second-guess the decisions made by the FCA or any other regulator. The regulatory bodies around the world are well funded and have the legal powers to enforce laws and listing rules as well as punish those who fail to comply.

FTSE aims to be as predictable as possible, but every now and again index providers can be caught out. It is not a problem peculiar to London. The Hong Kong-listed Chinese marble miner ArtGo Holdings caused a problem in 2019 for MSCI which blocked it from index entry after its shares skyrocketed to trade at an improbable 73 times sales.

How we police inclusion to the FTSE 100 continues to evolve. If companies meet the rules, they are included. Only where companies raise something the rules haven't considered do we get into discussions. And for the vast majority of constituents, transparency is high and reputations remain paramount.

6

Passive beats active

Valley Forge, a small town that lies a 40-minute drive to the north-west of Philadelphia, played a special part in American history. It was here just before Christmas 1777 that George Washington's army took refuge. The American War of Independence was not going well. The British had captured Philadelphia, and Washington's men were tired and hungry. But over the course of several hard winter months, they recuperated, retrained and, with the aid of the arrival of allied French troops, mounted a fightback that would see victory declared and the end of British rule of its American colonies by 1783.

From harbouring one founding father – Washington was, of course, named the first president of the United States – Valley Forge became synonymous with another two centuries later. Jack Bogle led not a political revolution, but a financial one. The company he founded, Vanguard, became synonymous with passive investing, which aimed simply to mimic the performance of a stock market index, not beat it. He began to strip humans out of the investment process, arguing that the outcomes he could deliver that way were for the benefit of the people.

At the forefront

Today, the figures are astonishing. As of January 2020, Vanguard had about $6.2 trillion in global assets under management, across more than 400 funds serving over 30 million investors in 170 countries. The vast majority of that money is passively managed, although more than $1 trillion is actively managed by in-house teams or appointed sub-advisers. Vanguard states its core purpose is 'to take a stand for all investors, to treat them fairly, and to give them the best chance for investment success'.

I first visited Valley Forge in May 2005. I had been spending half my time in the USA for about a year at this point. Rachel Rubenstein, FTSE's co-head of North American sales – and later my wife – drove us down. She had been building up the relationship with Vanguard and paving the way for this meeting with the chief executive.

You could be forgiven for thinking you were in the English countryside. Compared to the urban blare of New York that we left behind, the surrounding rolling fields and bustling main street packed with independent stores explained why Valley Forge served as a perfect weekend break destination. But as soon as I entered the largest of the clutch of buildings scattered across town from which Vanguard operated, it was clear to me that this was a company that worked hard and played hard.

Jack Brennan had been chief executive of Vanguard for almost a decade by this time but had worked at the firm since 1982. Brennan had served as Vanguard's president alongside Bogle, and when Bogle stepped down he was his handpicked successor. He shook me warmly by the hand and explained the company's philosophy and culture.

Then came a real treat. Bogle had stepped down as CEO in 1996 but still came into the office regularly, running a research centre on what felt like Vanguard's university campus. He was there that day and offered to show me around. His pride at what they had achieved was obvious.

Bogle's story was remarkable. He had been born into a wealthy New Jersey family, but his parents lost their inheritance and were forced to sell their home after the 1929 stock market crash. Despite reduced circumstances, he excelled at his studies, obtaining a scholarship from Princeton University where his subjects were economics and investment. For his thesis, Bogle alighted on the mutual fund industry, then a small branch of the savings industry based in Boston with $2 billion in assets under management. Mutuals were more flexible than the closed-end funds common at that time because they allowed retail investors to buy and sell shares as they saw fit and pool their money. It meant that the little guy was able to share the returns enjoyed by larger, professional investors.

In the thesis, 'The Economic Role of the Investment Company', for which he was awarded an A+, Bogle wrote: 'The investment company can realize its optimum economic role by the exercise of its dual function: to contribute to the growth of the economy, and to enable individual as well as institutional investors to have a share in this growth.' One other passage gave a clue to his path in life. Bogle said investment companies should avoid creating 'the expectation of miracles from management [...] and make no claim for superiority over the market averages.'

Bogle put his ideas into practice commercially at Wellington Management Company, whose first fund had been established in 1929 by the entrepreneurial Walter Morgan. In less than 20 years since joining Wellington Management in 1951, Bogle scaled the company and replaced Morgan as chairman, but a merger with the aggressive fund manager Thorndike, Doran, Paine & Lewis went sour and he was ousted in 1974.

Bogle fought back and won approval to maintain administrative oversight of the group's funds at arm's length from Wellington, creating a new parent company that the funds would jointly own. In casting around for a name, the keen sailor was inspired by the words of Lord Nelson, written on the deck of his flagship HMS *Vanguard* after a famous victory: 'Nothing could withstand the squadron under my command. The judgment of the captains, together with the valor and high state of discipline of the officers and men of every description, was absolutely irresistible.' Incorporated on 24 September 1974, Vanguard it was.

The nautical theme ran right through the firm. It doesn't have staff; it says it has a crew. Bogle was warm and engaging as he showed me the buildings and meeting rooms that were all named after famous sea battles and hung with paintings of ships. The meaning of the word 'vanguard', 'at the forefront', has proved to be apt, seeing as it has overtaken many other firms in its field to become a leading investment company. Bogle might have suffered from health problems – he suffered his first heart attack at age of 31 and was diagnosed with a rare cardiac condition at the age of 38 – but he had an iron will.

His simple idea was that a mutual fund company should not have outside owners because they cloud the mission. If the funds' shareholders owned the company, there was no one sitting outside the firm seeking profits. It became part of Vanguard's mantra to put investors' interests first. Initially, Bogle battled with critics who said it would not work. BlackRock, one of Vanguard's greatest rivals, once described the firm to me as the communists of the fund management industry.

Bogle was not the first to launch an index fund. Since the early 1970s, it had been a tool used by the big US pension funds. What Vanguard did was to adapt the format to a mutual fund format, so everyone could benefit. Created in June 1976, Bogle's First Index Investment Trust was heavily criticized in the investment industry as 'the pursuit of mediocrity' or even 'the devil's invention'. Charging a fraction of the fees associated with active funds, Bogle's board weren't keen either. Proposing to follow the S&P 500, Vanguard took three months to raise an initial $12 million. It was slow-going, but eventually, a decade later, when the fund had grown to $500 million, rivals began to launch copycats.

Vanguard was by this time well established and went on to launch similar index-linked funds for small-cap stocks, bonds and world markets. Their mission was simple: to constantly bring down the cost of fund management. I didn't mind falling fees for fund managers. Vanguard and its rivals created great demand for indices that could be a trusted to guide their money instead of more expensive and unpredictable human decision making. At the back of my mind that day in 2005, I wondered how we could begin working together.

The academics

The theory underpinning passive investing predated Jack Bogle. It can be traced to the work of at least half a dozen eminent economists who wrote on the range, rationality and reliability in investing.

First of all was the Chicago-born Harry Markowitz, whose work on portfolio theory beginning with his article 'Port-folio Selection' (1952) suggested that investors could reduce risk by diversifying their assets across a portfolio. Markowitz, who jointly won the Nobel Prize in Economics in 1990, writes on his website that his 'focus has always been on the application of mathematical or computer techniques to practical problems, particularly problems of business decisions under uncertainty'. He was influenced by John Burr Williams's theory of investment value, which proposes that the value of a stock should equal the present value of its future dividends.

This hypothesis that markets operate efficiently was picked up in the capital asset pricing model (CAPM) developed by Jack Treynor, Bill Sharpe, John Lintner and Jan Mossin during the 1960s. It explores how risk relates to return and the impact of diversification in a portfolio.

Then came Burton Malkiel, whose 1973 book *A Random Walk down Wall Street* suggests that stocks are rationally and efficiently priced and it is highly unlikely anyone can consistently outperform the market average. For many years, he was a director of Vanguard.

And finally, there is Paul Samuelson, whose 1974 article 'Challenge to Judgment' comes with the subheading: 'Perhaps there really are managers who can outperform the market consistently – logic would suggest that they exist. But they are remarkably well-hidden.' Samuelson also wrote *Economics: An Introductory Analysis*, a seminal textbook published in 1948 when Bogle was still a student. 'It opened my eyes to the world of economics, a world I never knew existed. I knew what earning and saving money was, but I never thought about economics as a body of lore, quasi-scientific or scientific,' Bogle later said.

The 'father of indexing'

Luggage company Samsonite was one of the first leisure brands, set up in 1910 when the concept of travel was reserved for the monied few. The founder, Jesse Shwayder, redesigned the basic wooden trunk with shiny metal studs and corner pieces making it more eye-catching and 'strong enough to stand on', or so said a marketing campaign that pictured five men balancing on one of them.

Sixty years later, the family-owned company was still innovating. It is believed to be the first company to have adopted an index tracker for its pension fund whose assets had previously been invested conventionally via mutual funds. The company devised the plan with the bank Wells Fargo, which had just hired the research manager Bill Fouse. His keen interest in portfolio theory and stock analysis had caused his last boss at Mellon National Bank & Trust to exclaim: 'Goddammit Fouse, you're trying to turn my business into a science.'

Samsonite was willing to try something off the beaten track. Rather than an index tracker following the S&P 500, it opted for a strategy of following every stock on the New York Stock Exchange, equally weighted. It was tough to administer so by 1976

Samsonite switched to track the S&P with a cap-weighting. In the meantime, the evangelical Fouse had convinced several other companies to give his method a try, including Wells Fargo's own pension fund. The quantitative analyst did not become known as the 'father of indexing' for nothing. But if Fouse began the trend for matching the market, Bogle popularized it to great effect.

More than most

On 22 January 1993 a nine-foot inflatable spider dangled from the ceiling of the American Stock Exchange (Amex) at 86 Trinity Place in Manhattan. It was not uncommon for frat-boy japes to spill onto the trading room floor but this decoration was no hangover from Halloween. Instead, Amex, which began as a market for small stocks and had long since ceded market share to the New York Stock Exchange and the technology-focused Nasdaq, hoped it had alighted on a new money spinner.

Standard & Poor's-500 Depositary Receipts – or SPDR, or Spiders, hence the gimmick of a giant blow-up arachnid – was launched on the world two days after Bill Clinton was sworn in as the 42nd US president. Passive investing caught fire in the 1990s, spurred on by Vanguard's efforts and rivals rushing to catch up. But just as Bogle's retail tracker – which became known as the Vanguard 500 Index Fund – took a while to catch on in the 1970s, this latest innovation that would once again transform the investment industry had a slow start.

SPDR was the first exchange-traded fund (ETF), a financial product that promised investors the portfolio spread they were used to getting from a mutual fund with the flexibility of a single stock. As with all new launches, potential customers just had to be educated about it so they were comfortable handing over their money. Rock-bottom fees – known in the business as the expense ratio of a fund – caused ears to prick up.

ETFs were the brainchild of Nate Most, a physicist by training who – among other things during a long career – traded cooking oil in the 1960s working for the Pacific Commodities Exchange. The trade was simpler than the transportation, so he became used to exchanging slips of paper in lieu of drums of oil – not dissimilar to futures contracts.

'You store a commodity and you get a warehouse receipt and you can finance on that warehouse receipt,' he said. 'You can sell it, do a lot of things with it. Because you don't want to be moving the merchandise back and forth all the time, so you keep it in place and you simply transfer the warehouse receipt.'

Most was cash-strapped Amex's vice president of product development when he fashioned ETFs as a way of generating more income for the company. He explored different classes of security that could be traded and alighted on mutual funds. ETFs might have launched sooner had it been for a painfully slow approvals process by the US Securities and Exchange Commission. That in itself was surprising.

Most and his colleague Steven Bloom were inspired after reading the SEC's report into what went wrong on Black Monday, the October 1987 trading rout. At a time when computerization was still in its infancy, regulators concluded that investors' elaborate hedging strategies and automated sell orders had exacerbated the decline. If only there was something as simple as a basket of stocks they could trade or use as a hedge against sharp falls that would doubtless reduce volatility. Most had taken the idea to Bogle at Vanguard but he wasn't impressed. Bogle said the model was more expensive than if you use a mutual fund to invest because of the rapid trading it encouraged.

In the foreword to Will McClatchy and Jim Wiandt's *Exchange-Traded Funds: An Insider's Guide to Buying the Market*, Most wrote:

To solve this problem, I returned to my commodity experiences and thought that we might separate the functions of fund management and exchange trading by using what would essentially be a warehouse-type operation.

Portfolios of stocks conforming to an established index would be deposited with a trust bank, which would then issue a depositary receipt to the depositor. The receipt would be divisible into a large number of pieces – 50,000 has become typical. The divided pieces could then trade on the Exchange as equity securities. These pieces would not be redeemable by the fund, but could be reassembled into the full depositary receipt and submitted to the trust bank in exchange for the underlying share portfolio.

Amex needed a partner so recruited State Street Global Advisers to effectively house the baskets of shares. Bogle had been absolutely right. There were additional trading, market impact and administration costs which would need to be borne by the investor and he felt it would encourage investors to take a short-term approach, buying and selling unnecessarily rather than holding the fund for the long term. Bogle thought it was not in the interests of investors, so Vanguard did not proceed. Whereas that first retail tracker in 1976 was inspired, his reticence this time was a big mistake. The simplicity and flexibility of ETFs made them a key weapon in the battle for investors' money – and responsible for a period of explosive growth for index providers.

A crowded market

It did not take long before more players crowded into the ETF market. Morgan Stanley and Barclays teamed up in 1996 to launch World Equity Benchmark Shares (Webs), a range of funds pegged to overseas markets that allowed easy access for retail investors. Not surprisingly, they chose to track Morgan Stanley's MSCI indices, which were fast becoming the global benchmark.

FTSE was still very new in the US market and Goldman Sachs was leading the introductions to potential clients and partners. They introduced us and S&P to Deutsche Bank who were developing a product called Country Baskets to go head to head with Webs. In fact, we launched a week earlier than they did. But it soon became clear that Barclays and Morgan Stanley had committed far more to marketing the products and Deutsche didn't have the distribution in the USA, which was the prime battleground. We lost out. 'Since their ignominious departure from the scene in late 1996, they have been known to many ETF insiders as the "country caskets",' McClatchy and Wiandt wrote in *Exchange-Traded Funds*. In their book, Herb Blank, the Country Baskets chief investment officer, attempted to explain why the venture failed:

> The main thing that went wrong, in my opinion, was the lack of long-term corporate commitment to the product. Basically, the larger the organization, the larger the politics, and the people who approved and believed in the venture when we started were no longer the decision markers when the plug was pulled. It's that simple.

Amex could not keep this good idea to itself as ETFs began to list on most of the major exchanges. As it watched competitors profit from its own ingenuity, I had to sit back and watch Barclays' success too. What was tougher was seeing MSCI without a rival streak away, on top of the early success enjoyed in the ETF field by S&P with the S&P 500 and its US indices.

As well as a new type of investment, ETFs conceived a new business model. When indices had been used by funds as performance benchmarks, there was an 'all you can eat' element to our contracts. Asset managers paid to use our data to measure their own effectiveness, but the price didn't vary depending on how large their assets were. With ETFs, we were the portfolio. It meant we could charge according to how much flowed in. As ETF funds grew in size, it stood to be very lucrative indeed. I had to work out how FTSE could bounce back and make a name for itself, too.

Barclays and passive investment

Barclays' leadership in index funds stood out. Here was a European company prospering early on in a field that had almost exclusively been driven by American finance firms. Its success can be traced in particular to two men: Donald Brydon and James Woodlock.

Woodlock might have gone into farming – he had attended agricultural college before heading to the City of London. His pride and joy was a Massey Ferguson tractor that rolled off the production line four days before he was born. At Barclays since 1972, the straight-talking Woodlock started out as a bookkeeper managing private client money before transferring to the corporate side where he was unimpressed by the twenty-something fund managers sitting around him boasting about what shares they had bought or sold that day with little regard to how their overall portfolio was faring. At this time, Barclays trailed some of the great old City names such as Schroders, Barings and Mercury. The money management mandates it picked up compared to theirs were scraps from the table.

Woodlock had been hearing how passive investment had been pioneered in the USA and wondered if it could work in the UK and stimulate more business. He reasoned it would suit Barclays' reputation, which – at that time – was boring and steady. With a responsibility for performance measurement, he carried out a study which came to the familiar conclusion that following an index would be cheaper for investors and probably perform better in the long run.

Brydon, who arrived at Barclays Investment Management in 1977, was immersed in this world, too. As an analyst at the British Airways pension fund from 1970 onwards, he created an 'inertia portfolio' of stocks. Short of computing power in those days, he adapted the airline's Boadicea booking system to create an investment model that automatically tracked the market – effectively creating an All-Share tracker fund before its time. BA's pension trustees were concerned at what Brydon was doing so he was sent to see Harold Rose, the eminent economist at London Business School. The message came back: 'He's doing no harm.'

United at Barclays, the pair had a memorable meeting with Barr Rosenberg, a California-based finance professor who had done some work with Fouse at Wells Fargo to set up an index fund. Rosenberg is best known for founding Barra, the quantitative investment consulting firm acquired by MSCI in 2004.

Encouraged by Brydon, who became the managing director of Barclays Investment Management in 1981, Woodlock became the firm's first passive manager. Barclays' first index pension fund client, the US industrial conglomerate Honeywell, was won in 1983 and began tracking the nascent FTSE 100 when it came to life in 1984.

Fast-forward to 1995 and Barclays was bolstered by the acquisition of Wells Fargo Nikko Investment Advisors, the antecedent of the firm where, a generation earlier, Fouse had helped Samsonite's pension fund first track an index. At a cost of $440 million, it was a marriage made in heaven. Wells Fargo Nikko was the largest manager of indexed assets in the USA and craved international growth. Barclays had grown to become the largest indexer in Europe but had struggled to break into the USA, the main market for these products. Together, they had assets of $205 billion. Barclays Global Investors (BGI) was born.

That early expertise in indexation explains the eagerness to launch into this new ETF market. The new millennium brought a new name for Webs when they were rebranded as iShares. Nate Most had been recruited along with some of his Amex team, but it was Lee Kranefuss who led the charge for Barclays as the bank threw money at this market opportunity with new product launches and heavy marketing. The iShares

S&P 500 ETF offered the lowest expense ratio so far, at just 0.095 per cent of assets. Computers were taking the strain, and their running costs were lower than human fund managers. Such tactics worked. A decade later, in 2009, when more than $1 trillion had been sunk into ETFs, iShares was the world's largest platform by a stretch, accounting for more than twice the assets of its nearest competitor, State Street. The investment pioneer Vanguard was a distant third.

That was the year Barclays agreed to sell BGI to BlackRock, a bold move so soon after the financial crisis. Tougher capital adequacy rules meant Barclays needed to raise cash. Numerous banks were hunting for non-core assets they could sell. Because of the runaway success of iShares, BGI was a valuable asset. Until he put it up for auction the bank's bookish chief executive, John Varley, didn't realize quite how valuable.

Barclays had previously agreed to sell its iShares platform to private equity group CVC Capital Partners for $4.4 billion in April 2009 but the deal contained a clause that left scope for a counterbid. By June, the investment manager BlackRock had pounced, offering an eye-watering $13.5 billion not just for iShares – which at this time had over $300 billion of assets in more than 350 funds – but for the whole of BGI. The deal at a stroke created the world's biggest asset manager, with combined assets under management of more than $2.7 trillion.

The BlackRock story deserves a book of its own. Only launched in 1988 as an institutional asset manager by a group of executives who had worked together at the investment bank First Boston, it went public in 1999. Through some tenacious deal-doing by chairman and chief executive, Larry Fink, it left other more established money managers in its wake. BGI made the enlarged BlackRock a leading player in both active and passive investment, creating a platform from which it was only going to get larger. Vanguard had a mountain to climb if it was going to catch up with its rival.

A long courtship

2 October 2012 was a pivotal day for FTSE. It was the day that we won a significant slice of business from Vanguard. The giant fund manager announced it was handing us the mandate for six international stock funds which had $170 billion of assets. To be phased in over several months from the following January, they would start to track FTSE indices. Among the half-dozen funds was a real plum: the Vanguard Emerging Markets Index ETF, which was to become the largest emerging markets ETF of them all.

I cannot understate the importance of this development. Together with acquiring Russell in 2014 and our early breakthrough in China – of which more in the next chapter – the Vanguard relationship has been pivotal to FTSE's success over the last decade. No wonder I was pleased.

'With the switch, FTSE will become the third-largest equity exchange traded product index benchmark provider globally, with more than $124 billion in ETF assets benchmarked to FTSE indices,' I said gleefully in the statement we put out. This announcement was the result of a seven-year courtship. Until this point, we had been a lowly number eight in the global league table of indices as measured by the value of ETF assets following them. This catapulted us to number three.

There was a degree of schadenfreude, too. Up to this point, MSCI's chief executive, Henry Fernandez, had always told the Wall Street analysts that made the weather for his shares that there was only one game in town. That wasn't true, but thanks to its involvement as the international benchmark for what became iShares, MSCI continued to dominate the ETFs market in particular.

Not anymore. On the analysts' call that day, the longer Fernandez spoke, the further his stock price seemed to fall. One key admission was that the choice made by ETF managers of a preferred index provider 'may not be as sticky as we all thought,' he said on the call. In heavy trading volume, MSCI shares closed down 27 per cent that day, to their lowest in over three years. No one was wearing the idea that such a significant loss was a one-off.

In total, Vanguard moved 22 of its funds that day. What was notable was that the other 16, US-focused funds, went to the Center for Research in Security Prices (CRSP) at the University of Chicago's Booth School of Business. CRSP had built its renown in this field since 1960, but this was the first time it had marketed investable indices. Its benchmarks up until this point had been used purely for academic purposes.

It had been a long haul for FTSE. After that initial meeting in 2005, up to once a month I would be down seeing Vanguard. They were really just getting around to thinking about how they could get into the ETFs market that Bogle had spurned early on. FTSE was, of course, running money for CalPERS and others and were growing our revenues at probably 15 per cent a year. It sounds a lot, but the market was exploding and we started from a low base. To win some work from Vanguard would have given us a visibility we couldn't achieve piecemeal.

The firm was very protective of its investors and would never introduce funds to them that were in any way risky. Often, they would research new ideas for many years, before offering them to their customers. In addition, this whole strand of investing was conservative. The whole point of passive investing was not to deviate from the norm, and for most of the ETF platforms, the norm was the indices that everyone else used.

However, the direction of travel worked in our favour. Vanguard's international funds were all with MSCI and its domestic funds used S&P. Its costs were rising as these index providers commercialized. How could they bring in competition so they did not have to pass these increased costs on to investors? It was not going to be easy because Vanguard had become very reliant on both firms, which were closely integrated with their operation.

My pitch to Jack Brennan and his colleagues was simple: try us. They eventually agreed to try out a new index we created. The breakthrough came when Vanguard was introducing a new world fund but MSCI had licensed the index they wanted to base it on to arch rival, BlackRock. Vanguard was stuck – and angry. I said that FTSE could step into the breach. It wasn't simple. Some of the terminology we used was different, and all of this would have to be explained to their investors. Still, it would be the first time they used an index provider other than MSCI to track the globe.

A partner of choice

Vanguard launched its Total World Stock ETF using FTSE, and BlackRock launched its iShares MSCI ACWI within a few months of each other in late spring 2008. Vanguard competed on lower fees, and iShares competed on the brand of the underlying index: MSCI versus FTSE. Vanguard with its lower fees policy won, and the majority of the funds flowed to them. As a relative unknown, it was a great toe in the water for us.

I was mindful of maintaining good relations. A clash between Vanguard and S&P a few years earlier (though ultimately resolved) reminded me how things could turn sour. In June 2000, S&P's parent company, McGraw-Hill, filed a lawsuit in the US federal courts against Vanguard claiming breach of contract, trademark infringement and unfair competition over a series of new ETFs.

This was remarkable, given their close ties forged right back in 1976 when Vanguard launched its first retail tracker that used the S&P 500. It grew to become the world's top mutual fund, the Vanguard 500 Index Fund.

But as far as I understood it, the longevity of their relationship was part of the problem. Early deals were struck before index providers learned how to make money. It reminded me of when I had licensing difficulties with LIFFE and others in the early days. As S&P woke up to the value of its data, it went back to Vanguard to ask for a larger licence fee. It was irked by the launch of Vipers (Vanguard Index Participation Equity Receipts), which Vanguard claimed was covered by their 1988 licensing deal and S&P claimed was a new product that required a new payment to them. It was reportedly earning just $50,000 a year in perpetuity from Vanguard for the 500 Fund. I can understand the frustration.

After establishing a single fund, I wanted to see if we could turn ourselves into Vanguard's partner of choice. For that I needed a lieutenant on the ground that I could trust. Bumping into Jonathan Horton and his wife, Acko, in the Eurotunnel terminal in Calais on a trip over to France was fortuitous. Jonathan and I have worked together on and off for many years, and we have become good friends. We complement each other, and I have huge respect for him and his abilities. He gets into the detail, understands complex issues and is very structured in defining the problem and in delivering the solution. He allows me to be more entrepreneurial and helps me turn my thoughts into strategies and plans. He challenges and forces me to turn vague ideas into something that is actionable. When I was setting FTSE up, I asked for very little from my two shareholders, but I did think I needed some help in getting to grips with the role. That is where Horton came in, as my executive coach, which really helped as I tried to develop as a leader.

I sent him out to New York, with the number-one task of taking forward the relationship with Vanguard. Horton stepped up contact and was at Vanguard every week for a period of a year. It was true that great sums of money were at stake, but this came down to relationships. They had to trust us.

Horton documented his first meeting at Valley Forge on 9 June 2011, confidently reporting back to me that the chemistry was good. On a second trip, the talk was much more explicit, covering Vanguard's relationship with MSCI and whether this could be the point where they were willing to think about alternatives. The timing was fortuitous. Vanguard was thinking of changing its benchmarks.

I needed some assurances. I didn't want FTSE to be used as stalking horse to get the incumbents to lower their price. Vanguard confirmed it would not begin a conversation with us on that basis.

There was also the South Korean issue to overcome. By this time, FTSE classified South Korea as a developed nation; MSCI did not. It sounds like a minor difference, but it would lead to significant variance in how we both calculated world indices. I will cover this in greater depth in the next chapter. Vanguard took the view it would only be a matter of time before MSCI would promote South Korea to its own developed category.

The Vanguard way is to get consensus before making a big move, so it brought back its former chief executive Jack Brennan to mediate. The process ensured everyone could express their views and challenge the decision. We were inundated with questions and requests for further research. It made for a nervous few months while the decision was thoroughly reviewed, but once the decision was ratified, we knew that everyone was brought into this very significant change and we could move forward together, united and with confidence.

Vanguard is a cautious company, but when it goes for something it does so at full throttle. We pitched for and won the international business. This agreement would mean a sharp uplift in revenue for us, and I wanted to make extra sure we built on it to uplift our brand in the USA, so I committed millions to marketing the FTSE brand and our indices to investors.

Vanguard's fairness is something to admire but it also worked against us. Vanguard had told us it was going to tender for its domestic business later on, but I discovered they had been working with CRSP in Chicago on designing a bespoke US benchmark for Vanguard. When we learned at the last moment that the firm was going to move both its international and domestic business at once, we went back and pitched again. We wanted to win the lot, but Vanguard had made its decision. It was a day for celebration, but if we had taken the domestic business too, we would have been the same size as S&P – which had entered this market almost two decades earlier – in terms of ETF assets.

Ongoing innovation

To some extent passive investing showed up active investing for what it was: overpriced and often overpromising. Even now, the fees that some funds houses attempt to levy on customers look egregious and the mysticism of the stock picker is not justified by some very ordinary results. But active has a place in global markets that undoubtedly benefit from variety.

For a time, passive investing had its downside, too. But the industry has continued to innovate. Because of two important meetings I had early in the new millennium, FTSE has continued to do so, too.

The first was with Roger Urwin, the global head of the investment practice at the pension consulting firm Watson Wyatt. I had got to know Urwin over several years. He was well regarded in the industry and very balanced in his outlook. What was intriguing on this occasion in late 2003, given that he sat on the MSCI advisory board, was that he was bringing me a business idea. Squeezing extra performance from a portfolio was very much on investors' minds at that time. If it could be done without having to adopt active investing that would ramp up costs, all the better.

In investing, 'beta' has always been used as a measure of risk relative to the broader market. As the name suggests, 'smart beta' seeks to apply an intelligent filter to the risk that investors are prepared to take on. In doing so, passive investors can more closely replicate the choices made by active managers. Urwin had taken his idea for smart beta funds to MSCI but they weren't interested. Could FTSE do anything with it? Through Urwin I was introduced to David Morris who ran a firm called Global Wealth which was experimenting in this area.

Then there was Rob Arnott. The common link here was Mark Anson, who was chief investment officer at CalPERS which we had worked with for several years. Arnott had earned himself a reputation as a big thinker who challenged conventional investment wisdom. He had run two asset management firms, First Quadrant and TSA Capital Management, and had also been global equity strategist at Salomon Brothers. In 2002, he set up on his own. Research Affiliates aimed to develop investment ideas and put them to work with leading financial institutions. Arnott was fast-talking and confident that his latest breakthrough would make someone a lot of money. The other two leading index providers were not interested, but I immediately saw an opportunity. Because CalPERS wanted to embrace the idea and it used FTSE indices, it was also important to maintain that relationship.

The concept of what Arnott described as a fundamental index was sparked by the sharp downturn experienced by investors in the aftermath of the bursting of the technology bubble in 2000. Portfolio weights that were linked to market capitalization suffered when the price of overvalued tech stocks was suddenly corrected.

Sitting on huge losses, some investors thought there had to be a better way. George Keane, the founding president of Commonfund, which managed $40 billion of university endowment assets, challenged Arnott and his team to find it without reverting to equal weighting, which would have been a backwards step.

A study of the problem threw up some startling results. Research Affiliates found that over an 80-year period to 2006, the top ten stocks in a cap-weighted portfolio outperformed the average stock just 31 per cent of the time. Even worse, over the same period they underperformed the average by 29 per cent. So much for upweighting larger stocks in a portfolio.

Arnott considered alternative metrics such as a weighting by sales value, the type of measure by which most business owners lived by. By putting emphasis on the biggest revenue generators in the USA, it was possible to create a portfolio that outperformed the S&P 500 by more than 2.5 percentage points annually over more than 30 years.

There were other factors that could be considered, too: earnings, cashflow, dividend, even the number of employees. Each of them broke the link between portfolio weight and a perceived pricing error. Combining many or all of these factors created a broad investment portfolio that ironed out individual weaknesses, such as that an index weighted according to dividends paid would rule out more than half of all US stocks including many growth companies.

There had been attempts to develop indices like this before but factoring in the new characteristics to a passive investment still defied convention for many. Speaking at the Information Management Network's Superbowl of Indexing in December 2005 in Scottsdale, Arizona, Arnott was heckled from the floor by an angry active manager who demanded to know: 'How dare you call this an index?' On hearing about his strategy, one chief investment officer of a largely passive house described it as 'active management in drag'.

Despite strong opposition from some of FTSE's cap-weighted index licensees, I was sold on the idea. We tried to back both horses – Global Wealth and Research Affiliates – but Arnott's marketing nous made it clear to me who we should side with.

Launched in 2005, the FTSE RAFI (Research Affiliates Fundamental Index) series brought smart beta to life.

Ten years on, investable products linked to the indices FTSE developed with Research Affiliates had approximately $75 billion of assets under management. To mark the anniversary, we launched a new FTSE RAFI Equity Income Index Series, this time to track high-dividend-paying stocks which are screened to target sustainable income. In the intervening years, ETF issuers – including many of these who were dubious at the outset – have adopted more factor-based approaches in an attempt to stand out from the crowd.

For a long time, indices all had similar hallmarks. They were a cap-weighted representation of a wider universe. Not anymore. The index envisioned to aid Harry Markowitz's port-folio diversification theory has morphed into whatever investors want it to be. Any prescriptive set of rules that govern respective weights and eligibility can be applied to a universe of companies.

Indexation didn't stop there. It grew again, not only by re-defining how it measures constituents, but what it measures. From a background tracking companies, FTSE's ambition to track the relative performance of countries was exciting – but fraught with geopolitical risk.

7
Countries not companies

An international drive was an essential element of the expanded FTSE I had sold to both of our shareholders when the company was created in 1995. It had two prongs, selling our services to the biggest asset owners and also going market by market, effectively bringing exchanges closer together with investors. As I explained in Chapter 4, winning mandates from the large asset owners began with the help of Goldman Sachs, pitching to the likes of the California Public Employees Retirement System (CalPERS).

And I could not have done any of it without the team I had assembled. We also pushed into Europe with a Paris office opened by Donald Keith, who became my deputy in November 2001, followed by Frankfurt and Madrid. Then we won a mandate from the French sovereign wealth fund in a pitch against MSCI, the first time that we had gone up against them and won. Norway was another big win. That told the fund management community that there was an alternative. From that basis we were able to grow by offering our world index – of which more later – or a customized model for the big asset owners.

In tandem, we also took our design and approach to other stock exchanges. Our pitch was that we could do for their market what we had done in London: upgrading the index series, widening classification, lifting operating standards. It was not flashy, but the markets chiefs could see that approach would help to improve liquidity by attracting international money flows to regional exchanges that might otherwise have overlooked them. We sat with their index bosses, helped them to install an advisory committee and eventually took over the calculation of their indices, which we ran from London.

Greece became a template for us, with the exchange operator entering into a commercial partnership with us in order to grow the pie. On 1 July 1997 we announced a new 20-share Greek stock index, the FTSE/ASE 20, which was designed to open the market to derivatives trading and increased international investment. Piraeus Bank and OTE Telecom were two of the founder members. These deals might not be thrilling but they were sensible and steady. Wherever it happened to be, I spent half my life on a plane for many years.

Because we could offer global redistribution and calculation of real-time indexes on systems managed by Reuters, the risk to us was negligible. Within a few years in the early 2000s, we had to build out a team in London overseeing overseas indices 24 hours a day, initially five and then six days a week. We were covering the Asian, Middle East, African, European and American markets spinning around the world, one team handing over to the next as the sun went down. Donald and I maintained contact with the clients, partners and our staff throughout the day, every day.

All this provides a backdrop for the three big international developments at FTSE I want to explore in this chapter: China, South Korea and Saudi Arabia.

China

The Mandarin Oriental has been a focal point for Hong Kong business life as long as I can remember. Opened in 1963, the 27-storey luxury hotel instantly became a landmark on the British colony's skyline, exciting guests with the first direct-dial telephones and a bathtub in every room. I love the lobby, stylish in black marble, where the chatter of commerce continues from morning until night. I have often repaired to the Captain's Bar, off to one side, when I needed to grab a gin and tonic to soothe my jet lag or meet contacts.

One morning in September 2000, I stood in the lobby awaiting my next appointment. I was in town for a gathering of the steering committee of Hong Kong's main stock index, the Hang Seng, and also to catch up with a few clients. Another opportunity had dropped into my diary: an invitation to meet an entrepreneur named Fredy Bush, who had a proposition for me.

With a name like Fredy, I naturally assumed he was a man. Instead, a few moments later, I was shaking hands with a woman, short with blonde hair pinned up and impeccably well dressed in the Chinese style. Loretta Fredy Bush, an energetic, razor-sharp, some would say controversial American, was one of a handful of partners that dramatically changed FTSE's fortunes over the years. She could offer something I thought we would never obtain: a path into China.

A land of opportunity

In 2000, China was not on many investors' radar. The Middle Kingdom was regarded by some as a communist backwater that hadn't even joined the World Trade Organization (WTO) by that stage. Besides, there was much more excitement around the first wave of dotcom stocks for whom boom had turned to bust that April. But international expansion had always been part of my game plan, and I was convinced there was an opportunity across the South China Sea.

Bush's life story, as she told it, was remarkable. I was never sure if I could believe every word. She told me she grew up in a Mormon family in Utah. When she became pregnant at 16, her boyfriend disappeared and her church leader father disowned her. She married soon after, but her husband died in a motorcycle crash. That's how at the age of 19 she came to be living in a trailer park in Mexico with two children in tow.

A chance meeting with a Chinese woman who befriended her saw the family move to San Francisco for office work. It transpired the woman was the daughter of the head of one of the main political parties in Taiwan, the island state off China that was in the process of liberalizing.

Remarkably, he needed an assistant in Taipei and Bush had impressed his daughter, so she relocated with her children to a country where she had never been and could not speak the language. She began working in a central approvals office that was fast becoming a free-market gateway, not just serving the island, but China across the Taiwan Strait. She learned how to marry Western private interests with Asian public government entities in joint ventures, with her in the middle first of all taking a consultancy fee and later a cut of future revenue as these ventures grew in scale. She earned her first million helping foreign banks secure trading rights to the new derivatives exchange in Taiwan.

What transformed her fortunes again was when the Xinhua News Agency came calling. The government news provider was China's official propaganda machine, a mouthpiece for the People's Republic of China, but that didn't stop it from having designs on becoming something bigger. It thought Bush could help it develop commercially. Xinhua first tried creating a Chinese Reuters inside the agency with Fredy's help. The bureaucracy made that impossible. So, bold as anything, and with talk of creating the Chinese Reuters it desired, she convinced Xinhua to set up a joint venture with her. Together, they could build a financial information business, a trusted source of news in preparation for the stock market opening up.

Bush was clever and charismatic. Whereas many investors were put off by China in those days because of its tight economic controls and lack of clear regulation, she saw an opportunity to help introduce the standards that investors required to invest. Just like more mature financial markets, that meant three information services with which to make well-informed decisions: financial news, market indices and credit ratings. Her powers of persuasion led to a 20-year exclusive agreement with Xinhua and scope to extend. The Xinhua Financial Network (XFN) was born.

Now, all she needed was a strategy. I was introduced to Bush by Mike Balaban, an American investment banker who had run the equity capital markets group for Citigroup in Japan and had reinvented himself as a business adviser helping entrepreneurs to tap Asian markets. Since April 2000, they had been shopping a business plan but failing to excite financial backers wary of China. They turned their attention to strategic investors who wanted to break into the market for reasons of their own business model. In financial news, that meant partnering with PR Newswire, which paid $7.5 million for the privilege. In the indices world, I was in no doubt that Bush was courting MSCI and Standard & Poor's at the same time as me. But the offer was compelling: did FTSE want to partner with Bush in bringing indexation to the Chinese market?

From the moment we sat down together in the Captain's Bar, I was interested but I had to make sure all of this was real. Some people praised Bush and several years later *The Wall Street Journal* listed her among the 'top 50 women to watch' globally and the American Chamber of Commerce in Hong Kong named her its 'entrepreneur of the year'. But others I consulted were less complimentary. 'She is a con artist. A constant liar. Be very careful,' said one banker to me. That's why I insisted that before I'd sign a deal I met the President of the Xinhua News Agency, a member of the Central Committee of China's Communist Party.

Just in time: XIN

That meeting couldn't have been further from the glamour of the Mandarin Oriental. It took place in an old army building in the back streets of Beijing. The lift was rattling so much I didn't think it would make it all the way up. Up until that point, my dealings in Asia had all been with men in suits who spoke perfect English. Now I was face to face with the president of Xinhua News Agency, Li Congjun, dressed in a high mandarin collar and surrounded by interpreters. But I was satisfied, and even more so when I persuaded Bush to collaborate with FTSE without us putting in a single dollar.

It was a whirlwind. Analysing the domestic markets in China and collecting and cleansing all the data we required was going to take time. We needed to persuade the regulator, the China Securities Regulatory Commission (CSRC), to allow us to operate in China and we needed the permission of the two securities exchanges in Shanghai and Shenzhen to use their pricing feeds. Bush seemed confident that, with the backing of Xinhua, she could help us achieve this. I had my doubts. We set up a dedicated team operating within mainland China, but we needed an accomplished Chinese national to lead the venture. Bush said she knew someone who was perfect for the role. And she was right.

Zhu Shan had been a high-flying officer in the Chinese army. His army career came to an abrupt end, through no fault of his own, when a senior official he was accompanying in the USA chose to stay there and not return to China, leaving Zhu Shan to return home alone. He was smart, well educated and trilingual, speaking English, Mandarin and Cantonese. He understood the complexities of China, the need to build a consensus, and how to gain support for change. I grew to trust and rely on his judgement, and he never let us down. Without him, we would never have made inroads into China.

While this work went on, we needed to show we could produce an early first product. There were just enough Chinese companies listed on the Hong Kong Stock Exchange for us to create our first Chinese index. On 21 April 2001, we announced the FTSE/Xinhua China 25, an index of Chinese stocks for international investors. We were just in time. iShares, the leading provider of ETFs and now part of the global fund giant BlackRock, was looking to launch an ETF on China in the US market. It had been examining MSCI's China Free Index, which was part of MSCI's global equity series and like ours compiled largely from stocks listed in Hong Kong. But the MSCI index had some issues that financial regulators in the USA were uncomfortable about. There was a high concentration in a small number of the biggest stocks, and some China listed stocks – known as B Shares – were included which foreigners were allowed to own but which were problematic to trade. We could custom-build our index to overcome these issues, so BlackRock chose us to launch with. Using the ticker name XIN, we launched BlackRock's first China ETF in the USA, and Fredy Bush, Zhu Shan and I rang the bell on the floor of the New York Stock Exchange to start trading. It was a huge success.

At the Great Hall of the People

In those days the mainland Chinese equities market was volatile and the preserve of retail investors. Disclosures were poor, there were no large companies setting standards, and most companies featured a government stake. We were bringing international standards to China, and the local fund managers and institutional investors who were just beginning to emerge supported and adopted us. In 2003, we launched China's first index tracking fund, the Bosera Fund, which was based on the FTSE/Xinhua A200. The FTSE/Xinhua indices were starting to get a wide following in mainland China.

Many of China's state-owned companies were being privatized, but the majority of shares in these companies were still held by the Chinese government. Listing rules and corporate governance standards were being written, but appropriate board structures and corporate cultures would take some time to develop. The CSRC was split between those who wanted to reform quicker and those who thought change was being pushed through too fast. The reformers supported us and our advisory committee was filled with local industry experts and chaired by Liu Hongru, a highly respected figure in China's growing financial industry. Bush had used her Xinhua connections to approach him, and I was keen to have an ex-chairman of CSRC heading our advisory committee. A graduate from the finance class of the People's Normal University of China, Liu Hongru got his associate doctor's degree in economics from Moscow University. Having started his career in the People's Bank of China, he had been the Vice President of the Agricultural Bank of China and Vice President of the People's Bank of China before serving as the chairman of CSRC from 1992 to 1995. Liu Hongru gave us credibility and a level of acceptance in the China market. He also guided us in developing our relationship with CSRC and ensured that we maintained a dialogue with senior government officials. CSRC were supportive and gave us a list of 'Manipulated Stocks' which they were keeping a close eye on and thought should not be included in our indices. Zhu Shan found sources of data and we built the first extensive domestic series of indices for the China market.

Unlike developed markets, where large-, mid- and small-cap stocks behave differently in economic cycles, we found no such trend in China where retail investors' speculation drove share price movements. But we believed the market would develop and change as it matured, so we built these indices to encourage the development of the market. We used our global industry classification system even though some sectors had few stocks as they were yet to privatize in China. And, very new to China, we calculated based on free-floating stock weights, removing the many state holdings and reflecting the shares that were available for trading. With the help of the CSRC reformers and local market experts, we built a series of domestic indices that would help investors in China navigate the growth and future development of the market. But China is an unpredictable centrally controlled market. When the centre changes its position, you can suddenly find yourself out of favour and on your own.

By 2001, FTSE was already in 77 countries worldwide and working closely with exchanges including those in Amsterdam, Brussels, Luxembourg and Madrid on their indices. But this launch was something special. Little more than six months after that initial meeting at the Mandarin Oriental, I had to pinch myself as I stood next to Bush in Beijing's Great Hall of the People. This grand building, on the western edge of Tiananmen Square, is lined with thick carpets, shining walls, traditional Chinese art and elaborate floral displays. As an emblem of the nation, it hosts the Communist Party's annual congress and state banquets at which visiting dignitaries such as Ronald Reagan and Margaret Thatcher have spoken. To mark the launch of the FTSE/Xinhua indices, which instantly made us the biggest provider of domestic indices to China, I had been invited to give an address, too.

To an expectant audience, I said it was a great honour to be there and made the point we were bringing international skills into China to help develop the Chinese market. Over time, I said, China had the potential to become a major financial player with influence on the global stage. What I didn't say is that I regarded entering new markets like any investor would: making a calculation that balanced risk with reward. China was still fraught with risk, but the Xinhua venture would prove to be extremely rewarding, for a time. However, it would not end well.

Souring relations

The innovations in China came thick and fast. After the initial launch, we added a wider family of indices covering domestic A shares, bonds and composites as well as foreign currency denominated versions of the main indices to support early foreign investor interest in China. Some progressives were trying to open up the market a bit faster than probably the Chinese government was ready for. And with our Xinhua partnership we were at the vanguard. We tried launching futures in mainland China, beginning with a trial with the Shanghai Futures Exchange. I went to Shanghai and spoke at an event organized by them to launch the trials. There was a lot of excitement, with over 300 people crammed into the hall to hear about the new futures contract and the index. When the government decided that that form of trading was too risky, it intervened and the trial was stopped. Then we did a deal with the Singapore Stock Exchange to launch Chinese futures with them in September 2005.

Initially, the reformers at CSRC had encouraged us to do this, but it was soon apparent that they were in the minority.

We pressed ahead, but relations soured quickly with the Shanghai Exchange and we were dragged to court. One of its divisions which gave us stock prices under contract sued us for providing the FTSE/Xinhua A50 Index to the Singapore Exchange. Bush correctly argued that we had previously signed licences with both the Shanghai and Shenzhen exchanges giving us permission to use their prices. She also argued that market prices were public property as soon as they were disseminated and we had done nothing wrong.

What also complicated matters was that Shanghai was preparing to launch its own futures index in a few months' time. The two contracts would end up competing for liquidity. On 31 October 2006, a Shanghai court ruled that FTSE/Xinhua had violated its price dissemination contract with the Shanghai

Exchange and we were ordered to desist and pay a fine of $25,000. We had gone from the highs of trialling futures contracts on our indices in Shanghai to the lows of being fined by the Shanghai courts. Then, to make matters worse, Bush stood on the steps of the court and told the world's media that we would be appealing.

Things had calmed down a little by the time the appeal was heard in Shanghai. The A50 index futures contract was trading on the Singapore market, but trading volumes were modest. The court found us in breach of our contract and we paid the fine.

And what became of Fredy Bush? XFN floated shares on the Japanese market in 2004, but the regular reporting and intrusive questioning of shareholders did not suit Fredy's style. She began devoting more of her time to developing an offshoot, Xinhua Financial Media, and the company started to get into trouble. Then the financial crises of 2008 struck. Bush stepped down from XFN, and FTSE bought out the index venture in 2010. The FTSE/Xinhua indices were renamed FTSE China and continue to be widely used today. Unfortunately, there was worse to come for Bush. In 2013, she was sentenced to one month in prison for a US tax violation. Knowing her entrepreneurial character she will be back doing deals around the world.

South Korea

It was hot under the lights as perhaps a hundred journalists and their assorted cameras faced us. Early mornings were never quiet on the trading floor of the Korean stock exchange in the heart of Seoul's financial district but on this occasion it was exceptionally busy. I was flanked by Lee Kwang-Soo, president of Korea Exchange's stock market division, and Lee Sung-tae, the governor of the central bank. Everyone seemed to know what I was going to say but they came along to hear it anyway.

I found out later that this press conference was carried live on the national morning news.

September 2008 was a torrid month for financial markets. A few days before my announcement, Lehman Brothers, the US investment bank, filed for Chapter 11 bankruptcy protection on 14 September. Numerous other lenders were in trouble, and share prices swung wildly for fear of exposure to collateralized debt obligations (CDOs), the slicing and dicing of low-grade mortgage debt, and other exotic financial instruments that few properly understood and were unravelling fast. The day I arrived in a steamy Seoul, the UK bank HBOS announced the terms of a rescue takeover by Lloyds TSB, a deal that would see the enlarged bank bailed out by the government within the month.

In this part of Asia, however, there was excitement of a different kind. South Korea, one of the region's tiger economies, was about to join a very exclusive club. After four years of negotiations, I was in town to confirm that it would become the 25th country to carry FTSE's developed market classification one year from now.

It wasn't exactly news on the day. A leak meant the story was heavily trailed in all the newspapers that morning. And in our review of market designations carried out a year earlier, FTSE had signalled the upgrade was likely to be approved in 2008 and implemented in 2009. But it was significant all the same.

A nation on the rise

South Korea was leaving behind the likes of South Africa and Mexico in our 'advanced emerging' category and joining the ranks of Japan, Singapore and Germany in the 'developed' group. In terms of sheer monetary value, at that point it was the most valuable decision FTSE had ever taken. Because our country classifications were a vital signpost for global investors, my announcement would lead to billions of dollars flowing into Korean stocks. The amount of global investment money following developed market indexes was more than six times as large as that in emerging-market funds at that time. The Korean bourse operator predicted a net capital inflow of about $8 billion to $16 billion in the medium to long term after investors adjusted their portfolios.

Those numbers explain the intense lobbying from the South Korean finance minister down and the saga of will-they-won't-they media coverage that had gone on for several years. South Korea was the largest emerging-market country that FTSE tracked and a key focus for mutual funds. Within its old grouping it accounted for 14 per cent of the index but that would drop to about 1.6 per cent in its new home.

Like nervous schoolchildren anticipating the start of the new term, September had become an annual event for ministers and central bankers around the world. That was when FTSE published its annual update of country classifications which complemented the day-to-day work we did collating stocks into categories of size and industry. Much rode on deciding which country, if any, was up and which was down. It involved a programme of year-round engagement and the measuring of many criteria including the size and liquidity of markets.

In some ways, FTSE's South Korean decision was a case of playing catch-up. The nation's economy had recorded one of the most remarkable growth stories in the second half of the 20th century, the 'Miracle of the Han River' as it was known. The nation had been an agricultural backwater hobbled by the Korean War, but had laid the groundwork to become a key exporter by investing in its industrial capacity. Having joined the Organization for Economic Co-operation and Development (OECD) in 1996, South Korea suffered a setback in the Asian financial crisis of 1997 when markets suffered steep downturns. It had to turn to the International Monetary Fund for a $60 billion bailout to which there were strings attached to offer more flexibility around exchange rates and increased access for foreign investors. World-renowned brands such as Samsung in electronics and Hyundai in automotive guaranteed it a place on the global stage, and the World Bank already qualified it as a high-income country.

What made it easier for us was that three years earlier, the stock exchange, futures exchange and the newer Kosdaq electronic trading market united into one company. But a continuing point of contention was around the convertibility of the Korean won. Trading volumes were much greater outside South Korea. The central bank wanted to control that trade through the major Korean banks and we wanted an open door to foreign investors. There were also questions over stock transfers and the ability for foreigners to trade among themselves in securities.

Because of the numerous large Korean companies whose shares were traded I instinctively felt this should be a developed market. But some investors were resistant to change. They liked having such a large, mature market in their emerging portfolios and smoothing out some of the volatility they experienced. It was a negotiation, just as the job has been since before we created the company in 1995. In the end, we pressed ahead.

The decision to promote South Korea had only been confirmed late the night before. I flew in and reached my hotel room about midnight. I felt like I was a visiting local dignitary. The room was over two floors with great views of Seoul and a baby grand piano to occupy me. I had no time to attempt to play it.

The market response that day was underwhelming, with the local Korea Composite Stock Price Index (KOSPI) falling 3 per cent in early trading. I suspect that was more to do with the havoc being wrought in financial markets. The after-effects of the financial crisis are still being felt more than a decade later, with ultra-low interest rates, economic stimulus and tougher banking regulation. Arguably, my announcement that day had just as much of a ripple effect in South Korea itself but also among those countries that aspired to win promotion, too.

A little more background

The reach of FTSE around the world goes back to 1987. Not wanting to be caught out again after the LSE set up the SE 100 on its own, the *FT* created its own world index. Under the guidance of Richard Lambert, the deputy editor, the newspaper teamed up with the Institute and Faculty of Actuaries with whom it had worked on indices since 1962. Policy decisions were taken by a 12-person committee of which the chairman, Richard Pain, and its auditor, John Brumwell represented the Actuaries Investment Committee. But because of the obvious international dimension, the *FT* needed other partners who could contribute overseas data. For the FT-Actuaries World Index, it also teamed up with the investment bank Goldman Sachs to obtain American data, and the Edinburgh broker Wood Mackenzie contributed further-flung information to create an index that would take a view than merely of domestic stocks. Pointedly, the LSE, which had acceded to demands for the *FT* to put its name on what became the FTSE 100, was not involved in this launch.

There had been some market capitalization-weighted indexes that tracked global markets since the 1960s, but it wasn't until investment portfolio managers began looking across borders in the 1980s that demand for better data took off. Just like investors often choose an asset class or an industry segment to back, they could choose a country to favour, too.

The FT-Actuaries World Index was early to recognize this opportunity but was remarkably thorough. It covered 70 per cent of the market capitalization of 23 countries. This was done by targeting 70 per cent coverage of the aggregate market value of all listed equities in each local market and at least 10 per cent by number of the available companies in each market. Published daily in the *FT* in four currencies – sterling, US dollars, Japanese yen and the local currency – the indices quickly won a strong international following.

To be included, countries needed an established stock market with reliable stock prices and companies. Compilers gauged the relative wealth of countries as the distinguishing measure plus some subjective judgements about the quality of the market. It threw up some surprising results. For example, Finland didn't qualify for inclusion for the first year because of concerns over its company data.

A system of weightings reflected the relative importance of different countries – and how that has changed over time as economies have risen and fallen. At inception, Japan represented about 35 per cent of the FT-Actuaries World Index and the USA was 37 per cent. Thirty years later, Japan had dropped to 8 per cent and the USA had grown to more than 51 per cent.

What was lacking early on was a distinction to reflect the different nature of each of these markets. For instance, the Indian market might be showing fantastic growth compared to the UK market, but relative performance does not take into account diverse characteristics such as how developed each economy was.

Ownership of the FT-Actuaries World Index changed in 1995, when Wood Mackenzie sold its stake to Standard & Poor's, giving rise to the FT/S&P Actuaries World Index just as the *FT* stake was injected into the nascent FTSE company I set up. Initially, Interactive Data Corporation (IDC) that was part of the FT Group at the time took over the Edinburgh-based

Wood Mackenzie staff and their calculation responsibilities. S&P took over the calculation of the US indices from Goldman Sachs. In 1997, when FTSE took over the calculation of the non-US indices from IDC, the index was renamed as the FTSE/S&P-Actuaries World Index. As well as disparate ownership, there was no consistency with methodology or the classification of companies that read across to FTSE's UK and other domestic country indices. FTSE bought out Goldman Sachs and S&P in 1999, and the index was renamed as the FTSE World Index. However, it was now a mix of developed markets and a handful of significant emerging markets. But many important emerging markets were missing.

Defining categories

This was quickly resolved in 2000 when FTSE bought the Baring Emerging Markets Indices and merged them together with the FTSE World Index Series. The deal coloured in much of the globe for us, adding 20 countries. That resulted in an index covering 49 countries with some 2,300 constituents. At this point, we needed to get organized. I thought it important to start distinguishing between countries depending on how developed their economies were, while ensuring that only countries that met high-quality standards for international investors should be included in the 'developed' – the highest – category. Investors made the distinction and we needed to on their behalf, too. It was precisely how we had developed the other indices: expanding coverage and smoothing out our methodology as we went.

We were starting to compete with MSCI on the quality of the product, and institutional investors were showing more interest in us. We took the opportunity to classify countries in the existing World Index into 'developed' and 'advanced emerging' categories, adding the Barings countries not already covered by the

World Index to create a third, 'secondary emerging', category. By the time the family was renamed as the FTSE Global Equity Index Series (GEIS) in 2003, coverage had been deepened to include small-cap companies. There had been so much change that we stepped back to explore how our classifications could be as objective as possible and based around a clear set of rules. Now we had categories we had to make it simple for investors to gauge the likelihood of countries moving between them. We also needed to make clear to countries that we didn't yet classify how they could qualify for inclusion – or indeed gain promotion.

What emerged was a quality of markets assessment that is key to any country that wants to progress in the index. For each country it includes information on the gross national product per capita as calculated by the World Bank, one of the original mechanisms used to help distinguish between the different classifications. More recently, the country's credit rating was also added. After that, there are four pillars covering regulation, the dealing landscape, custody and settlement, and the presence of a derivatives market, which combine to make up 21 criteria in total. Developed markets should not fail in any category, while advanced emerging markets are those that fall short in areas such as free settlement, stock lending and short selling. Secondary emerging countries are deemed not to have a developed foreign exchange market and might place some restrictions on foreign ownership. 'Frontier' nations, a fourth grouping introduced in 2008, have the most basic markets provision. For example, they might suffer from poor liquidity, high transaction costs and insufficient competition between brokers.

There are other measures, notably a watch list that was instituted so that investors could see which country is under consideration for promotion or demotion from a particular category. We help the countries understand what they need to do to improve their chances of promotion – or avoid demotion.

Those decisions are ultimately taken by FTSE's internal Product Governance Board, taking into account the advice from the FTSE Country Classification Advisory Committee – consisting of market practitioners with technical expertise in trading, portfolio management, and custody – which advice is itself subject to comment by the FTSE Russell Policy Advisory Board.

Changes to country scores are recommended and published twice a year in March and September. It is a gradual process because investors need plenty of notice in case their portfolios have to be altered. A country must stay on the watch list for at least a year, and could remain there for several years, before it can be reclassified. An additional check was added in March 2020. To ensure that countries have sizeable and liquid markets, to gain entry to 'developed' will from now on require at least five qualifying stocks and a combined investable market capitalisation of $25.5 billion as of the end of 2019.

Country classification has become a year-round event. Every September, FTSE announces movements or potential movements. But the schedule of assessment begins the preceding October, starting with those countries that have been freshly placed on the watch list. What evidence is there of improvements or deterioration in a country's scores? Such evidence is actively sought through engagement with the central banks and markets regulators in each case.

As of September 2019, the FTSE GEIS includes 49 countries with a further 30 countries classified as 'frontier' markets. Although the index series still covers only one in four countries, it does capture more than 90 per cent of all global equity markets. That breadth of coverage of what is already there is what concerns international investors, not prospecting in new markets. We have sought to classify those countries that are going to have an impact. Markets that were too small would just add cost. And then we have pursued markets in regions where investors have a strong interest, such as the Middle East.

South Korean success

South Korea's inclusion is the tale of two countries. Ever since 2004, it had been on our watch list alongside Taiwan, another significant destination for emerging-market investment, for a possible upgrade. Whereas South Korea worked towards promotion, Taiwan pushed back. Its central bank wanted two things: to retain much greater control over their currency than we would have countenanced, and to preserve the influence that local brokers had over the market. That restricted access to foreign investors, and we could not allow it. After numerous FTSE meetings with the central bank governor and finance ministers, Taiwan is still in the 'advanced emerging' category. One year after inclusion, in 2010, South Korea became the first Asian and non-G8 host of the G20 summit of the world's largest industrialized economies. Of course, that had nothing to do with FTSE, but every little bit helps.

In the event, the financial crisis delayed the expected final improvements from South Korea. In a white paper in 2013, Chris Woods, who joined FTSE in 2010 to further develop our structure for assessing countries, reviewed our decision on South Korea. He wrote: 'Unlike some other indexers, FTSE does not regard country classification as merely an exercise in box-ticking. Broader considerations of a country's overall standing in the global economy, and the perceptions of investors, are also essential to the final decision.'

More than 10 years on, our closest rival, MSCI, still classifies South Korea as an emerging market, making a sharp point of difference between our respective indices. This makes the transition costs bigger for any client we win from MSCI, but it's a one-way street. One day, MSCI will need to promote South Korea, and its clients will have the choice of bearing the cost of this change at a time of MSCI's choosing or moving to FTSE ahead of this change at a time of their own choosing. Vanguard has already done this.

Saudi Arabia

Out of the elevator and down a long, thickly carpeted corridor, I picked my way through a detail of security guards talking discreetly into head microphones. The vast suite into which I was ushered contained white-gloved butlers busying themselves at the table and chairs fanned out in a crescent shape for an earlier cabinet meeting. After waiting for a few minutes, in strode a beaming Mohammed bin Salman (MBS), the 32-year-old crown prince of Saudi Arabia, who greeted me warmly with a hug.

It was 28 March 2018 and there was much to discuss. The Saudi Arabians had taken over the entire floor of New York's Plaza Hotel, a 20-storey monument to luxury that occupies the corner of Fifth Avenue and Central Park. This was the venue where the movie star Marlene Dietrich booked in for a month and the playwright Truman Capote hosted his famous Black and White Ball. And now one of the richest men in the world was in town keen to make his own splash on the global stage.

A new vision

FTSE was helping him to do so. After years of work, we confirmed that morning that, following our latest country classification review, Saudi Arabia would be granted secondary emerging market status. To be ranked alongside Colombia and Chile did not appear to be worth crowing about, especially for a fantastically wealthy nation that boasted the 12th largest stock market in the world by market capitalization. But to win our nod was a crucial step forward in MBS's plan to open Saudi Arabia up to the world. His 2030 Vision, announced two years earlier, set out ambitions to diversify the kingdom away from its reliance on oil, open the company to greater foreign investment and boost productivity. FTSE accreditation meant that billions of dollars of capital would begin pour into the kingdom in a year's time when membership was slated to begin.

I was as pumped up as the Saudi team after conducting a packed-out press conference across town followed by some upbeat client meetings – all good promotion as I continued to grow FTSE's reputation on Wall Street. From an arcane activity that took place in a newspaper back office to capturing the interest of a world leader, surely this was the pinnacle for the indexation industry. It certainly excited me – even though I knew many thought Saudi Arabia's human rights record should automatically rule it out of the investment conversation.

Lined up next to me was Saudi's finance minister, Mohammed Al-Jadaan, regulatory chief Mohammed El-Kuwaiz, who was chairman of Saudi Arabia's Capital Market Authority (CMA), Sarah Al-Suhaimi, the first woman to chair Tadawul, the Saudi stock exchange, and Khalid Al Hussan the Tadawul chief executive. Also in attendance was David Warren: LSE's finance director who had raised doubts about the Russell acquisition four years earlier was now interim chief executive after the departure of Xavier Rolet.

It was a brief audience. An imposing man dressed in opulent robes – in contrast to most of his team who had been across New York that day dressed in their Western-style dark suits – I found MBS somewhat reserved. Here was the great reformer who was changing Saudi society: lifting the ban on women drivers, reopening cinemas and touring the world to meet fellow world leaders. Under his rule, Saudi had also imprisoned many of its own elite, in a crackdown on corruption, as well as made a bloody intervention in its neighbour Yemen's civil war.

MBS was nowhere near as outgoing as senior business and political figures usually are. He didn't feel a need to dominate the conversation and warmly greeted his team, talking to each of them in a friendly and very personable manner. For about 10 minutes, we talked about how pleased he was at being accepted into the index and how the decision fitted with his vision for the kingdom. At least he was in a light-hearted mood. The renowned workaholic laughed and joked about whether his assembled retinue, including Al-Jadaan, was working hard enough.

Saudi did not qualify for FTSE just because of the photo opportunity, however. It had succeeded in improving its model for share administration and agreed to open its stock market further to overseas investors. We calculated that the kingdom would immediately become our largest market in the Middle East, accounting for around 2.7 per cent of FTSE's Emerging Index.

What some will find surprising is that this entire programme of events was choreographed without any input from the UK government. It is important to me that FTSE largely operates autonomously, impartially, but some of these major inclusions felt like acts of diplomacy all the same. It was always useful to receive briefings and guidance from the UK government, but I tried to steer clear of asking for help as we worked with sovereign state investors and departments worldwide.

In the case of Saudi, ministers were kept informed but never tried to get involved. That was despite our meeting taking place just three weeks after MBS had enjoyed the pomp and ceremony of a three-day state visit to London. He dined with the Queen, Prince Charles and Prince William, while a blanket advertising campaign in UK newspapers proclaimed to sceptical commuters that: 'He is bringing change to Saudi Arabia.'

The UK's defence industry had long relied on Saudi as a free-spending customer for weapons and expertise. But after the Brexit vote the previous summer that had estranged the UK from its leading trading partners around Europe, the prime minister, Theresa May, was intent on shoring up and broadening other international partnerships. In April 2017, May's first foreign trip after triggering Article 50 that began the Brexit countdown was to Riyadh. She said building a relationship with Saudi Arabia was better than 'standing on the sidelines and sniping' about humanitarian issues. May was joined by Rolet, as the pair tried to land one major prize in particular: to play host to the upcoming flotation of the giant Saudi state oil company Aramco in London.

Aramco was vast, accounting for 10 per cent of global oil production and dwarfing London's long-standing oil majors, BP and Shell. Not only would its listing in London mean a fees bonanza for Square Mile banks and brokers, it would send a signal to the world that the City was still at the centre of world finance post-Brexit. The powers that be were bending over backwards to win the business that was another plank of MBS's 2030 Vision. By proposing a new category within its premium listing regime for state-controlled enterprises that would make it easier for the Gulf oil giant to comply, the Financial Conduct Authority (FCA) had aroused the concerns of the Treasury Select Committee, the Institute of Directors, and City investors. The Square Mile's reputation for good governance was once again brought to the fore.

A new category

By this point, I had been visiting Saudi Arabia for several years. In that time, the kingdom's ambition to be a global business centre had grown up like the Riyadh skyline. Construction of the Tadawul Tower in the King Abdullah Financial District began in 2012. This 42-storey edifice has become a gleaming

glass-and-steel blade at the heart of a development on the out-
skirts of the city that is still largely deserted. As the name suggests, the top seven floors of the tower have been given over
to the Saudi Stock Exchange. It epitomizes a strategy unlike
anything in the West – a vast building programme intended to
stimulate demand over the next two decades.

Its very existence marked a big change. At first, the Saudi
market was very closed off and they had no intention of opening up. After China, it was the next biggest market that wasn't
covered by indexation, so it was a great prize. However, it fell
a long way short of our country classification rules. At FTSE, I
decided we needed to find a solution, in part to get our people focused on this market and engaging with Saudi. As with
China, the inclusion of Saudi Arabia in the 'frontier' index
would – as a result of its sheer size – have dominated the cap-
weighted index. In 2008, I announced that, because of the size
and significance of Saudi Arabia, FTSE would introduce a standalone index for the market for those international investors
who wanted to add it to their global portfolios. It was a way of
opening the door to them and FTSE meeting growing investor
demand. It was also important to me to keep pace with our
rival, MSCI, which had done a lot of work in the region. The
Saudi-specific category meant that we took all their prices to
do our calculations and all the time learning about this market.

When the 2030 Vision was published, there was a sea change
in attitudes. I saw the opportunity to influence the Saudis, and
they were willing to engage with us much more. The kingdom's
development programme for its financial sector set out targets
to increase the size of financial assets as a ratio of GDP, increase
the share of SME financing offered by its banks, open up the
financial services sector to emerging competitors, and fully
comply with international standards for financial stability. They
were keen to develop a mature capital market, deepen liquidity, create a better debt market and introduce more financial

instruments. MBS saw to it that businessmen were appointed to key positions to get things done.

In places, suddenly Saudi Arabia was going too fast. It was building the latest systems for real-time, same-day transaction settlement. It was too fast because most international investors were not able to buy stocks and transfer currency – the cash to buy stock – in the same time frame. International investors needed two days to put everything together. They needed our guidance to meet international standards, not exceed them.

I spent a lot of my time dealing with Mohammed El-Kuwaiz, who had been chairman of Saudi Arabia's Capital Market Authority (CMA) since July 2017. He was a former McKinsey management consultant who had a considered view of the world, having obtained his MBA from New York University's Leonard N. Stern School of Business – the same school my son Dominic attended. That meant we had things in common from the off. El-Kuwaiz was impressive. A natural leader, he was engaging and clearly respected by all those around him. He didn't avoid problems but rather sought solutions, built consensus and understood the detail, always focusing on the bigger aims. Most importantly, he delivered. Confidence grew when he became involved.

I met the local brokers and fund managers because I wanted to understand how they were trading and what their issues were. The market users always tell me more than the officials. Two things surprised me. Everyone was very young – about two-thirds of the population are under 30. And they were quite desperate for change. Some of them described what we were involved with as Saudi Arabia's last chance to reform. I was surprised by how strongly many of the younger workers felt and how open they were to the changes being championed by the ambitious Vision 2030.

But everything had to be reviewed in detail – the exchange, the trading, the clearing, the central bank, the currency – and modified to meet our standards. El–Kuwaiz and the finance minister coordinated all the departments of government to achieve that goal. Chris Woods and his team, particularly Joti Rana, one of our leading governance analysts based in New York, met frequently with El–Kuwaiz, Khalid Al Hussan and their teams. We applied pressure but made sure we did not move too quickly for fear that investors would not follow us.

The Saudi Stock Exchange opened to foreign investors in 2015, and in September that year we put Saudi on our watch list. Thirty months later, its promotion was confirmed. El–Kuwaiz and Al Hussan coordinated and delivered the most impressive change programme we have experienced in dealing with governments around the world. They also built enormous goodwill with the major institutional investors who we rely on to vet and accept the market infrastructure and regulatory and financial policy changes we require. We led the way this time and beat MSCI with the announcement, although it fast-tracked it own inclusion on the back of what I suspect was our pioneering work.

These are not box-ticking exercises. We have rules and a committee of the big users and experts in this field, who were making judgements and helping us determine whether Saudi had done enough. Usually, we insisted on the committee being unanimous. But there were times when two or three members on the committee dragged along the rest. We would not promote until we had the vast majority of users with us. The biggest institutional investors around the world have a huge say and influence on us, and it would be foolish to introduce any significant change without their backing.

Facing a dilemma

Disaster struck on 2 October 2018. Jamal Khashoggi, a US-based journalist and stern critic of the Saudi Arabian regime, was murdered in the kingdom's consulate in Istanbul. He had gone to collect papers to prove his divorce so that he could remarry, but did not leave the building alive.

The incident was roundly condemned by the international community, and MBS was implicated in its arrangement, although Saudi officials said the killing was a 'rogue operation'. Speaking in the House of Commons, Theresa May condemned the killing 'in the strongest possible terms', adding 'we must get to the truth of what happened'. Donald Trump described it as the 'worst cover-up in history'.

It was undoubtedly an unacceptable illegal act and a great tragedy – and for FTSE it created a dilemma. Six months earlier we had given our blessing to the reforming Saudi regime. In six months' time, the kingdom would be admitted to our world index.

I have always been very nervous of introducing political issues into our process. We exist to capture the investment opportunity – by that I mean to include in our indices all meaningful countries and stocks that can be reasonably bought and sold by international investors – not to selectively pick and choose which countries or stocks should be included in global portfolios. That is the role of the asset owner or fund manager. We had got this far without judging countries beyond the transparency and effectiveness of their markets, so for us to change now would challenge a core principle and raise difficult questions. Maybe this is an area for sustainable investing experts to consider, but rules will need to be developed so that a consistent approach is taken that is globally acceptable.

It is the role of the market to price risk in and for us to demonstrate what can be invested in. Clearly, developments in Saudi meant there was a greater risk attached to that market, but it did not mean investors had to withdraw if they wanted to take that risk. That said, I am sure that, if the Khashoggi incident had happened before FTSE made its decision, we would probably have deferred. Having already made the decision, reversing it would have been very difficult. This was not an investment issue — it was a behavioural issue for the leadership of that country.

Our advisory committees and the investors were supportive of us. At the exchange, Xavier Rolet understood the regulatory issues and did not get involved or offer a view. It was a FTSE matter for us to decide. There were no grounds in our rules to review the decision for such a matter, and neither did we think new criteria should be developed. We accepted that we would be criticized for this approach and decided to press ahead.

The first test was a seminar for institutional investors we held in New York in mid-November to brief users of our indices. I opened the event, but El-Kuwaiz was the keynote speaker. To the surprise of the 200 hardened Wall Street fund managers in the room, he addressed the killing at the outset. El-Kuwaiz spoke passionately about his upbringing and his values and made no attempt to excuse what had happened. It was clear to all that he held the same strong beliefs about human life and societal change as the best of us. There were no questions on Khashoggi in the room at the end, but I think a number of investors pressed him further during the coffee break.

The Aramco flotation

After the audience with MBS in New York, there was a celebratory dinner that night at Le Bernardin, a French seafood restaurant with three Michelin stars. The crown prince wasn't there, but many of his cabinet were. I was notionally the guest of honour, although it felt as though that accolade had been reserved for the Saudi Arabia's energy minister, Khalid Al-Falih.

The minister sat opposite me and was clearly a powerful man around whom all conversations seemed to centre. Not only did his ministry oversee more than half of the Saudi economy, it having been expanded on his appointment in 2016, he was also

a prime mover in the Organization of the Petroleum Exporting Countries (OPEC) cartel. Al-Falih was also the chairman
of Saudi Aramco (officially the Saudi Arabian Oil Company),
having worked his way up through the company since joining in 1979. The finance minister, Mohammed Al-Jadaan, knew
his place, describing Al-Falih as the one who generated all the
revenue.

The conversation over Aramco's flotation was continuing
between the LSE and the Saudis, and I had stayed out of it.
FTSE had been clear from the very start. Aramco was a Saudi
company, and no matter where it listed it would be included in
our Saudi index and priced off the Saudi exchange price.

Al-Falih asked me what I thought of the Aramco flotation. He
was cautious and clearly not fully convinced the listing would
be the success hoped for. Others had well-telegraphed doubts.

The Investment Association in the UK was concerned about
Aramco going into the FTSE 100 if the company listed in London, and even though we had been explicit with them that
this would not happen, they raised their concerns with several
newspapers.

Some 18 months after the New York dinner, Al-Falih was
stripped of both his ministerial and Aramco roles, seemingly
because he was lukewarm on a fast IPO plan. It doesn't pay to
stand in the way of progress. But the power he exuded had not
totally dimmed despite appearing to fall out of favour. In February 2020, he bounced back when he was appointed to lead
Saudi's new investment ministry.

In the end, Aramco shares did not list in either London or
New York. The flotation was fraught with difficulties and it
became a far smaller event than the kingdom – and salivat-
ing investment banking advisers – had first envisaged. When
the shares began trading on 11 December 2019, Aramco did
become the most valuable listed company in history and soon
passed the $2 trillion mark for market capitalization. But

because of a mixture of heightened geopolitical risk, low oil prices and the climate change lobby that was causing some investors to rethink putting their money behind fossil fuels, it was a debut more muted than had been hoped when the prospect of a flotation was first announced in 2016. Aramco sold only 1.5 per cent of the company. It raised $25 billion, but most of the money that bought shares came from Saudi companies, government agencies and loyal retail investors. FTSE, after consulting international investors, decided to allow Aramco to join its world indices and MSCI followed it. Only a tiny proporion of Aramco was included in the FTSE and MSCI world indices but this will only increase over time as Aramco floats further shares. The benefits for the Saudi market will spread beyond Aramco itself and will be felt across the whole market and the wider workplace, touching and influencing all Saudi citizens.

China again

23 March 2020 was one of the biggest days in the history of FTSE. And yet for many market observers – certainly retail investors – it passed without incident. Billions of dollars flowed between emerging markets at our instigation that day. The financial world shifted subtly on its axis.

That Monday marked the end point of inclusion for both China A shares and Saudi Arabia in FTSE's emerging market indices, concluding a phased process that had run since we announced their qualification in 2018. Large countries are introduced to our indices in stages to limit disruption and spread the outflows from those markets being sold down to make way in portfolios for the new constituents. 23 March marked the fifth and final tranche of the reclassification of Saudi, representing 25 per cent of the weighting of its securities. At the same time, the last 40 per cent of China A shares – those in more than 1,000 mainland companies traded in renminbi – were admitted, too.

For investment banks and brokers, this realignment presented a huge technical challenge. Expanding the investment universe is seen as a positive, firstly because it creates a flurry of trades which all need to be paid for by clients. But much work goes into making it as streamlined as possible and that the infrastructure is in place to process trades at volume. As soon as we published our guidance on what would happen when, preparations get under way to transfer the passive money. Hedge funds also pay attention to see if they can game the system by getting ahead of the transactions.

It is not the end of the story for either nation. The Saudi Arabian exchange Tadawul said that foreign investors were net buyers of more than $20 billion of locally listed shares in the first eight months of 2019. When the oil giant Saudi Aramco achieves a 5 per cent free float, it will be admitted to our indices and international investors that follow them will be required to buy the stock, too.

In China, there are still capital controls that stem the amount of money that flows in. They will lift over the next decade, rebalancing portfolios further so that China accounts for almost 50 per cent of all emerging markets – dominating in a way that the USA dominates developed markets. As much as $400 billion could flow into the Chinese stock market over the next decade if the amount tracked by all the three of the main index providers are combined.

Ongoing issues

Admitting China A shares was not as easy as Saudi Arabia where the establishment put its weight behind compliance. In China, the relationship between the China Securities Regulatory Commission (CSRC) and the two exchanges in Shanghai and

Shenzhen is more complicated as the regulator owns them and its senior executives are often drawn from the two exchanges. I often thought this created a problem in that the regulator was concerning itself with the commercial interest of the exchanges rather than focusing purely on the interests of the market. And there were other issues, too, such as the quality of companies and the way they reported and the over-involvement of the government in the market, but China has improved greatly and I always thought it was worth persevering because the A share market was the biggest in the world outside the USA. As a start, a growing number of Chinese companies were listed in Hong Kong, which is well regulated, so we started including those companies, grouped into the global indices, but the vast majority were A share issues in China to which international investors could not get access.

Every quarter, I went to Beijing to remind CSRC of the benefits of FTSE inclusion. But in China it's not a negotiation. When the government finally decided that this was something it wanted to do, it would do it. We were often stuck between the Chinese authorities and international investors. We would get close to having the authorities introduce the changes the international investors demanded but could never quite bridge the gap and get agreement. This went on for many years. When we got close in spring 2015, we created the China inclusion indices and Vanguard adopted these. That was a huge step forward, but very few fund managers would follow them and we could not build a momentum for change and nor could we convince the CSRC to meet our requirements.

I met a couple of the CSRC chairs and vice chairs over several years. Two stood out for me. Qi Bin was one executive I would class as a modern thinker. He was educated at Tsinghua University and the University of Chicago and was director general of the CSRC's international affairs department, among other roles. He understood that improving the quality of the market was in interests of China but he met resistance, too. He worked with us in taking our quality of markets criteria and establishing a programme of positive changes in China's capital markets. His work laid the foundation for us being able to create the China inclusion indices. I was not at all surprised to see him promoted to become executive vice president of the Chinese Investment Corporation, the country's powerful sovereign wealth fund.

Another is Fang Xinghai. I first met Fang back in the early 2000s when he was a promising senior manager at the Shanghai Stock Exchange. He joined CSRC as vice chairman in October 2015, and in that position sought to bring all parties together and open up and improve the quality of China's capital markets step by step. His work together with the support of Dr Huang Hongyuan, the chairman of the Shanghai Stock Exchange, enabled us to finally announce in September 2018 the inclusion of up to 25 per cent of all eligible China A shares. At a ceremony at the Shanghai Stock Exchange, I joined Fang and Huang to celebrate the beginning of China's inclusion into global benchmarks. Both Fang and Huang are committed to continuing to open up China to overseas funds, but the journey has a long way to go before completion.

Towards the future

It was clear that one tactic of the CSRC was playing FTSE off against MSCI, our closest rival. It knew how competitive we both were. That rivalry will ensure that both will seek to increase the percentage of China A shares included in the global indices at a pace international investors will accept. If either goes too fast or too slow, they will lose clients to the other. It will be a tricky path for them to tread. This competition manifested itself in the summer of 2018 when I bumped into my opposite number, Henry Fernandez, on the steps of the CSRC in Beijing. He was leaving the building as I was parked outside waiting to come in to a meeting where the CSRC hoped to finalize China's inclusion. It could not have been choreographed better. To defuse a tense situation, I shook Fernandez by the hand and said: 'Henry, for once you're ahead of me.' We all laughed together.

This shrinking investment world is not popular in all quarters, especially as a trade war has raged between the USA and China since Donald Trump moved into the White House. In June 2019, Senator Marco Rubio accused MSCI of letting China gain unprecedented access to US capital and granting it a legitimacy it did not deserve. In a letter to Fernandez, he wrote:

> Given China's willingness to openly flout US laws and its stated
> intentions to displace American industrial leadership, MSCI's decision
> to include Chinese companies in its indexes raises serious questions
> and concerns about the quality and depth of the diligence undertaken
> throughout its decision-making process.

Increasingly, the index providers will find themselves subject to political pressure. I experienced my own taste of this when I was presenting to the US Securities and Exchange Commission (SEC). The Democrats on the SEC were all in favour of what we were doing. And the Republicans seemed to be down on most things: our admission of China, quality controls and restrictions around customized indices, the exclusion of non-voting shares which affected companies such as Snap. They wanted us to remove as much regulation as we could. We were just a private company and should know our place.

I could never have predicted that FTSE would find itself entangled in political debate all over the world. The financial world will keep evolving, and we have to evolve with it. If we get it right, and only if we get it right, the investors that use us will continue to do so. We don't take lightly our influence over capital flows, but it comes as a result of the trust put in us by the world's largest investors. We will only maintain this if we keep standards and transparency high, so that investors and policy-makers can understand and trust what we are doing.

8
Doing good

As the veteran film star Roger Moore stood up to address the room full of diners, my mind was whirring. It was late 1999: a banqueting hall in Zurich. Investors and bankers who had spent the day in the Swiss city at a FTSE conference pushed back their chairs to listen, sated from the delicious three-course meal that was being cleared away.

'I've just given them an idea,' said Moore, with a conspiratorial lift of his eyebrow and gesturing to the top table where I was sitting. Best known for starring in seven James Bond films, the debonair actor was here performing a very different role. Moore was spending less time on screen these days, and had become devoted to the United Nations Children's Fund (UNICEF), for which he had been a goodwill ambassador since 1991.

The quintessential Englishman always joked that he never tried too hard in front of the cameras, but in this guise he relentlessly worked a room. In his very charming way, Moore was always trying to get UNICEF's corporate partners and their guests to do more for the charity that worked to save children from malnutrition, violence and trafficking. Tonight was no different. As he was wont to do, he pledged all of our future efforts to UNICEF before retaking his seat to a round of applause.

I had met Moore a few months earlier on an overseas trip, but over dinner had been the first chance I had to properly explain to him – when asked – what FTSE did. He took in my answer and considered it for a while before posing a question. 'Look, Mark,' he said, 'I really think FTSE should be able to do something more to raise funds. Can't you create an index of all the good companies?'

It was an idea that sparked some laughter around the table. After all, how on earth could you tell the difference between a good and not-so-good company? But, besides the merriment, Moore had struck a chord. I had been thinking we needed to do something that was different for a while and had looked at how we could apply our expertise to aspects of company performance other than financial. After all, FTSE had spent more than a decade classifying stocks by their size, industry sector and domicile. Why not other metrics, such as how well they were run or their environmental impact?

After his speech, and over brandy and cigars at the end of the evening, Moore and I continued the conversation with one or two others. I sounded out some of the big investors present that evening. They gave the idea a muttered welcome, but they, like me, thought it would be very difficult to achieve. This was how capitalism operated according to those who were suspicious of big business – closeted chats in smoke-filled rooms. And it's true that in those ornate surroundings the world's ills could not have felt further away. Little did I know that what began as a chance conversation would develop into the part of FTSE of which I am most proud.

Indexing the good

Soon after we set FTSE up in 1995, I began thinking about the values the company should have. I never thought that would be something important to me. My early motivation was purely commercial: pulling a proper business together from the loose alliance of the *FT* and the LSE and doing my best to outflank the competition.

However, I knew that standing for something other than profit would become more important the larger we grew. I wanted a close culture and there were already little things that we did to foster that. Our executive team handed out chocolate to everyone else on Fridays. Our family days out and summer outdoor team-building events brought everyone together outside the office. We supported a special needs theatre group, but I knew there could be something more. As a starting point, I asked FTSE's marketing director, Alastair Herbert, to think about which charity we could adopt as a primary cause.

UNICEF leapt off the list he came back with. The United Nations Children's Fund, to give it its full title, was long established, having been set up in the aftermath of the Second World War to provide relief for children devastated by the effects of the conflict. It was hard to argue with its ongoing mission: to promote the rights and wellbeing of every child, providing medicines, clean water, nutritious food and basic education to millions. I wanted to support something that undertook vital works and was as global as we aspired to be.

The charity became our philanthropic partner in 1996. It was a relationship that worked both ways. We raised funds internally and did our best to act as a gateway for UNICEF to reach donors. It saw us as a great brand that would raise its profile in big business cities around the world as well as refresh relationships with numerous financial services supporters from years gone by. Herbie Skeet, my close contact at Reuters, hosted parties to raise funds on several occasions.

Compared to where we are today, these were the early days of corporations working closely with charities. We were still a tiny company compared to our brand name, but every little helped. And as we hired staff it was a great cause to unite recruits around. I didn't forge the relationship to impress clients particularly, but I think some of the bigger City firms thought about their own charitable efforts when they saw us rattling the tin so hard.

I got to know David Bull, who was UNICEF's chief executive in the UK, as well as Gordon Glick, the charity's UK corporate relations manager. I regarded Glick as its chief fundraiser, always gently pushing us to do better. One of the first campaigns we mounted together was the UNICEF perpetual zero-coupon bond in December 1997. It was an inside joke for bond traders: this was a financial product that was never going to mature – and in the meantime, it was going to pay out nothing for ever. Some investment. But as a method of opening wallets it attracted a lot of interest because UNICEF succeeded in talking traders' language.

Actually, this product was way ahead of its time. Social finance – where good causes seek investment, not donation – is everywhere today but back in 1997 nobody was doing this kind of thing. To gain even more attention, UNICEF registered the bond in Spain, denominated in euros, more than a year before the introduction of the new currency. It was thrilling to raise $500,000 for an educational project in Bolivia and get the likes of Credit Suisse, Goldman Sachs and Santander to back us.

'Flights to Reality'

The relationship between FTSE and UNICEF became close, and soon I had the opportunity to visit some of the projects that the funds we raised were paying for. It was on a trip to Morocco in September 1999 that I met Moore for the first time. The story of his involvement in the charity was slightly more glamorous than mine. In true Hollywood fashion, he had been introduced to UNICEF by Audrey Hepburn and became a goodwill ambassador at her request before she died in 1993.

The trip was UNICEF's first Flight to Reality, a concept developed to take a group of privileged one-percenters – chief executives, fund managers, donors and potential donors – to see at first hand the developing world from which they were totally removed. Funded jointly by FTSE and British Airways, another of UNICEF's supporters, the idea was to see how people at the bottom of the pyramid lived and how our money could best be applied to give them and their children a helping hand without lecturing or patronising.

In the Al Hauouz Province around Marrakech, we saw how the daily search for water kept girls out of school and meant literacy levels were at rock bottom. What a difference simply installing taps had made in these remote villages. In the ancient town of Ighil, kids cared for their younger siblings while their parents toiled in the fields. UNICEF ran trips so these children could see the sea for the first time. And it trained proud mid-wives to adopt better hygiene standards at a provincial centre in Ikherkhouden so maternal mortality rates improved.

We travelled high into the Atlas Mountains. It was 14 years since Moore had last played James Bond but his fame had not dimmed. Even when we turned up in a remote village, some-one would have hung out signs to welcome the world's most famous secret agent. Warm and engaging, he charmed them all. Bill Deedes, the legendary *Daily Telegraph* editor who was the inspiration for William Boot in Evelyn Waugh's novel *Scoop*, was also on that trip. He was the last person to go native. In 40-degree heat he refused to take off his three-piece wool suit in favour of something cooler. Deedes even kept it on when we took to mules to trek up a final, vertiginous stretch. Moore, in a crisp linen suit, refused the offer of a ride. Picking our way alongside the sharp cliff face, he just did not trust the animal.

A year later, in October 2000, I joined Moore in the slums of Accra, the capital of Ghana, to launch a fundraising campaign for polio vaccination. Earlier that year, we had drummed up support from City firms, asking for £5,000 to £20,000 each to pay for a National Immunization Day when 500,000 children would be vaccinated. It wasn't expensive to prevent the spread of a potentially crippling illness. By immunizing children under the age of five, UNICEF was intent on making polio the second world disease to be eradicated after smallpox.

On that trip, a handful of us took a flight across Ghana in a private jet to visit a remote UNICEF project. We got caught up in a thunderstorm flying over Lake Volta. The pilot told us he was going to try to outpace it. At one point, the lights cut out and the aircraft began to lose altitude. People were shouting and clinging on to their seats. Amid the panic, Moore reached across to the fridge, pulled out a beer and sat their sipping it, just as unflappable as one of his on-screen characters.

I was pleased to get further involved in UNICEF: in 2002 I was awarded an honorary fellowship of UNICEF and I became a vice president of UNICEF UK in 2011. There were other trips, such as going down the drains in Bucharest, the capital of Romania, with the Manchester United finance director, as we tried to get the famous football club on board as a supporter. The images of the orphans hiding away down there in atrocious conditions will never leave me.

In 2015, David Beckham launched a new fund to mark his 10th year as a UNICEF goodwill ambassador. It was called 7: The David Beckham UNICEF Fund – after the number on his famous England and Manchester United football shirts. UNICEF asked if I could help with fundraising, so I set up a dinner with prospective donors at one of our favourite Italian restaurants in New York, Carbone in Greenwich Village. I later found out that it was a favourite of David's, too. I had met Beckham before, at Old Trafford during his Manchester United playing days, when he gave my daughter a huge cuddle. He was very approachable and self-effacing that night, too, talking to everyone. He gave a little speech telling everyone he was not good at speaking. He was charming to everyone and made time for each and every guest, making them feel special. The wives each had their pictures taken with him while their very accomplished husbands grumbled that they were never going to be able to impress their wives ever again.

Aid organizations continue to evolve. Some get criticized today for how they deploy their support, especially when developed nations seek to intervene in the developing world – what the World Bank now calls the Global South. What I saw on the ground because of UNICEF only ever convinced me to redouble my efforts to raise funds. Moore's kernel of an idea over dinner in Zurich proved to be one of the best ways to do just that.

FTSE and socially responsible investing

By the time FTSE began exploring this area, socially responsible investing (SRI) had been around for a long time, although it didn't always go by that name. Religious investors such as the Methodists and Quakers had clear guidelines on which activities they would steer clear of bankrolling – such as slavery or war –several centuries ago. In the second half of the 20th century, the civil rights movement and other pressure groups targeted what they saw as 'bad' companies, often through their shareholder bases. One memorable example is Barclays – which incidentally has its roots in the Quaker movement. The bank suffered from a student boycott during the 1980s because it was invested in apartheid South Africa.

Two environmental disasters focused minds on companies' behaviour and how they affected the world around them. A leak from Union Carbide's pesticide plant in Bhopal, Madhya Pradesh, in India, in December 1984 exposed an estimated 500,000 people in surrounding villages to highly toxic gas. In 1989, the *Exxon Valdez* oil spill deposited almost 11 million gallons of crude oil into water around Alaska. Over time, steering funds into those companies that behave better – while trying to persuade laggards to improve their performance – became an industry in its own right.

All of that history did not make it any easier to assemble our 'good' index in 2000. Companies were beginning to make commitments around behaviour, but these corporate social responsibility (CSR) policies had not really led to asset allocation changing. There were some ethical or socially responsible funds, mainly targeted at retail investors. For institutional investors, there was limited understanding how these issues became sources of risk and return along with everything else they had to consider before deciding where to place their resources. And, despite having an inkling that profit should not be the only thing that mattered, they still had to beat their benchmark.

We needed to pull together some principles for determining our criteria. Unlike the indices we already ran, there was nothing much we could borrow, so we pulled them instead from various UN agreements that had been arrived at for the investment world. None of it was obvious, and it became a far larger piece of work than I had ever thought it would be. I was clear from the start that this was uncharted territory. We had to do the best we could, including navigating that subjectivity, and hope to encourage firms to do better.

Two developments helped our cause during development. The 1999 revision to the UK Pensions Act meant that pension fund trustees were required to declare to what extent they took social and environmental considerations into account in their investment policies. In addition, the UN launched its Global Compact in 2000, a high-level initiative encouraging corporate leaders to commit to following sustainable policies according to 10 principles covering areas such as anti-corruption and human rights.

We wanted to be totally transparent so we made sure the criteria we worked from were made publicly available. In the same way the actuaries had given credence to the early indices, we recruited a group of experts to oversee this product, too. The committee formed to develop the overarching SRI principles and selection criteria for constituents was led by Mervyn Pedelty, the chief executive of the Co-operative Bank, which prided itself on its social conscience. I also brought in Craig Mackenzie, one of the leading experts in this field in the UK. He ran the SRI operation at Friends Ivory & Sime which had launched the UK's first ethical fund in the 1980s. I was very grateful for how active Mackenzie was in developing our framework. His knowledge and understanding of the issues were indispensable.

Tobacco, weapons and nuclear power companies were immediately excluded from the new index. The remainder were then tested on three criteria: their environmental record, human rights and social issues such as how they dealt with a broad base of stakeholders. If they failed in any of these areas, they did not make the cut.

FTSE couldn't do all of this on its own so we searched for help. The Ethical Investment Research Service (EIRIS) was a charity set up in 1983 to help churches and charities work on their ethical investments. It became our research partner. In the USA, we needed extra partners because we didn't have the reach to sufficiently assess overseas companies at that time. EIRIS worked with the Council on Economic Priorities (CEP) and the Investor Responsibility Research Center (IRRC) to provide data on US companies.

They hunted through annual reports for policies and practice that was followed. Really, most companies didn't have anything like that, other than perhaps a corporate charity they supported. We would go back through all the information they threw up, check it, ask questions and then present to the overall committee. I could see the risk attached to getting this wrong. It was only five years since FTSE had begun to grow and promote its brand, and I wasn't about to throw that away on a project where we were trying to help.

Distinguishing the good from the bad

It was a big departure for us. Our indices to date measured a company's market capitalization, which was determined by investors' view of future profitability or dividend payments. We also looked at liquidity, in other words how many shares were available to trade. Now we were examining metrics that reached far beyond the finance department and assessed how a company was performing at this precise moment. This was probably the first time anyone on this side of the Atlantic had attempted to codify SRI. We weren't just calculating an index, we were establishing industry standards.

It took a few attempts to get it right. After we set what we thought were fair criteria, we discovered we didn't have enough qualifying companies to make the index. Of the ten largest stocks in the FTSE 100 at that time, only two or three met the criteria. It wasn't ideal. To achieve any kind of critical mass, we had to lower the standards we had envisaged, with a view to driving them up over time.

A further complication was that what constituted 'good' and 'bad' differed from Wall Street to the Square Mile or wherever an investor happened to be. This challenge came up time and again as we tried to create something with global appeal when such deep cultural differences existed. Take animal testing, which was the source of fierce debate. In Europe, people were dead against it. At that time, Huntingdon Life Sciences, a firm that tested drugs on animals, had been targeted by animal rights protestors, who attacked staff and shareholders. But in the USA, such activities stirred far less emotion. The opposite was true for alcohol. It was still a contentious investment for some in the

USA, the land of prohibition, but in Europe, where a glass of wine with lunch was de rigueur, there was no problem at all.

UNICEF felt these differences strongly. It was a global organization – something that had attracted me to it in the first place – and was fearful of falling foul to local sensitivities. We welcomed their involvement in choosing criteria. For them, one issue ranked above all others: classifying those companies involved in producing baby milk, which is officially termed 'breast milk substitute' (BMS). It became a whole theme of its own, of which more later.

The launch of a 'good' index of companies required a big leap of faith for UNICEF. To begin with there was a lot of resistance at its New York headquarters – even though it was one of their ambassadors who had been so keen in the first place. The charity's leaders could see ample reputational risk, and they were worried about not being seen as endorsing or punishing corporations either way. Don't forget they were taking money from some of these companies, and they ran the risk that suddenly FTSE, seemingly with their blessing, was going to say they weren't a suitable investment.

In New York, I was invited in to see Carol Bellamy, UNICEF's executive director. She was clued up on the investment world, having served a few years earlier as a managing director at Bear Stearns, the Wall Street bank, as well as Morgan Stanley. But she was nervous, and I could see our conversation ending with her politely declining to go forward. But we had put a lot of effort in, and I had the bit between my teeth. I was told later it was the strength of my conviction that got this project over the line with her. The projected financial contribution from our new index helped. By the time she left UNICEF in 2005, Bellamy had transformed the organization's finances. But I still had to reassure her that we could tread a fine line with this project.

Clara Furse, who arrived as the exchange's chief executive in February 2001, just as we were preparing to announce the new index, wasn't keen either. I should point out that the LSE was nervous because its responsibility was for representing listed companies. This was an extension of its mild concern over how we classified some of those firms anyway. Anything that ranked good and not so good was bound to be sensitive.

When we launched our new index on 27 February 2001, I hadn't quite reckoned with the reaction. Some saw it as an opportunity to joke. 'Thoughts of pin-striped investment managers knitting their own muesli conjures up immediate delight, although the prospect of seeing political correctness police on the march is less appealing,' wrote *The Times*. Another newspaper labelled it the 'silly index'. The normally staid Reuters newswire wrote that our name was closely linked to Britain's biggest businesses 'and they are as unlikely a bunch of activists as can be imagined'. Convincing the world that we honestly wanted to do the right thing would be an uphill battle. At least, it began a debate.

FTSE4Good

Most took our debut very seriously and that seriousness began with the name of the index: FTSE4Good. We were inspired by the Change for Good fundraising partnership that UNICEF had run with British Airways since 1994. Passengers were encouraged to donate foreign notes and coins left over from their overseas trips as flights neared their destination. The name was fine as a call for people to dig into their pockets and give. It proved to be more divisive in the context of an index.

If the name had involved language such as 'responsible', 'green' or 'ethical', I think it would have been easier to take by those we were classifying. It spoke to how SRI remained on the fringes of the investment world – and the fringes of company bosses' thinking. But 'good' as distinct from 'bad' was so black and white as to cause offence in some quarters.

We had constructed a family of indices, consisting of both a tradable and a benchmark index for four regions: the UK, Europe, the USA and global. We explained that the series was designed to be used by brokerages and investment managers in their investment strategies through the creation of FTSE4Good Index mutual funds, ETFs and other index-linked investment products. In the UK, Close Fund Management, part of the merchant bank Close Brothers, supported the initiative on day one with the launch of FTSE4Good funds that were available to both retail and institutional investors.

Roger Moore joined me in London at the launch of the criteria, and we were pictured together laughing at one of Moore's many jokes outside the Bank of England on the front page of the *FT*. He had kept himself informed of our progress, sending the occasional email. That was enough: he told me he didn't stray into areas where he was no expert.

We also took the opportunity that FTSE4Good threw up to extend our relationship with UNICEF into the USA. That alliance was announced by the veteran US television anchor Hugh Downs, who used to be the presenter on ABC News's weekly magazine programme, *20/20*. These days he was emeritus chair of UNICEF's US fund. Speaking at a lunch held at the UN in New York that day for UNICEF's corporate sponsors and FTSE clients at the UN, Downs said. 'UNICEF is the gold standard of social responsibility in action and FTSE4Good demonstrates economic efficiency in action.'

There was a big turnout that day in New York. I think there was a curiosity about what we were doing. The USA was particularly poor on these issues at that time, so the sensitivity over how companies were going to qualify came later. There was, however, an established index that did not take too kindly to our launch. The Domini 400 Social Index had begun in 1990, becoming the first SRI index to be calculated on a real-time basis in May 2000. It was set up by Amy Domini, an American investment adviser and co-founder of KLD Research & Analytics, a firm that had been early into the SRI field, screening out alcohol, tobacco and weapons among other contentious areas. I knew how Domini felt. What became a friendly competitor for us in this field, the Dow Jones Sustainability Index, had been launched in autumn 1999. Initially, it collected together the top 10 per cent of the best-scoring companies among the largest 2,500 firms listed on the Dow Jones.

I was content that we weren't just doing good, we were raising funds, too. Our fee structure for FTSE4Good meant that UNICEF would receive any licensing fees we charged passive funds based on the indices as well as 50p every time a computer terminal was used to access the real-time FTSE indices. In total, we expected a $1 million donation to be generated in the first year of operation.

That day we also dropped our bombshell: as it stood, more than half of the 762 companies in the FTSE All-Share index would not make the cut for inclusion in FTSE4Good. The same was true for every other region we measured. What infuriated companies more is that we wouldn't reveal who was included and who wasn't until the indices went live that summer.

I hoped the February announcement would be a call to arms for companies to get their houses in order because I wanted as few exclusions as possible. However, I conceded that some industry sectors, such as tobacco makers, would always struggle to gain approval. We thought it could be helpful to fire a warning shot that would give firms time to improve their chances. We published the criteria, setting out what we hoped to do, with the intention of working with companies on what they were required to do to gain entry. In some cases, it was a lack of information, not necessarily bad behaviour, that kept them out. I was clear this was the first step on a journey and our framework would evolve. We had to make sure we took companies with us by encouraging them to adopt solid SRI principles.

This mission did not go down well. The Confederation of British Industry (CBI), the powerful lobby for big business in the UK, was particularly concerned. It took the view that FTSE-4Good would just be used to embarrass companies that did not want to be coaxed into line. Sir Nigel Rudd, the well-connected industrialist who had graced the boardrooms of the Williams conglomerate, glassmaker Pilkington and car dealer Pendragon and chaired one the CBI's main committees, came to see me to try to change my mind. Scanning the media, I could see a campaign was brewing against us.

A landmark moment

When FTSE published the list of constituents for the FTSE-4Good index on 10 July 2001, the media attention was considerable. Reporters combed through our list and were quick to point out what they thought were anomalies. For example, BP and Shell won inclusion despite questions over their environmental and human rights records, while BG Group, a smaller gas explorer that was part of the same sector, was excluded for its failure to publish a human rights policy. Lack of disclosure was punishing companies, not lack of strategy. In many cases, they just had to tell the world what they were up to.

One of the most public spats developed between warring supermarket chains Sainsbury's and Tesco. Sainsbury's was included in FTSE4Good, but Tesco – along with a third grocer, Safeway – was not because it did not at that time publish an environmental report. Competition was fierce between the two. Only in 1995 had Tesco overtaken its rival to become the largest supermarket group in the UK. Sainsbury's was still struggling, so any opportunity to go one up on its rival was enthusiastically grasped. It took out a full-page advertisement in the *Financial Times* to celebrate meeting the new standard when many of its peers had not.

Tesco was irate. The chief executive, Terry Leahy, called me to complain. In the media, a spokesman for the group pointed out its good works, including the recycling of 155,000 tonnes of card the previous year, an amount roughly equating to 3 million trees. We were used to pushback – such as when we classified a company in one industry sector and it lobbied to be transferred to another – but this took matters to a whole new level.

FTSE4Good was a landmark moment for the company. We weren't just creating something new, we were really sticking our neck out. The dial had shifted a little since February. Still, only 64 companies from the FTSE 100 made the grade on day one. The ratio was poorer among smaller companies. In the FTSE All-Share, just 288 out of 757 companies qualified for FTSE4Good.

Some investors liked what we had created because it was easier for them to select stocks for their SRI portfolios. I thought FTSE4Good would be more valuable to investors if we kept exclusions to a minimum. That meant we did not go as far as some funds groups, such as Henderson Global Investors, which already screened out alcohol, gambling and pornography from its own SRI funds. The National Association of Pension Funds was not so welcoming. 'We are not in favour of drawing a line in the sand, with the good companies above and the bad companies below,' said David Cranston, the organization's director general.

A new club

What I worked out is that we had created a new club. The FTSE 250 index had showcased mid-cap stocks beginning in 1992, and the Techmark index sought to do the same for technology stocks when it was launched in September 1999. But here was something that drew attention to responsible stocks. It had the cachet of the FTSE 100 – not because membership was limited to a fixed number of companies, but because it judged those companies on their status as corporate citizens. Nor was it simple to get in. Our ratings were reassessed twice yearly by EIRIS and companies were warned they could just as easily be relegated as promoted if they slipped up. Because of the experience of Tesco and Sainsbury's, we knew we could leverage the competition between companies in each industry to keep raising standards.

For the first and only time while we were part-owned by a newspaper, I picked up the phone in the hope of generating some coverage that would snuff out the negativity. Richard Lambert, the journalist who had been so irate at the creation of the LSE's 100 index without the *FT*'s involvement, was by this time the editor. Lambert offered no promises, but at least said his journalists would listen to my story. The leader column they produced on the back of our meeting was balanced and fair and gave us the benefit of the doubt for now. With so much sniping, it was just what FTSE4Good needed.

The article pointed out that SRI funds appeared to perform well, suggesting there was a link between responsible management and higher profits. However, many of these funds happened to be overweight in technology stocks, which caused less environmental damage anyway. It asked what investing in responsible companies would do to change the behaviour of the irresponsible ones, whose exclusion from SRI indices would be unlikely to drive up the cost of capital for them.

The *FT* summed up:

> Rather than passing absolute moral judgements, FTSE is trying to get around this problem by creating a number of objective benchmarks with which to compare companies with their competitors. That brings its own problems. If a company does not meet the required reporting criteria it is automatically excluded. And if all companies comply, the exercise becomes redundant. Pressure groups will, in any case, apply their own standards. Ethical investors are perfectly entitled to try to

improve corporate behaviour. That may be – as some argue – a case of
sentimentality getting the better of rationality. But if there is a demand,
the market will follow.

By now, I was convinced the demand was there. But not everyone was so welcoming. On the same page in the *FT* that day
was a letter from Michael Hopkins, chair of the International
Centre for Corporate Responsibility and Business Performance at Middlesex University Business School. He wrote that
our indices were 'screening devices and not indicators of corporate social responsibility (CSR). Simply eliminating companies whose products you do not agree with is half-baked social
responsibility.' Our system would become more sophisticated
over time.

The milk of human kindness

I never imagined that embarking on the FTSE4Good project
would have involved me and many of the FTSE team spending
so much time on the topic of breast milk substitute (BMS).
The issue can be traced back to 1977 when the Nestlé boycott
was launched in the USA by INFACT (Infant Formula Action
Coalition) to protest against unethical marketing. The company
was accused of inhibiting the development of millions of babies
in the developing world by aggressively targeting new moth-
ers with formula milk when breast milk was a healthier and
cheaper option.

It had been an issue for UNICEF for years, so when we set
out we effectively screened out all infant formula makers from
the index because they all failed the World Health Organization
(WHO) code that insisted on no marketing to sell products for
the under-twos. This exclusion continued for the first five years.
By then we knew we were having an impact in other areas
where we could introduce incremental changes and encourage

those firms that made the index to improve their standards to remain members. In the area of nuclear power generation, for example, where firms had been totally screened out, we were able to have sensible conversations on standards with Friends of the Earth and Greenpeace about including companies that published better data on radiation levels.

In BMS, the atmosphere was deeply entrenched and poisonous. How could we begin some engagement? We set up an advisory committee which could pick a middle way through the issue. It was led by Reg Green, a veteran of the trade union movement who was used to difficult negotiations. Reg had been responsible for Health, Safety and Environmental Affairs at the Brussels-based International Federation of Chemical, Energy, Mine and General Workers' Unions (ICEM), which represented over 20 million workers in some 120 countries around the world. He was a seasoned negotiator and knew how to deal with senior corporate executives. The committee tried to codify the WHO guidelines so that companies could relate to them better. It consulted with companies, investors and relevant charities. The biggest issue was cutting marketing in the USA, which would have represented a big commercial hit especially for the company that went first. Rather than a worldwide ban, David Bull at UNICEF accepted our idea of including just those countries with the highest malnutrition and infant death rates.

This got the companies talking. Nestlé, the world's largest food company whose brands included Kit Kat chocolate bars, Cheerios breakfast cereal, Perrier mineral water and Stouffer's frozen food, was the most engaged. Little headway had been made in this area under chairman Helmut Maucher, a diffident German. But when Peter Brabeck-Letmathe was chosen to succeed him in 2005, becoming solely chairman in 2008, the culture changed. Still, Nestlé spent a long time calculating the cost and weighing it against the value of being included in FTSE-4Good. One sticking point was that the marketing ban would extend to Russia, which was another big market for them. Over lunch with Brabeck-Letmathe in autumn 2010 at Nestlé's headquarters in Vevey, Switzerland, I persuaded him to comply.

On 11 March 2011, we announced that Nestlé was the first company to have met the selection criteria, after it had made some important changes to how it operated. It had been a long process to get this far. The criteria covered lobbying, reporting and management systems and concentrated on 149 countries with the highest rates of child malnutrition and child mortality with an aim to apply eventually a single global approach. We made clear that the independent verification we required was not a one-off assessment but an ongoing annual requirement. Manufacturers needed to demonstrate on the ground that practices followed the policies, such as by opening up their global headquarters, at least two country operations and site visits to clinics, hospitals and health centres where their product was used. Whistle-blowing procedures, the training of sales and marketing staff and responding to allegations would also be looked at. Nestlé committed to not promoting infant formula, follow-on formula for babies less than 12 months' old and complementary foods for babies under six months in all of the 149 countries.

This was a significant step, but just the beginning. BMS was a small category with six or so companies in it. But without more than one company in the index, we could not set about raising standards. FTSE was caught in the middle. Companies grumbled our measures were anti-competitive, handing market share to firms with lower standards. And charities thought we had undermined the WHO code and were driving down acceptable levels of behaviour.

We thought we had some leverage over Pfizer. The drugs giant was a member of FTSE4Good, but when it bought Wyeth, the infant formula maker, we informed it that it had to comply with our BMS standard as well. It didn't, and so Pfizer was excluded. However, Nestlé's rival Danone entered the FTSE4Good index in June 2016. The pair of them withdrew from the Infant Formula Manufacturers Association, the lobby group, because its standards were not high enough. It collapsed soon after. Another positive development came when Reckitt Benckiser, the maker of Durex condoms and Vanish cleaning fluid, acquired Mead Johnson, the US baby milk firm that performed poorly according to our assessments. Reckitt was far more willing to comply than Pfizer and upped standards significantly.

Then came the question of who was going to pay for this independent verification. FTSE did at first. I was conscious this was a big commitment to monitor a handful of companies when we had thousands of which to keep track. For a time, David Harris, FTSE's director of environmental, social and governance practices (ESG), was spending 20 per cent of his time on this area. But we had come this far. I was grateful that the Global Alliance for Improved Nutrition, a Swiss foundation funded by numerous development agencies, stepped in to share the cost of verification. Then along came the Bill and Melinda Gates Foundation with $2 million of funding that has lasted for several years. FTSE is exploring how to expand the criteria to more countries, and in the meantime WHO has tightened its own standard to exclude any firm from BMS marketing to children under the age of three.

Raising the bar

A decade on from the FTSE4Good launch, times had changed. In April 2011, we celebrated our 10th anniversary with a party at East Wintergarden in Canary Wharf. Vince Cable, then Business Secretary, for whom profit with purpose had become a particularly popular cause, had been meant to speak. His prepared comments said that:

> It is crucial for investors to encourage and support long-term thinking in the companies in which they invest. To facilitate this there is a great need for a focus on broader corporate performance, rather than a narrow focus on near term financials. Environmental, social and governance considerations are an important part of this.

In the event, Cable was stuck on a train travelling back to London, and his press team called in his apologies at the last minute. He sent along a Liberal Democrat colleague, Ed Davey, who rushed to be there in his place. At the time, Davey was Under Secretary of State for Employment Relations and Postal Affairs, so it was not a natural fit with the theme of the evening. However, he was promoted to become Energy Secretary in early 2012.

In the intervening years, SRI has been overtaken by ESG. It takes a broader view of the work we began in 1999, but it also has financial performance at its heart. Whereas behaving better was seen by some as in conflict with delivering enhanced shareholder returns, now the conversation is designed as a win–win: can those companies that do good increase value, too?

There was evidence that our approach of engagement had worked. A study led by Craig Mackenzie, now a senior lecturer in sustainable enterprise at the University of Edinburgh Business School, assessed our efforts to upgrade the criteria for environmental management in 2002, the first time since FTSE's creation we had attempted to tighten inclusion. At that point, around 40 per cent of eligible companies from the largest 2,000 in the world met our standards. On strengthening those criteria, some 388 – around half of those members – were likely to be expelled if they did not improve. Rather than ousting them immediately,

I wrote letters to them all, warning they had until 2005 to make appropriate changes. The Edinburgh study found that 49 per cent of the 388 firms complied. Of another group made up of 658 firms that were not part of the index, 23 per cent stepped up.

These statistics bore out what we had found over the years. There is often an internal champion in a company trying to improve standards. It is amazing how a letter from FTSE threatening exclusion puts these topics on the boardroom agenda. Over the years, we have probably deleted 500 companies for not keeping pace as we raised the bar. We had to practise what we preached. When the LSE bought the *FT* out of their joint venture in 2011, Harris noted that our new owner was ranked in the lower half of the FTSE 100 for ESG. When I raised this issue, Xavier Rolet and the executive committee agreed with me that we needed to get into the top quartile.

I wanted us to go further. We used the 10th anniversary as a platform to launch another tool, FTSE4Good ESG Ratings. This data service offered a full, transparent and objective system to measure the ESG practices of over 2,300 public companies worldwide. Once again, we looked for expert help. Representatives from the investment community, academia, the business community, trade unions and charities oversaw what we were doing.

ESG had become increasing important to understand how companies were able to achieve long-term, sustainable investment returns. I knew that in the following decade they would matter even more. The UN's Principles for Responsible Investment (PRI) had been launched in 2006 to provide a voluntary framework by which all investors could incorporate ESG issues into their decision making and ownership practices. So far, 227 asset owners and 496 asset managers around the world had signed up.

Our ratings provided a scoreboard of companies based on their overall ESG rating set against a broad pillar as well as six specific ESG criteria, including environmental management and climate change. High scorers on day one included British insurer Aviva, French media group Vivendi and Bank Hapoalim of Israel.

The climate crisis and sustainable investment

Sustainable investing has continued to climb the agenda. On 2 July 2019, John Glen, the UK's City minister, announced a major initiative at the Green Finance Summit held at the Guildhall in London. One month after Theresa May, the prime minister, pledged to end the UK's contribution to global warming entirely by 2050, Glen set another target for corporate Britain. By 2022, he called on all publicly listed companies and large asset owners to disclose details of how they are mitigating climate risk. It is part of an effort for businesses to contribute more to hitting the binding target of creating a net-zero carbon economy by 2050. While Brexit paralysed much of the government machine, it is one of the few areas where the UK government made progress.

In a speech delivered in Tokyo on 8 October 2019 at the annual summit of the Task Force on Climate-related Financial Disclosures (TCFD), Mark Carney, the Governor of the Bank of England, said: 'Firms that align their business models to the transition to a net-zero world will be rewarded handsomely. Those that fail to adapt will cease to exist. The longer that meaningful adjustment is delayed, the greater the disruption will be.' He is, of course, right.

In his annual letter to chief executives at the start of 2020, BlackRock's chairman and chief executive, Larry Fink, declared he thought that 'we are on the edge of a fundamental reshaping of finance' and that climate change was almost invariably the top issue that clients around the world were raising with his firm. Fink drew lines between climate risk and investment risk, such as the difficulty in offering 30-year mortgages without a viable market for flood or fire insurance in impacted areas, or modelling economic growth in emerging markets where extreme heat hits productivity. He predicted that, 'because capital markets pull future risk forward, we will see changes in capital allocation more quickly than we see changes to the climate itself'. Fink signed off: 'Companies must be deliberate and committed to embracing purpose and serving all stakeholders – your shareholders, customers, employees, and the communities where you operate. In doing so, your company will enjoy greater long-term prosperity, as will investors, workers, and society as a whole.'

As of the end of 2019, 2,370 investment institutions have become signatories to the UN's Principles for Responsible Investment, with just under $90 trillion of assets under management, a figure that has almost tripled since 2011. Since 2014, 118 investors with over $10 trillion have signed the Montreal Pledge, committing to disclose the carbon footprint of their investment portfolios every year. It took years to shift asset allocations, but now the trickle is becoming a torrent.

Efforts by governments, central bankers and investors have forced companies to act. In August 2019, the US Business Roundtable, a group of chief executives from major American corporations, committed to stakeholder value in place of shareholder value – a momentous shift if words are backed up by deeds. 'The American dream is alive, but fraying,' said Jamie Dimon, the chairman and chief executive of Wall Street giant JPMorgan Chase and also the chairman of Business Roundtable as he acknowledged that corporations had to up their game.

In February 2020, the new chief executive of BP, Bernard Looney, set a target to reduce the oil firm's carbon footprint to net zero by 2050. It is a target that means it will have to take more than 400 million tonnes of carbon emissions a year out of its business. The Irishman, who has spent his entire career at BP, insists he can plant the seeds of change while maintaining BP's $8-billion-a-year dividend. He has to try. Some doubt that fossil fuel firms have a future, and some investors have been ridding them from their portfolios, including US university endowments which have faced protests on campus.

Despite clamour to do more, many companies around the world do not disclose externally their performance and practices in most ESG areas. Where it is reported, it can be disjointed, with different statistics emerging from different locations in formats that do not map onto each other. Compiling and comparing this information is where index providers come in.

Into the mainstream

FTSE4Good's 15th anniversary in 2016 was a momentous day, with the stock market opened by Sir Mark Moody-Stuart, who had become chairman of FTSE's ESG advisory committee. As a former chairman of Shell and Anglo American, his appointment said a lot about how these issues had moved to become mainstream business concerns.

To point out that inconsistencies still existed, FTSE published a country-by-country league table. Based on 34 quantitative indicators, it ranked 46 countries according to the disclosure levels of the 2,923 companies in the FTSE All-World Index. Greece came top – based on only five companies that achieved an average 69 per cent ESG disclosure – followed by Finland and Portugal. At just 5 per cent disclosure averaged from eight companies, Egypt came bottom of the table, with the United Arab Emirates and China little better. Another way to emphasize the range that exists is to take one popular metric, the reporting of greenhouse gas emissions. Of the same 2,923 large- and mid-cap stocks, 60 per cent were found to disclose their carbon emissions. But while 80 per cent of European companies published the relevant data, only 51 per cent did so in the Asia–Pacific region.

As policymakers have put more emphasis on ESG, index providers have been racing to track and evaluate this investment strand more closely than ever. On 21 November 2019, S&P Global announced it was acquiring the ESG ratings business of RobecoSAM, an affiliate of the Dutch investment management firm Robeco. It included the widely followed SAM Corporate Sustainability Assessment (CSA) – an annual evaluation of companies' sustainability practices – and cemented a relationship that went back 20 years to the launch of the Dow Jones Sustainability Index.

Today, FTSE4Good includes more than 15 benchmarks based on ESG ratings for over 4,000 securities in 47 developed and emerging markets. It still measures metrics in the same areas, only with a far greater degree of sophistication. Across a grid of pillars and themes, more than 300 individual indicators are used to assess each company with an average of 125 applied each time. Areas of interest now extend to water security, labour standards, anti-corruption and tax transparency. Membership is still reviewed twice yearly, with a lower threshold applied to companies in emerging markets. Coal firms are now excluded, but conglomerates that produce coal as part of their output are not.

FTSE4Good continues to make headlines. In December 2019, it was criticized for adding Russian state oil producer Rosneft to its list among other polluting energy firms. The inclusion process has always trodden a fine line. My view is that dropping the entire oil and gas sector makes it harder to apply shareholder pressure. Better to have these firms inside the tent where it is easier to agitate for change. FTSE4Good helps to guide investors but also sparks the conversation for improving behaviour. We don't want to simply reward the trailblazers. My aim has been to effect real change among that middle band of companies.

Other organizations are doing their bit, too. Tortoise, the news website launched by the former BBC News chief James Harding, created the Responsibility 100 Index, a ranking of the FTSE 100 companies as measured by their commitment to social, environmental and ethical objectives such as carbon reduction, gender equality and good business practice. It began publishing its findings every quarter from January 2020. Its initial findings were that 61 of the FTSE 100 companies reported lower emissions than the prior year, while 39 reported increases. One in ten of subsidiaries to FTSE 100 companies was registered in a tax haven, it found.

Religious investors continue to put their money where their mouth are, just as the Quakers and Methodists did of old. In January 2020, the Church of England launched a passive index aligned with the Paris climate change goals. It put £600 million into the FTSE TPI Climate Transition Index, having previously used a version of the MSCI World Index for its passive portfolio. Companies with public emissions targets, such as Shell and Repsol, were given a higher weighting in the index, while those without, such as ExxonMobil and Chevron, were excluded.

The TPI (Transition Pathway Initiative) was launched at the LSE on 11 January 2017. It marked a coming together of 18 asset owners and managers with over £2 trillion under management. It was designed to track how individual companies were preparing for the transition to a low-carbon economy. The Church of England and Environment Agency pension fund led the initiative, in partnership with the Grantham Research Institute at the London School of Economics. FTSE contributed its climate data on the 350 companies that together easily account for two-thirds of all global, corporate emissions. From here has come Climate Action 100+, a grouping that is actively pressing companies to cut their emissions. It could be the most effective way of achieving global climate targets. Companies can see that as they shift on this, the money follows.

There is always more work to do. FTSE4Good has encouraged companies to perform better and make it easier for investors to hold them to account. It also helped take sustainable investing mainstream. FTSE4Good and other forms of sustainable investing today attract over $30 trillion of money. The profit and dividends that once drove stock market performance are still necessary but not sufficient. A permanent change has taken place.

And the work goes on ...

It is funny to think so many years later that FTSE's partnership is touted as one of the best that UNICEF ever struck. FTSE-4Good alone has raised over £6 million for them, and our association with UNICEF has raised many more millions. And all from a chance remark over dinner in Zurich.

Without FTSE4Good, investors would not have been able to start making those informed choices. I am proud that we played our part. Sir Roger Moore, who was knighted in 2003 and sadly died in 2017, was proud, too.

9
Rivalry and responsibility

Bob Diamond marked the 16th anniversary of his arrival at Barclays in the public glare. As chief executive of the one of the UK's leading banks, and before that the risk-taking leader of its investment banking arm, the American has never been able to shun the spotlight. The ambitious Boston-born executive, who spent his formative years on Wall Street at Morgan Stanley, always stuck out among the straitlaced British banking bosses. None of his peers were bold enough to snap up the US assets of Lehman Brothers, one of the highest-profile casualties of the financial crisis. It was a pivotal deal in growing Barclays Capital in the USA.

Diamond's renown also contributed to his downfall. Dubbed 'the unacceptable face' of banking in 2010 by the then Business Secretary Lord Mandelson, he was a tall poppy waiting to be beheaded when the banking industry blundered into its next scandal. It is why on 4 July 2012 – when most Americans were gathered with family and friends to mark Independence Day – Diamond was being quizzed for three hours by the UK Parliament's treasury select committee over Libor rigging, the burning issue that had forced his resignation from Barclays one day earlier.

The Libor scandal

The Libor scandal was one of the unedifying aftershocks of the financial crisis. It reminded the public that while banks' balance sheets had been cleaned up with bailouts and write-offs, their culture had not. The London Inter-bank Offered Rate (Libor) was a benchmark that tracked the rate at which banks lent money to each other for the short term in a particular currency. It was calculated once a day by the financial data firm Thomson Reuters based on interest rates provided by members of the British Bankers Association (BBA). It was a crucial metric in the determination of trillions of pounds of financial transactions. And, along with its European equivalent, Euribor, it was systematically manipulated for years by dozens of bankers at numerous institutions eager to boost profits or create the false impression of financial health during the crisis.

Andrew Tyrie, the select committee's forensic chairman, was spot on when he remarked that day to Diamond that Barclays had suffered from 'first mover disadvantage'. The lender was one of the first banks to come clean over its Libor activities. In late June that year, it agreed to pay fines of $200 million to the US Commodity Futures Trading Commission (CFTC), $160 million to the US Department of Justice and £60 million to the Financial Services Authority (FSA). But the payments were just the start of a public furore. Libor might have been an obscure but vital part of the financial system but it had a role in pricing UK residential mortgages and commercial loans to businesses. Within a few days, the Barclays chairman, Marcus Agius, had resigned. Diamond and Agius both denied knowledge of manipulation, but Diamond's resignation followed soon after. Only 18 months before, appearing in front of the same committee, he affirmed hopefully that the time for banker remorse was over.

In retrospect, the Barclays duo unfairly carried the can for what was widespread industry malpractice. Over the following three years, almost every major bank paid Libor fines in a scam that revealed traders from New York to Tokyo had invented prices for a rate, even though trading volumes had evaporated in the financial crisis. A very similar collusion over foreign exchange rates was exposed, too. As well as financial penalties, the aftermath led to tougher regulation for all the organizations involved in the calculation and use of benchmarks to do business – and that included independent commercial index providers such as FTSE.

Ramifications of a scandal

Keen for the City of London to restore its reputation, the UK Chancellor of the Exchequer, George Osborne, called for a probe to consider whether the revelations around Libor required a wider policy response. That task was handed to Martin Wheatley, my former LSE colleague and one-time chairman of FTSE International. Since departing the exchange in 2004, Wheatley had made a name for himself in Hong Kong as a tough chief executive of the Securities and Futures Commission. He had returned to London to lead the newly formed Financial Conduct Authority (FCA) – a consumer-focused watchdog created in response to the financial crisis – which came into force at the end of 2012.

Published in September that year, the Wheatley Review set out a new regulatory framework plus the new institutions required to administer and oversee Libor in order to regain trust in the system. The same month, the BBA, which acted as a lobby organization for the same banks that submitted data and which it nominally oversaw, gave up oversight of the benchmark. Free from that conflict of interest, a tender process to produce Libor was won in July 2013 by NYSE Euronext, which was acquired by IntercontinentalExchange that November. Still the benchmark for $350 trillion of financial transactions, Libor is due to be decommissioned by the end of 2021 when it is being replaced by the reformed lending rate Sonia (the Sterling Overnight Index Average).

The ramifications of Wheatley went wider. From Libor, he extrapolated to benchmarks operating elsewhere in the City in markets for equities, commodities, credit and money, where conflicts of interest and weak governance had in some cases the potential to be a problem. The review recommended that 'the UK authorities should work closely with the European and international community and contribute fully to the debate on the long-term future of LIBOR and other global benchmarks, establishing and promoting clear principles for effective global benchmarks'. It suggested that 'an international organisation should act as a co-ordinator and information-sharing platform for work undertaken globally in relation to benchmarks'.

That body proved to be the Madrid-based International Organization of Securities Commissions (IOSCO), a broad grouping of the world's securities regulators and a global standards setter. Wheatley chaired a taskforce for them along with Gary Gensler, the chairman of the CFTC. Up until that point, there had been little oversight of stock indexation. There were far racier City activities to worry about and fine rather than including FTSE and its like which had not got into any difficulty.

At a time when the EU wanted to regulate everything, Wheatley and Gensler did a pretty good job of finding a middle ground. In July 2013, they published a set of principles for financial benchmarks designed to protect the integrity of how benchmarks are determined, address conflicts of interest, promote quality, set out some basic information about methodologies, and introduce audit reviews and complaints procedures. Benchmark administrators were required to comply within a year and state publicly that they did so.

'Given the known problems with LIBOR, EURIBOR and other significant market benchmarks, I am pleased that the IOSCO Principles issued today require that benchmarks be anchored by observable transactions and subject to robust governance processes that address potential conflicts of interest,' Gensler said.

Keeping to the right side of the line

The scrutiny did not end there. IOSCO's principles were built on by the European Union's Benchmarks Regulation (BMR) whose provisions came into effect in January 2018. This framework was meant to ensure indices are accurate and have integrity. It regulates not just those that administer indices, who must be registered with the relevant national watchdog, but also contributors and users. The US Securities and Exchange Commission has adopted a much more relaxed stance on indices, but because all the main groups operate in Europe as well as on Wall Street, today there is regulation that covers the entire industry. If the USA has concerns over the index providers, it stems from two issues. The first concerns the concentration of funds tracking the indices of the three largest index providers – FTSE, MSCI, S&P – giving them the influence to be able to establish industry standards which drive investment behaviour. The second is that it worries the line between index provider and fund manager is becoming blurred, with the sneaking suspicion that we have morphed into entities that give investment advice. There is no intention on the part of index providers to give investment advice, but there needs to be clearer guidance as to where to draw the line so that we can ensure we stay on the right side of that line.

I can quibble with how we got here – Libor was a very distant relative of our work – but regulation was necessary for an industry that had grown up fast. For some operators, I know that internal controls were not of the standard required for their size. Clients didn't mind. They were always pushing us to launch new products as soon as possible. When we explained how long it would take to do with due care, they still said they would take the risk. Now we have more process and documentation, more independent checks and more eyeballs on our work, both internal and external. FTSE thinks much more carefully as it takes on any new benchmark for a client to ensure that we have full oversight of calculation and dissemination. We will often decline work.

The consequence of regulation was that we had to be crystal clear about taking responsibility for our actions. We were getting there anyway. The consensus, committee-led decision-making of old was initially a function of being a small business with limited in-house expertise. At first, FTSE didn't know how a portfolio manager would deal with certain events. Today, we welcome feedback from clients but we don't need it to function. We have our own strategic insights.

Regulating the indices

Some of our critics argue that FTSE Russell, MSCI and S&P Dow Jones have a 'private authority' which they use to influence how billions of dollars of investments are managed worldwide. Much is being spent on academics and lawyers to explore just how much influence we wield. These index providers draw their authority from different sources. S&P Dow Jones gets it from the huge derivatives market that is built around the S&P 500, which gives it a clear advantage in the US ETF and mutual funds markets. MSCI and FTSE Russell draw their authority from the billions of dollars of assets from pension funds, sovereign wealth funds and other institutional asset owners that use their global equity benchmarks as an essential component of their decision making processes. These authorities are not impenetrable, but they do provide significant barriers for others to overcome. Most importantly, if they are complacent this clout will be lost.

Moving forward, instead of enforcing the same level of regulation for everyone I have urged regulators to identify the benefits of indexation for investors to ensure these are maintained or enhanced and to think about where the risks really lie. If the key benefits to investors are lower fees, greater transparency and reduced investment risk through diversification, how do we ensure that these benefits are uppermost of mind when advising clients. Where risks are concerned, being clear about conflicts of interests and holding senior executives to account for managing these properly is essential. Whether prices are anchored in transactions or not misses the point. Many types of assets cannot be properly valued on transactions as they are traded too infrequently. Regulation that addresses conflicts of interest openly and helps foster the right culture and behaviours is good for the market and to be welcomed.

Libor remains the prime example of what happens when culture fails and conflicts of interest are not addressed. Banks and their traders were free to set prices, from which a benchmark was created that informed the price of their products and therefore the value of their bonuses. To make matters worse, the whole governance process was overseen by the banks. It is no wonder the prices were found not to be accurate.

Ongoing changes

The index industry continues to consolidate and grow. On 30 May 2017, I made another significant acquisition. The LSE agreed to acquire The Yield Book and Citi Fixed Income Indices from the investment bank Citi for a total cash payment of $685 million. These two assets were both leading providers of fixed income indices and analytics globally for hundreds of institutions including central banks, insurers and broker-dealers. The deal also included the World Government Bond Index

(WGBI), a broad benchmark which measures sovereign debt from over 20 countries in a variety of currencies.

It was timely. My industry had grown up in equities, but as banks withdraw from non-core activities and institutional investors look to increase their exposure to other assets, in both public and private markets, here was an expansion opportunity into a parallel activity. It also showed how the value of index businesses had moved. Here was essentially a bolt-on deal with a price tag greater than what the LSE had paid to buy half of FTSE from the *FT* less than six years earlier.

MSCI, S&P Dow Jones and FTSE are all strong in the equity index business. It is where our roots are. Previously, the banks had dominated the bond markets but as an asset class its indexation was still much more opaque. Like Libor, the banks had a conflict of interest to manage. They determined which bonds were to be included in their indices, they priced the constituent bonds, and they calculated and controlled the distribution of the indices. In addition, they usually offered the indices free to institutional investors so long as those investors traded through that bank. The regulators challenged the banks and most banks decided to exit the business.

After equities, bonds were the next biggest asset class and the major ETF providers wanted to extend their offering to include bonds as well as equities. The bond markets slowly began to change. Bond ETFs began to grow in popularity, and trading platforms such as Tradeweb and MTS started to gain traction as volumes grew.

Bond indices

As the index providers continue to expand, we have tried to apply our expertise to all the asset classes. The Libor scandal highlighted the benefits of putting index calculation into trusted third-party hands. Citi announced it was going to sell and told the major index providers there would be an auction. I was determined not to lose out this time.

Eighteen months earlier, the financial data firm Bloomberg had snapped up Barclays' index unit including the widely used Barclays US Aggregate Bond Index. It remains the most popular bond index in the world, tracking around 17,000 bonds, including corporate, municipal and US treasury bonds. Until 2008, it was known as the Lehman Agg and was one of the assets that Bob Diamond cleverly acquired when Barclays purchased Lehman's US unit.

Any plans Barclays had for wringing the best price out of the index providers ran into trouble when it emerged that some of the bond pricing data essential to its indices actually belonged to Bloomberg. After that, there was only one buyer. Bloomberg is now a strong fourth place in the industry, with an expanding family of indices.

My consolation prize was that many of the management team of Barclays' indices did not want to join Bloomberg. I hired them, led by the chief executive, Waqas Samad, with a view to either expanding our bond indices business dramatically or acquiring another one of the existing bond index providers. Samad was knowledgeable and understood the bond and credit markets. Before Barclays he had already spent time as head of Deutsche Bank's index research team in Europe and Asia and also in various technology roles at Credit Suisse. When The Yield Book and Citi Fixed Income Indices became available, one of the challenges for Citi was disentangling the unit from the rest of the bank. MSCI, S&P Dow Jones and FTSE were all competing for the business. The one advantage I had was that Waqas and his team had untangled the Barclays bond indices from their research operations so we offered them our help. It was complicated and took time, but during this time we built relationships across Citi that would help us negotiate buying the business.

Future competition

Bloomberg is not the only index provider to watch. Many firms have ambitions to enter the index market or grow existing index businesses. Set up by former stock analyst Joe Mansueto in 1984, financial data firm Morningstar is renowned for its investment research for asset managers. Mansueto has done very well out of it. He still owns more than half of the company, business magazines *Inc.* and *Fast Company*, and the Chicago Fire soccer club. Morningstar also has its own investment management arm with $233 billion under advisement and management at the end of 2019. Over the last decade, it has built up an index division, covering equities, fixed income and commodities. In the last quarter of 2019, the company reported that assets linked to its own indices grew by 45 per cent.

Mansueto is eager to grab business from FTSE, MSCI and S&P Dow Jones. It will not be easy. In December 2019, Morningstar hired Ron Bundy as the managing director of its indices business. Bundy used to work for me. He is affable and a strong relationship builder, and is well liked by clients and staff. When FTSE acquired Russell, he was chief executive of the index side of the business and most recently ran our North America benchmarks and strategic accounts. Morningstar's ambition drives on the three leading index providers to hunt for new asset classes and new methods of calculation. They also face competition from a range of start-ups and will need to keep innovating if they wish to maintain their market share.

In January 2020, MSCI struck out in a new direction, taking a stake in the Burgiss Group at a cost of $190 million. Burgiss is one of the market leaders in indexing and analysing privately held assets. It sounds counterintuitive, but growth in this area is expected to boom as investors hunt harder for better returns that are not pegged to market conventions. They will sink more funds into private assets as long as they have the confidence they can understand them. Burgiss was founded in 1987 by James Kocis, whose involvement in private equity began in the late 1980s when he was a consultant at PaineWebber. He built one of the first database systems to help investors manage their private equity assets. Now the firm collates information covering close to 10,000 private asset funds representing nearly $7 trillion of committed capital.

Two days later following that deal, the Singapore Exchange (SGX) acquired a 93 per cent stake in smart beta index provider Scientific Beta, paying €186 million in cash. The Singapore-based venture was set up by Noël Amenc and his very well-respected team of finance professors from France's EDHEC Risk and Asset Management Research Centre at the EDHEC Business School in 2013 to provide asset owners and asset managers with factor indices and strategies. As at 30 September 2019, some $55 billion of assets from more than 60 asset owners and asset managers replicated Scientific Beta indices, up more than 10 times the amount four years ago. The investment complements SGX's own thematic and custom index capabilities.

Newcomers

This flurry of deals is a reminder that the index industry is not static. Frankfurt-based Solactive has marked itself out as an innovator and prospered without running a flagship index. It was set up in 2007 by Steffen Scheuble just before the financial crisis hit. He worked in Deutsche Bank's derivatives department for several years and then created what became Solactive while at a Swiss consulting firm. Today, it employs 250 people and has carved out a market for itself creating indices for ETFs as well as real-time calculations such as indicative optimized portfolio values (IOPVs).

The list goes on. There is Moorgate Benchmarks, IndexOne and ALLINDEX, a Swiss start-up which is a white-label platform that plugs into its clients' own data sources. This vibrant market goes some way to explaining why the combined market shares of FTSE, MSCI and S&P are falling. Global index revenues grew 8 per cent to $3.7 billion in 2019, according to Burton-Taylor International Consulting, a division of TP ICAP, with FTSE in third place accounting for 20.5 per cent of the pie, having occupied top slot in 2018. More than half of all income now comes from asset-based fees, driven by the ETF boom. Factor and ESG indices are growing fast. But, behind the headline rise, it is notable that the leading trio jointly account for 70 per cent of the market, down from 78 per cent in 2017.

I still think some of the greatest disruption will come from the longest-standing market participants and the wisest heads. In April 2019, Deutsche Börse announced a clever deal. The exchange group, for so long a will-they-won't-they partner for the LSE, struck a partnership with private equity group General Atlantic to transform its index business. Deutsche Börse would create a new company into which it would inject its STOXX and DAX assets, plus the $850 million acquisition of Axioma, a provider of investment portfolio and risk management software to asset managers and hedge funds that it had dealt with for many years. The transaction was underwritten by General Atlantic, which took a minority stake in the venture that was initially valued at €2.6 billion. Axioma already has over $10 trillion in assets under management. There is also room for a comeback from big brands such as the *FT*. John Ridding, its chief executive, has been quietly building FT.com into a powerful digital platform that has a loyal following among investment professionals worldwide. The Japanese media group Nikkei purchased the *FT* from Pearson for $1.3 billion in 2015 and is the provider of Japan's globally followed Nikkei 225. Similarly, Chinese index company CSI, the China Securities Index company jointly owned by the Shanghai and Shenzhen Exchanges, will want to expand internationally.

Self-indexation

Fees have been falling for so long in the investment industry, it was only a matter of time before they disappeared altogether. That expected move eventually came on 1 August 2018 from an unexpected source: Fidelity Investments, the family-controlled funds giant that was founded in 1946.

Fidelity is famed as an active fund manager with star stock pickers down over the years including Peter Lynch in the USA and Anthony Bolton in the UK. However, it has also built up a large passive business. In an announcement headlined 'Fidelity Rewrites the Rules of Investing to Deliver Unparalleled Value and Simplicity to Investors', it said it would offer two index funds with a zero expense ratio – essentially, no fees – to US investors.

'We need to find other ways to get people to give us a try,' said Fidelity's chief executive, Abigail Johnson, in an interview with Bloomberg in November 2018. 'Having a no-minimum, no-fee offering seemed like a pretty good way to get people to consider us with the minimal amount of friction possible.'

Fidelity was banking on the two diversified trackers to act as loss leaders it could offset against other products it hoped new clients would buy. With over $7 trillion in total client assets at that point, the firm was large enough to experiment. But what was also notable was that Fidelity avoided using the big three index providers as benchmarks to keep costs down. The launch was judged a success: within the first month it attracted $1 billion of inflows and saw shares in its closest rivals drop.

Competitors didn't welcome the move but called it out as a warning to index providers. 'It's a reaction to the fees that the index providers continue to impose on money managers and investors,' Ron O'Hanley, the former boss of State Street Global Advisers who now runs the wider State Street group, told the *FT* in September 2018. 'If you look at where costs have been coming down, it's the management fees. Where they have not is the cost of using indices.'

But is this true? Are the big index providers charging too much? Fund managers are having to compete for business like never before. Many have chosen to reduce management fees to attract investment flows, and the big index providers have accommodated these players. Others are looking for ways to differentiate their products and want to own and control the index they choose to use. The biggest fund managers are combining these approaches. For a long time, the big funds houses have spread their business around and looked for alternative ways of creating investment products. As I noted in an earlier chapter, Vanguard began using indices from the Center for Research in Security Prices (CRSP) at the University of Chicago's Booth School of Business for 16 US-focused funds as far back as 2012.

The rebellion over index charges – which still remain a typically small portion of a fund's overall expenses – has given rise to a trend for funds trying to replicate our service themselves. There are any number of start-ups, as listed above, which can provide low fixed fee indices or lend a hand with so-called self-indexing. They calculate an index according to a fund's requirements and will for a small additional fee handle implementation and ongoing management. Crucially, this means that the funds control the intellectual property, retain exclusive use and can sell the product under their own brand. The Deutsche Börse venture has pursued this option. From autumn 2019, it was rebranded as Qontigo and began offering tools for self-indexing.

It is a trend that should keep FTSE and the other major index providers on their toes. An index such as the FTSE 100 is simple enough to compute but managing the underlying data is more complex than many think and getting wide market adoption requires an open inclusive approach. FTSE also seeks to be as transparent as possible and freely discloses the constituent weights for many of its indices. The prices can be sourced from anywhere.

For broader, more diversified indices, the real value we offer still lies in managing the indices. Every day index managers receive a set of forward-looking files from FTSE, which acts as an effective running commentary on the index: stock splits, buy backs, share issues, deletions, fast entries, the lot. These professionals don't need the latest index value from us. They care about what they need to trade today to match the index tomorrow. Rivals have tried to replicate this service but not got very far. Turning out that data reliably day after day is no mean feat from a universe of more than 60,000 companies with more than 230,000 listings that equates to hundreds of millions of pieces of data processed every year.

What the big investment platforms must carefully navigate if they dive deeper into self-indexation is conflicts of interest. It would be all too easy to cover up a mistake in the management of a portfolio by adjusting their benchmark index to compensate. Or, worse, make the same mistake in both the index calculation and investment fund. Unwinding a mistake is expensive. Investors welcome low fees, but not if they are the price of a compromise in governance standards. Once appropriate Chinese walls have been installed and investments have been made in people and systems, I wonder how much cheaper than using an external index provider it will really be.

I think the future lies in direct indexing, which is still taking shape. This will be a technology that sits on an investor's desktop. They will be able to choose exactly what they want to do with their portfolio using all the tools we have created. Rather than going to one of the large investment platforms, they will be able to design their own benchmark, or have one custom-made. The independent index provider would still do all of the calculations and hold the data. This will appeal to pension funds and other institutional investors, particularly if the index providers can provide the database and tool set to create and customize indices across all asset classes, investment strategies and themes such as ESG. This will suit those with in-house research skills where they can be rewarded for the value they add.

Given the direction of travel, I can only imagine that at some stage our biggest clients will start to compete directly with us. BlackRock must be considering to what degree it calculates and manages its own indices. Vanguard, too. If that happens, it is not impossible to see MSCI and FTSE moving in the opposite direction. The boundaries between fund managers, investment advisors and index providers will blur. Technology and data will allow investment in a broader set of assets and give us all much greater flexibility and choice in how we choose to construct and manage our portfolios and the indices which they seek to replicate. Despite questions over conflicts and how to best apply regulation, firms which once had a discrete role in the world of investment will coalesce all the same.

Departure

22 January 2019 was a day of mixed emotions. It was time for me to depart. After spending the vast majority of my career

involved with FTSE, it was announced that I was stepping down from day-to-day involvement with the index business. Waqas Samad, whom I hired from Barclays three years earlier, was appointed by LSE as group director for the information services division. I was made non-executive chairman of the division on my way to leaving the group after almost 35 years at the end of 2019.

The kind words in the official statement were gratifying. David Schwimmer, the exchange's chief executive since August 2018, said:

> As the founder of FTSE and a founder and inaugural chairman
> of the Index Industry Association, Mark has been a pioneer in the
> development of the global index industry. Mark has successfully built
> a world class global business with m*f*ore than $16 trillion assets under
> benchmark to FTSE Russell Indexes.

Sir Donald Brydon, by now the exchange's chairman, said that I had 'made a huge contribution to the evolution of indices and the development of the asset management industry'. I couldn't resist a smile when I saw the rest of his comment. More than anyone else, as the chairman of FTSE's first steering committee, Sir Donald knew from what modest roots we had grown – and how modest were the hopes of our two shareholders as I attempted to create a new business. He added: 'Having been chairman of FTSE in the 1980s and a party to his initial CEO appointment, I can truly say that he has more than exceeded everyone's expectations at the time.'

Much had changed in the intervening years, but as I prepared for the next chapter of my career, I reflected on how much had stayed the same, going right back to the time of Big Bang. That vast deregulation was born out of defensiveness – and it didn't go exactly to plan. This latest changing of the guard – with Xavier leaving – was sparked by another strategic step backfiring. The LSE, and to a lesser extent FTSE, continues to be a dramatic thread that runs through life in the City of London.

On 23 February 2016, a sharp move in the LSE's share price forced a statement to the market. Almost five years to the day since the announcement of its abortive merger with the owner of the Toronto Stock Exchange, it was having another go at pairing off. With this partner, it had an even longer history. Some 16 years after first discussing a combination, the exchange revealed that once again it planned to merge with Deutsche Börse.

It was not an altogether popular move in the Square Mile, especially as the exchange would be the junior partner, with LSE shareholders holding a 45.6 per cent stake in the enlarged firm and Carsten Kengeter, Deutsche Börse's boss, lined up to take the top job. But critics need not have worried because this deal would be scuppered by an unlikely source. Following the Brexit referendum, and because of stiff demands for sell-offs from the combined group to appease the European Commission, the proposed merger was abandoned the following March.

Because Xavier Rolet had promised to retire on completion of the deal, there was a lingering uncertainty over what came next. Activist investor Sir Chris Hohn campaigned for his reinstatement and the ousting of Brydon instead. In the event, 79 per cent of shares voted went against Hohn's motion, but Brydon had already pledged to depart in 2019 to defuse the row.

Brydon was brought in as a strong character who could rein in Rolet. By this time, the Frenchman had been chief executive for many years and had enjoyed many successes, broadening the exchange out in post-trade, by taking a majority stake in the clearing house LCH. Clearnet, and of course in information services with FTSE and Russell. The downside was that, although he was strategic and a strong leader, in my opinion he was decisive rather than someone who would build a consensus before taking action. What came after Rolet's exit and in the months following the merger collapse was another bout of soul searching for the exchange. You could draw parallel lines with how it cast around for direction in the aftermath of Big Bang.

Rolet was hugely ambitious and had been a big fan of the Deutsche Börse deal. If he had sealed that combination and secured the top job, I know that within a year or two he would have been looking for the next big deal to cement the role of the LSE as a leader within the global securities markets. I would not have been surprised if some sort of tie-up with the Shanghai Exchange was next on his agenda.

I remember pushing back against him on this point at one of our executive away days at Coworth Manor. This five-star grand mansion house surrounded by polo fields and tennis courts sits in the rural countryside south-west of London and close to the Ascot racecourse. To my mind, exchanges were no longer the valuable part of the business we were in. Either clearing or data was where we should be continuing to make our investments. FTSE had been a success in spite of being inside an exchange, not because of it. I could see that others, such as Stoxx, buried in Deutsche Börse, had been inhibited by the exchange environment.

After all these years, scale was still what mattered. There were those sitting around the table more concerned that the LSE was going to fall victim to a takeover, with either ICE or the CME the most likely suitors.

Nevertheless, in the aftermath of Rolet's departure, the board made it clear it wanted a successor with deep exchange experience who would continue on the same path as before. I had thrown my hat in the ring, but the choice was a newcomer, David Schwimmer, who had spent 20 years at Goldman Sachs including serving as chief of staff for the bank's future chief executive Lloyd Blankfein, when he was COO. I felt Schwimmer was different to Rolet. A natural consensus builder, he had advised derivative exchanges in the USA and preferred to keep a low profile. He was young and ambitious and very much a Goldman Sachs role model. Educated at Yale with a law degree from Harvard, he is a native of New York. The board was keen that Schwimmer and I got on, but it was clear to me that this appointment was my cue to leave. We reached an amicable agreement, but the exchange insisted on a long non-compete clause that would keep me out of the market for some considerable time. It was enough time to write this book and think about how the industry would change over the next few years.

Changes and challenges

Schwimmer put his firm imprint on the business in little over a year. In August 2019, the LSE announced it was paying $27 billion for Refinitiv, the rebranded Reuters data business that was owned by private equity group Blackstone and Thomson Reuters. The news and journalistic side of the business continues under Thomson Reuters, as before. Refinitiv is a large provider of financial markets data and off-exchange trading infrastructure to more than 40,000 institutions in approximately 190 countries. A generation on, it is essentially the same business that lent FTSE vital international distribution in the early days.

The deal created huge value immediately, as investors saw from the soaring share price on day one. Clearing the competition hurdles and then modernizing Refinitiv will not, however, be without its challenges and comes with significant risk. But the strategic thinking was right. Exchanges will become critical market infrastructure providers across the different asset classes built on data and technology. Trading floors are a thing of the past and many intermediaries – banks and fund managers – must learn to connect and service their client base differently in this new digital world. Exchanges must learn to work with both the banks, their traditional clients who once controlled them as members, and with the institutional investors, who will be suspicious of them. The biggest challenge however will come with regulators and governments. Infrastructure providers need to operate at scale to be able to pass on the benefits of lower costs and greater connectivity to their users. This will be a tricky challenge as exchanges have, in the past, been national champions. Like the telecoms and technology industries, global success will bring greater political scrutiny and challenge. Rolet had the right vision and almost got there. Schwimmer will need those consensus building skills to complete the job.

Postscript

An index is nothing more than a more systematic approach to investment management. I have dedicated the best part of 35 years to bringing order to markets, encouraging money flows, transparency and falling costs. It is an intoxicating activity and, as the amount of data we collect on the form and function of all manner of asset classes multiplies, so too do the options for investors that rely on our work.

It was ever thus. The FTSE 100, a world-famous index today, was created in 1984 in response to a need for better performance measurement and to stimulate activity in the futures and traded options markets. Who would have thought that the painstaking activity of newspaper backrooms and actuarial logarithm tables would have grown to become the backbone of the global investment industry?

I am proud that FTSE sits at the heart of a network that connects US investors with Chinese assets, chief executives of the largest companies in the land and the most careful pensioners.

We are trusted to deliver accurate, predictable and transparent data to our clients around the clock.

The team I led only succeeded by managing carefully what every investor keeps their eye on: risk. It was a risk to partner with Fredy Bush to enter China for the first time. It was a risk to pioneer FTSE4Good, classifying whole new areas of corporate activity and championing sustainability. It was a risk acquiring Russell, the deal that transformed our fortunes in the USA. It was a risk working with Rob Arnott who challenged the perceived wisdom of what an index was or could be. As I look back, these were all risks worth taking.

Now, to the future. As I came to the end of writing this book, it was clear that coronavirus was going to change all of our lives. Away from the political and medical emergencies, the major indices measured the sharp economic jolts that the planet will be recovering from for a generation.

This pandemic fast-tracks the digitally connected future and the ensuing financial crisis will place even greater emphasis on driving reliable investment returns. The unprecedented financial stimulus packages unleashed by the US Federal Reserve, European Central Bank and others will keep interest rates lower for longer and corporate earnings growth will struggle to recover.

Indexation that powers low-cost investing will continue to prosper. It will spread across markets, asset classes, investment themes and geographies. China will grow in importance as an investor and an investee country. The world will tip further on its axis.

The public markets will continue to shrink unless public policy dramatically changes to increase their attractiveness to both investors and entrepreneurs. In their place, private markets will grow and index providers will follow them, shining a light on assets that for a long time have been the preserve of a privileged few.

Aided by intelligence gathered by index providers, the large passive managers will come under increasing pressure to engage with companies across markets to improve governance stand-ards. Sustainable investment will become a must-have, not a nice-to-have, and countries as well as companies will be held to account by investors.

Computer-driven trading will be further automated and asset allocation models will be refined. Direct indexing will put the tools in the hands of every investor, enabling them to do the same thing. Indexation – impartial, transparent and trustworthy – will be more important than ever.

Glossary

active An investment strategy determined by human intervention, ie fund managers.

actuary A business professional involved in the measurement and management of investment risk.

Actuarial Tuition Service Training service for actuaries run by the Institute and Faculty of Actuaries.

aggregate market value The total value of a company's outstanding shares.

Amex (American Stock Exchange) An early US stock exchange that developed a reputation for trading alternative assets, including the first exchange-traded fund (ETF). Bought by NYSE Euronext in 2008.

Benchmarks Regulation The European Union's framework of index regulation which came in to force in 2018.

Big Bang The sweeping deregulation of London's financial markets, effective October 27 1986.

Black Monday Stock market crash of October 19 1987 when US markets fall more than 20% in a single day.

Bloomberg US news, financial data and indices company established by Michael Bloomberg in 1981.

blue-chip index Nickname for the FTSE 100 or any other flagship index. Blue chip denotes highest value companies as constituents.

broker An intermediary working for an investor who is buying shares listed on a stock exchange.

CAC-40 France's premier share index; the French equivalent of the FTSE 100.

CBOE 100 The Chicago Board Options Exchange 100 was the most popular stock option trading product in the world.

China A-shares Domestic shares in Chinese companies denominated in renminbi and listed and traded on the Shanghai and Shenzhen stock exchanges in mainland China.

collateralized debt obligations A financial product derived from a pool of loans that is sold to institutional investors.

commodities In markets, a tradeable raw material such as gold, wheat or copper.

Daily Official List The definitive and legal record of daily trading activity on the London Stock Exchange.

depositary receipt A type of share issued locally representing an investment in a foreign company.

derivatives A contract that derives value from another underlying asset.

Deutsche Börse German stock exchange based in Frankfurt.

Dow Jones Industrial Average Also known as the Dow 30, the Dow Jones Industrial Average is a closely followed stock index first calculated in 1896 and expanded to cover 30 stocks in 1928.

Epic (Exchange Price Information Computer) The original computer system used by the LSE to collect and disseminate share prices.

equity In markets, the ownership of an asset that might have debt or other liabilities attached to it.

exchange-traded fund A basket of shares collated like an index but traded like a share.

factor investing An investment approach that involves targeting quantifiable characteristics or "factors" that can explain differences in stock returns.

Faculty of Actuaries Scottish professional body for actuaries until 2010 merger with the London based Institute of Actuaries.

Financial Conduct Authority UK financial services regulator since 2013.

Financial Services Authority UK financial services regulator from 2001 to 2013.

FT 30 First calculated in 1935, the oldest continuously-compiled index of 30 stocks was overshadowed when the FTSE 100 launched in 1984.

FTSE All-Share Formerly the FT Actuaries All-Share, this index is the widest aggregation of London-listed shares, begun in 1962.

FTSE Global Equity Index Series (GEIS) International indices family that includes 49 countries. Launched in 1987 as the FT-Actuaries World Indices.

FTSE 100 The UK's flagship index of the 100 largest stocks listed in London, launched in 1984.

FTSE 250 UK index covering the next-largest 250 stocks, launched in 1992.

FTSE Eurotrack 100 Index tracking 100 companies listed on exchanges in Continental Europe.

FTSE Research Affiliates Fundamental Index (RAFI) Index that tracks not price movement but company fundamentals such as sales and cashflow. Launched in 2005.

FTSE4Good ESG index series launched in 2001.

FTSE/ASE 20 Index created in 1999 in partnership with the Athens Stock Exchange to track performance of the top 20 Greek stocks by market capitalisation. Now part of the FTSE/ATHEX Index Series.

FTSE/Xinhua A50 Index Launched 2001 as an index of Chinese stocks on which ETFs and derivatives could be created. Now FTSE China A50 Index.

futures A futures contract is an agreement to buy or sell something at a predetermined price and a specified time in the future.

G20 International forum for 19 leading nations plus the European Union.

gilts Gilt-edged securities are bonds issued by the UK government.

Hang Seng Index The primary index for the Hong Kong Stock Exchange.

hedge fund An investment fund that utilises complex and sometimes risky techniques such as short selling and derivatives.

index (pl. indices) A tool that tracks the performance of stock markets or a subset of their constituent companies.

initial public offering Share sale when a privately-held company is launched onto the stock market.

Institute and Faculty of Actuaries The professional body for actuaries, created in 2010 when the Faculty of Actuaries in Scotland and Institute of Actuaries agreed to merge.

International Commodities Clearing House London-based institution that fulfilled commodities contracts. Pre-cursor to LCH.Clearnet, which was acquired by the LSE.

International Monetary Fund Washington-based international organization that champions monetary cooperation and financial stability.

Jobber Firms and individuals who made the market in shares bought and sold on the London Stock Exchange before Big Bang in 1986.

Kosdaq South Korea's electronic stock market.

large-cap A market's most valuable shares – those with a large market capitalisation.

Libor (London Inter-bank Offered Rate) An interest rate average calculated from estimates submitted by leading banks in London. Due to be phased out by the end of 2021 in favour of Sonia.

liquidity The volume of a particular asset that is readily available to be bought or sold.

listing The availability of a company's shares on a public market.

Markets in Financial Instruments Directive Swathe of regulation designed to harmonise treatment of financial services across the EU that became law in 2007.

mid-cap The middle-sized tranche of shares listed on a stock market.

MSCI US indices company originally created by Morgan Stanley bank acquiring the rights in a global equities index owned and operated by Capital Investment.

mutual fund A professionally-managed pool of assets contributed by numerous investors.

Nasdaq US electronic stock market, heavy with technology stocks.

Organization for Economic Co-operation and Development An intergovernmental organization designed to stimulate economic progress and world trade.

options An options contract is an agreement that gives the right to buy or sell something at a predetermined price and specified time in the future.

passive An investment strategy that tracks a stock market index with little human intervention.

SE 100 Original name for the FTSE 100 during the first four months of its life in 1984, before accord reached with the Financial Times to co-brand.

Securities Another term for shares or equities.

share portfolio A set of investments assembled by a fund manager or retail investor.

small-cap The least valued companies traded on a stock exchange.

S&P Dow Jones Indices US indices company, owner of S&P 500 and the Dow Jones Industrial Average.

Sonia (Sterling Overnight Index Average) The interest paid by banks for unsecured overnight transactions in the sterling market.

Square Mile, The London's financial district.

stock exchange Market place for the purchase and sale of shares in public companies and related derivatives.

Taurus (Transfer and Automated Registration of Uncertified Stock) Intended to replace paper share certificates with computerised share settlement, this IT project was abandoned by the LSE in 1993 at great cost.

Topic (Teletext Online Price Information Computer) The LSE's televised share information service. Now replaced by Bloomberg, Refinitiv and other data vendor terminals.

trust bank A bank that acts as a transaction trustee, transferring assets from one client to another.

UK Listings Authority A unit of the FCA that regulates admissions to the London Stock Exchange.

World Bank International organization providing loans and grants to poorer countries.

World Equity Benchmark Shares (Webs) Early name for a range of ETF funds launched by Morgan Stanley and Barclays in 1996 that evolved into iShares.

World Trade Organization Intergovernmental organization concerned with the regulation of trade between nations.

Bibliography

Arnott, R., *The Fundamental Index: A Better Way to Invest*. London: John Wiley & Sons.

Channel 4 News (1984). Produced by ITN. 13 February.

Clarke, R., (reprinted 1985). Formula for success of a simple daily indicator. *Financial Times*. 1 July. p15.

Cole, R. (2001). Opportunities and risks as FTSE starts ethical share index – Tempus. *The Times*. 3 March. p51.

Dimson, E. and Marsh, P.R. (1984). Hedging the Market: Performance of the FTSE 100 Share Index. *Journal of the Institute of Actuaries*. 111(2), 403–430. Available from: https://www.jstor.org/stable/41140693

Douglas, C.M., (1928). The Statistical Groundwork of Investment Policy [with DISCUSSION]. *Transactions of the Faculty of Actuaries*. 12(112), 173–228. Available from: www.jstor.org/stable/41218123

EFT Express (2010). Standard & Poor's licenses S&P 500 to Vanguard. *EFT Express*. Available from: https://www.etfexpress.com/2010/06/27/52091/standard-poors-licenses-sp-500-vanguard

Fleet, K., (1984). Sharpening the stock exchange picture. *The Times*. 3 May. p21.

Haycocks, H.W. and J. Plymen, (1964). The Design, Application and Future Development of the "Financial Times"–Actuaries Index. *Journal of the Institute of Actuaries (1886-1994)*. 90(3), 267-324. Available from: www.jstor.org/stable/41139790

Investegate, (2020). Update regarding independent review. *Investegate*. Available from: https://cf-cdn.nmc.ae/Uploads/InvestorRelations/nmc-health-plc-update-regarding-independent-review-12-mar-2020-fd7f2999-a9d0-42e1-9eac-e4171e9e15ab.pdf

Kynaston, D., (1997). *LIFFE: A Market and its Makers*. London: Granta Editions.

Lauricella, T. and Luchetti, A. (2001). McGraw-Hill Wins Suit Over S&P Fund. *The Wall Street Journal.* 26 April. Available from: https://www.wsj.com/articles/SB988235944273318913

Leader column. (2001). Good investment. *Financial Times.* 11 July. p18.

Lucchetti, A. and Lauricella, T. (2001). Feud Between Vanguard, S&P Shows How Lucrative Indexing Has Become. *The Wall Street Journal.* 23 August. Available from: https://www.wsj.com/articles/SB998512100682891414

Malkiel, B. (2020). *A Random Walk down Wall Street.* 12th ed. London: W.W. Norton & Company.

Markowitz, H. (1952). Portfolio Selection. *The Journal of Finance.* 7(1), 77–91.

McClatchy, W. and Wiandt, J. (2001). *Exchange-Traded Funds: An Insider's Guide to Buying the Market.* New York: Wiley.

McDonald, M. (2001). Court Rebuffs Vanguard's Bid to Launch ETFs Tracking S&P 500. Available from: https://www.thestreet.com/investing/funds/mutual-funds/court-rebuffs-vanguards-bid-to-launch-etfs-tracking-sp-500-1405877

Merrifield, R., (2001). UPDATE 1-FTSE goes "green" with new ethical indices. *Reuters.* 27 February.

Michie, R., (1999). *The London Stock Exchange: A History.* Oxford: Oxford University Press.

Moore, J., (1984). Index based on 100 top companies begins. *Financial Times.* 14 February. p1.

News in brief. (1983). New index to start in January. *The Times.* 18 November. p19

(1984). Now it will be the FT-SE 100 index. *Daily Telegraph.* 12 February. p18.

Pain, D., (1983). New stock market index planned. *The Times.* 27 October. p15.

Pain, R. (1995). Introduction. The Actuaries' Investment Index. p3.

Prest, M., (1984). Liffe looks for global appeal. *The Times.* 21 February. p17.

Reuters, (2020). UPDATE 1-NMC founder Shetty considers selling UAE-based drugs firm, sources say. *Reuters*. Available from: https://www.reuters.com/article/neopharma-divestiture/update-1-nmc-founder-shetty-considers-selling-uae-based-drugs-firm-sources-say-idUSL-4N2AW40N

Samuelson, P., (1974). Challenge to judgment. *The journal of Portfolio Management*. 1(1), 17-19. Available from: https://doi.org/10.3905/jpm.1974.408496

Samuelson, P. (1948). *Economics: An Introductory Analysis*. New York: McGraw-Hill Education.

Shares, (2020). Unilever announces cross-border merger to create single parent company with more 'strategic flexibility'. *Shares*. Available from: https://www.sharesmagazine.co.uk/news/market/6956816/Unilever-announces-cross-border-merger-to-create-single-parent-company-with-more-strategic-flexibility

Short, E. and J.C.H. Brumwell, (1974). Composition of the F.T.-Actuaries Share Indices. *Journal of the Staple Inn Actuarial Society*. 21(1), 1-35. Available from: https://doi.org/10.1017/S0020269X00008744

Slater, R., (1996). *John Bogle and the Vangaurd Experiment*. Burr Ridge, Illinois: Irwin Professional Publishing.

The Lex Column, (1984). Taking stock by the minute. *Financial Times*. 14 February. p40.

Walker, O., (2018). State Street chief takes aim at high-cost index providers. *Financial Times*. 10 September.

Wathen, J. (2017). Forget BlackRock and State Street – S&P Global Is Making a Fortune From Index Funds. *The Motley Fool*. 6 June. Available from: https://www.fool.com/investing/2017/06/06/forget-blackrock-and-state-street-sp-global-is-mak.aspx

Wiandt, J. (2004) Nate Most, Exchange-Traded Fund Inventor, Dies at Age 90. *ETF.com*. Available from: https://www.etf.com/sections/features/281.html?nopaging=1

Acknowledgements

When I began work on this book in summer 2019 I knew it would be a team effort, just like the creation of FTSE itself. This is the story of the creation of a global brand but also of my career so far. So many of the friends and colleagues who helped to shape FTSE have contributed to the narrative and aided my recollections.

Many who helped build the brand are named in the text. To those I have not named but who contributed over the years I must apologize. I shall always be incredibly proud of our collective achievements.

When I joined the London Stock Exchange in 1985 to help prepare for Big Bang I knew nothing about the financial world and I am grateful to my boss at the time, Philip Danton, for teaching me and to Patrick Mitford-Slade, Hugh Armstrong and George Hayter for giving me the chance to show what I could do. Special thanks also to Michael (Mick) Newman and Daniel (Dan) Sheridan who led many of the changes at that time and recalled them for this book, along with Peter Jones, who sparked my interest in indices.

It would have been a very short story without the original nine members of FTSE International (in addition to myself) from November 1995: Maryann Bolland, Michael Caulfield, Anthony Cloke, Melvyn Lee, Nikki Oakes, Will Oulton, Gareth Parker, Peter Sterlini and Steven Vale. Paul Grimes joined us full-time before long. All but one are still in touch.

We needed experts to thrive, including the actuarial nous of John Brumwell and Richard Pain and academic insight of

Elroy Dimson, Paul Marsh, Steve Ross (who very sadly died far too young in 2017) and Bill Sharpe. Also: Gordon Bagot, Nick Fitzpatrick, Jack Wigglesworth, Reena Aggarwal, Andrew Ang, Michael Brandt, Keith Brown, David Chambers, Jennifer Conrad, George Constantinides, Will Goetzmann, Marty Gruber, Campbell Harvey, Roger Ibbotson, Donald Keim, Geert Rouwenhorst, Richard Roll and Laura Starks.

I owe a lot to Sir Donald Brydon who shared my vision for the creation of FTSE International and was fittingly the chairman of LSEG when I stood down. Other advisory committee chairmen and independent directors who offered counsel and support include Keith Percy, David Hobbs and James Woodlock, who sadly died soon after he was interviewed for this book.

At Pearson and the *Financial Times* I was encouraged by Dame Marjorie Scardino, John Makinson, Sir Richard Lambert, Sir David Bell, Stuart Clark, Alan Miller, Philip Hoffman, Peter Martin, Martin Dickson, Michael Gardner and John Ridding. A special thank you to Baroness Rona Fairhead for her guidance as chair of FTSE International for several years.

At the LSE, Christine Dann took me under her wing when I was young and headstrong and Giles Vardey did much to establish FTSE International. Also: Jonathan Howell, Martin Wheatley, David Lester and, as we expanded overseas, Stuart Leckie, Tim Batho and Simon Hookway.

We had fun at FTSE and the chief fun maker was Donald Keith, my deputy for many years. Together with Nick Teunon, Imogen Dillon-Hatcher, Jerry Moskowitz, Paul Hoff, Jessie Pak, Jean Li, Caroline O'Shaughnessy, Victoria Davies, Jo Roberts, Julie Fawcett, Ceri Richards, Geoff Flynn, John White, Kevin Hardy, Peter de Graaf, Brian Rosenberg, Toby Webb, Joti Rana, Catherine Long, Janet Cumberpatch, Guy Warren, Lance Fisher, Graham Colbourne, Gavin Day, Tim Ward, Reza

Ghassemieh and his talented research team including Philip Lawlor, Peter Gunthorp, Andrew Dougan and Dominic Stone, we created many successful relationships around the world. Jonathan Horton was my original coach and a colleague off and on for many years, Chris Woods, who superbly led the operational development of our indices and Philip Anderson coached and guided. You have been an inspiration.

Thanks also to the Russell team ably run by Ron Bundy, Richard Burns and the Yield Book team and Waqas Samad and the bond index team from Barclays.

FTSE has been blessed by having so many great partners. Those that deserve a special mention are: Research Affiliates: Robert Arnott, Jason Hsu and Katrina Sherrerd. EPRA/NAREIT: Dominique Moerenhout, Steven Wechsler and their teams. Xinhua Finance: Zhu Shan, Dan Connell and Michael Balaban. SGX (Singapore Exchange): Loh Boon Chye. Singapore Press Holdings: Patrick Daniel. Johannesburg Stock Exchange: Russell Loubster, Nicky Newton-King and Ana Forssman. HSI (Hang Seng): Vincent Kwan. TMX (Toronto Stock Exchange): Thomas Kloet and Eric Sinclair. It has also been a pleasure working with Kenneth Baronoff, Jeffrey Jacobs, Chris Moynihan and Edward Dweck at Peter J Solomon.

FTSE4Good was a kernel of an idea pushed on me by Sir Roger Moore. David Bull, Gordon Glick and everyone at UNICEF supported us and challenged us to do more. Sir Mervyn Pedelty, Sir Mark Moody-Stuart, Jack Ehnes, Reg Green, David Harris and Jayn Harding willingly gave so much of their time – and especially Craig Mackenzie who more than anyone led the development of FTSE4Good.

Christopher Gibson-Smith, the chairman of the LSE, warmly welcomed me back to the LSE in 2011. Without his support I would have struggled to acclimatize. Thanks also to Xavier Rolet, David Schwimmer, David Warren, Nikhil Rathi,

Daniel Maguire, Raffaele Jerusalmi, Catherine Johnson, Tim Jones, Diane Cote, Gavin Sullivan and the rest of the leadership team from whom I learnt so much. Also: Patricia Cuddy, James Nevin and Luca Filippa and the Milan team for introducing me to the delights of Italy.

A special thank you to my co-writer James Ashton who has turned my thoughts into a clear and compelling story through many hours of enjoyable conversation. We have been ably supported by our agent Toby Mundy and Iain Campbell, Emily Frisella and the team at Hodder and Stoughton. Martin Nielsen and Bhavna Patel at the FT and David Raymond at the Institute and Faculty of Actuaries also gave vital research help.

Finally, I offer post-dated thanks to those who are joining me in the next venture. Hopefully we will fill another book in time!

Mark Makepeace
July 2020

Index

Makinson, John, 78, 80, 82, 83, 85, 86, 87, 88, 114, 272
Malkiel, Burton, 155
Markowitz, Harry, 155, 172, 268
Mayhew, David, 132
MBS, 193–6, 200–1 (*see also* bin Salman, Mohammed)
McGraw-Hill, 101, 166, 268–9
Moody-Stuart, Sir Mark, 234
Moore, Sir Roger 209–15, 221, 237, 269, 273
Moorgate Benchmarks, 250
Morgan Stanley, 9, 91, 102–3, 105, 135, 159–60, 219, 239
  MSCI (Morgan Stanley Capital International), 99–121, 150, 159–66, 168–70, 173, 177, 179, 189, 192, 197, 199, 203, 206–7, 236, 243–4, 249–50, 254
Morningstar, 7, 248
Murdoch, Rupert, 98

Nasdaq, 89–90, 120, 157
Nestlé, 226–9
Nikkei, 2, 251
Nixon, Richard, 43
not-for-profit
  CBI (Confederation of British Industry), 223
  FTSE4Good, 15, 20, 220–6, 229, 231, 234–5, 237, 260, 273

Obama, Barack, 1

passive funds, 5, 7, 9, 72, 101, 106, 110, 138, 146–7, 151, 161, 169, 222, 251
Pearson, 25, 79, 83, 86, 93–4, 112–15, 251, 272
pension funds, 69, 92, 106, 118, 124, 131, 145, 154, 162, 216, 244, 254
  National Association of Pension Funds, 141

Pitkethly, Graeme, 146–7
PJ Solomon, 117

Qatar Investment Authority, 89

religious investors, 236
Reuters, 79–80, 85, 104, 110–11, 174, 176, 211, 220, 240, 258, 268–9
Robeco, 235
Rolet, Xavier, 89–91, 99–100, 112–17, 120–1, 140, 194, 196, 201, 231, 256–9, 273
Royal Dutch Shell, 139, 147
Royal London (prev. Scottish Life Assurance Company), 32
Russell, 117

S&P
  S&P Global, 2, 9, 16, 34, 68, 80, 100–1, 104, 110, 114, 116, 118, 121, 154, 156–7, 160, 163, 165–9, 188–9, 235, 243–4, 246–50, 267–70
  S&P Dow Jones Indices, 9
  S&P 500, 2, 16, 34, 68, 118, 154, 160, 163, 166, 171, 244, 267, 268
Saatchi & Saatchi, 78
Scardino, Dame Marjorie, 94, 112, 272
Schwimmer, David, 255, 257–9, 273
SE 100 Index, 20–4, 46, 47, 48, 49, 50, 52, 86, 269
SEAQ (Stock Exchange Automated Quotations), 61
SETS (Stock Exchange Trading Service), 76
SGX (Singapore Exchange), 91, 249
Shanghai Futures Exchange, 182
Shetty, Bavaguthu Raghuram, 149
Silicon Valley, 108, 144
Smith New Court, 62
Solactive, 249
Sonia (Sterling Overnight Index Average), 241

Would you like your people to read this book?

If you would like to discuss how you could bring these
ideas to your team, we would love to hear from you.
Our titles are available at competitive discounts when
purchased in bulk across both physical and digital
formats. We can offer bespoke editions featuring
corporate logos, customized covers, or letters from
company directors in the front matter can also be
created in line with your special requirements.

We work closely with leading experts and organizations
to bring forward-thinking ideas to a global audience.
Our books are designed to help you be more successful
in work and life.

For further information, or to request a catalogue, please
contact: **business@johnmurrays.co.uk**
sales-US@nicholasbrealey.com (North America only)

Nicholas Brealey Publishing is an imprint of
John Murray Press.